R. E. O. White

BIBLICAL ETHICS

John Knox Press
ATLANTA

Library of Congress Cataloging in Publication Data

White, Reginald E   O
   Biblical ethics.

   Bibliography: p.
   Includes index.
   1. Bible—Ethics. I. Title.
BS680.E84W45 1979   241   79-18058
ISBN 0-8042-0787-9

First published 1979 by The Paternoster Press,
Exeter, England.
First American edition published through special
arrangement with The Paternoster Press
by John Knox Press, Atlanta, Georgia, 1979.

Printed in the United States of America.

CONTENTS

The Question is . . .

THE FUNDAMENTAL QUESTION for Christian ethics today is whether there can be, strictly speaking, a "Christian" ethic at all. A second question, as fundamental and almost as provocative, is where a Christian ethic might be found.

A truly ethical decision, we are told, must be spontaneous, undirected, free – the individual's unfettered and uncoerced response to each new decision-demanding situation. "Rules" of behaviour, "laws" (whether divine, natural, or customary), edicts of conscience, philosophic "principles", a scale of "values" – all are abstractions: they have no place in mature morality. "Any ethical system is unchristian" says Joseph Fletcher, all system being opposed to life, liberty, and variety.[1] Thus, an adult reaction to the ever-changing kaleidoscope of experience rejects all legalism, scorns all second-hand responses to life, will have nothing to do with decisions preformulated by commitments already made, or preconditioned by inherited beliefs, traditions, conventions. Instead, the adult faces each novel and unique situation in unhampered freedom to make original experiments in living, and so to discover for himself toward what norms of behaviour – if any – he desires to move.

To some, this emphasis upon the individual's spontaneous response to each unprecedented situation in life will recall an ancient verdict upon another age in which "every man did that which was right in his own eyes" (Judges 21:25). How far "situationist" ethics is new, and what degree of truth lies within it, are questions to which a history of Christian ethics must give attention in due place; but – to clear the ground – it must be said at once that ethics cannot be entirely situational without ceasing to be ethical. Any individual's reaction to a presented situation may be irrational, impulsive, automatic, even instinctive: unless it imparts to the situation some specifically moral quality, good or bad, it is not an *ethical* response at all.

Some existentialist theories, it is true, suppose that an individual can reach a wholly original resolve, unconditioned by experience, by social obligation, culture, hope, or fear, and trans-

cending all former choices by a totally new act of will. In such a
decision, no standards of behaviour are assumed; any action can
be justified, either personally or pragmatically, but not judged;
there is no over-all viewpoint from which reactions can be assessed; and since no continuity binds such isolated acts into consistency, no evaluation of character is possible. It is doubtful if such
decisions are practicable at all: even Fletcher concedes[2] that "the
situationist enters into every decision-making situation fully
armed with the ethical maxims of his community and its heritage." But even if such capricious, inconsequent, characterless
responses are possible, they clearly fall outside the scope of moral
judgement, and so of ethics.

Certainly they have no place in any identifiable ethic. To speak
of "Christian", "Buddhist", "Communist", "Humanist" ethics
implies that the behaviour thus described exhibits some distinctive quality or form, observes such norms, is preconditioned by
such outlook, presuppositions, and ideals, as justify the description. To speak of "Christian" ethics implies that the form exhibited, the norms observed, the presuppositions and ideals expressed in the behaviour which Christians approve are related
directly to what Christians believe about the world, about God,
Christ, each other, the history of Christian salvation, the hope of
eternal redemption. "If Christianity is a living and organic unity,
and not a mere amalgam, plastic to the handling of each generation or group, then Christian experience as a whole must show
characteristic features"[3] – and so must Christian thought, and
Christian conduct.

While, therefore, some wholly new, unprecedented, concrete
situation always provides the occasion, and the content, of every
Christian moral decision, its form and direction, its nature and
moral quality derive from a paradosis of history, scripture, tradition, and accumulated experience, which becomes the inheritance
of each Christian convert through the corporate life and teaching
of the Christian fellowship. The modern Christian confronts
twentieth-century problems and situations with nineteen centuries of experiment, mistake, experience and development
behind him to illumine his circumstances, his self-understanding,
and the teaching of the Master.

Here at once the second fundamental question emerges: where
is any consistent and relevant "Christian" ethic to be found?
Christian history speaks with the same confused voice on moral
questions as it does on theological ones. On the one hand, all
formulations of Christian thought are born of particular circumstances, shaped by the background and problems of a particular
age. It follows that when the circumstances change and the age
passes, such formulations, whether of theology or of ethics, become traditional, archaic, to many minds irrelevant. On the other

hand, if we seek to escape the relativism of history by appealing to the scriptures, we are confronted not only by a historical context still more remote from our own, but by a considerable variety of insights and ideals.

The difficulty has been forcibly expressed by J. H. Houlden[4] as that of first enquiring, of any proposed topic of New Testament study, whether that topic can be isolated from the whole theological outlook of the New Testament without distortion; and then of asking whether there is, strictly speaking, any one view which can be identified as "the New Testament view" – in the present instance, any identifiable "New Testament ethic" – when each scriptural writer thinks in his own way, on the basis of his own concerns. "There can be no initial assumption ... that they necessarily sing in unison or even in harmony."

It will be contended that there is no possibility, without distortion, of isolating the ethic either of the Old Testament or of the New from the religious *experience* there described, an experience of which the theology on the one hand and the ethic on the other are but concomitant expressions. This is not to make a "Christian" ethic impossible for us: it is only to keep it "Christian". Moreover, the "Varieties of New Testament Religion" have been familiar at least since E. F. Scott expounded their differences in 1943,[5] and they are taken into consideration in any competent survey of New Testament theology or ethics. They lend a stimulating richness to New Testament thought, and to study each strand against the background of the individual writer's situation and purpose illumines not only his words but the whole process by which Christian ethical judgements are formed. When, further, New Testament ethical thought is seen in its true historical setting, as the flowering and fulfilment of the long development of Jewish morality, the indebtedness and the distinctions alike contribute to fuller understanding, although the gulf that separates biblical times from our own is thereby widened still further.

Nevertheless, neither the variety of biblical teaching nor its historical relativity must be exaggerated. Though, as Scott says, "Liberty is inherent in the Christian faith, and liberty always makes for difference", yet it is a liberty *within* the Christian tradition, a variety that testifies to the living creativeness of one ethical inspiration extending through Jewish and Christian experience. The slow sifting and ultimate canonisation of the scriptural sources was itself a recognition both of their inner unity and of their felt authority. And the treasuring of these writings for so long by two great world religions underlines their experienced value in the nourishment of broadly consistent moral ideals. There is little doubt that if the Bible had presented a single moral code, unrelated to concrete historical circumstances, that fact would have been urged against its validity for today – it would then have been dismissed as too abstract, too stereotyped and limited in range of application, to serve succeeding generations. Certainly we must avoid imposing on the biblical material a uniformity that it does possess; equally, we must avoid if we can interpreting ancient documents by modern presuppositions: but these are tasks to be accomplished, not excuses for abandoning the attempt.

Of course there are dangers in looking backwards. Biblical ethics slips easily into nostalgic escapism, content to perceive the scriptural insights and to remain irrelevant to modern problems, never getting out of the Bible's world into the twentieth century. It slips as easily into unhistorical exegesis, making the Bible answer *our* questions instead of letting it pose and answer its own. Yet Christian ethics must begin with the Bible, because – for good and sometimes for ill – biblical examples and precepts, laws and ideals, promises and warnings, revelations of judgement and assurances of grace, have been, and for most Christians still are, the foundations of morality, upon which all subsequent discussion and adaptation are mere commentary. "He has showed you, O man, what is good; and what does the Lord require of you but to do justice, and to love kindness, and to walk humbly with your God?" declares the Old Testament. "All scripture is inspired by God and profitable for teaching, for reproof, for correction, and for training in righteousness," answers the New.

At the same time it must be emphasised that, for the modern Christian, *biblical ethics is not enough.*

The very remoteness of that biblical milieu from our own, and the endless unprecedented questions posed for ethics by the modern world, is almost argument enough for supplementing the ethical study of the Bible by an exploration of what has happened to Christian morality since Bible times. Whatever effort of historical imagination we bring to our scriptural study, the intervening centuries have left their mark on the way we read the Bible. It is perpetually tempting to define Christian morality as the high ethico-religious tradition of Judaism, criticised, illumined, and universalised by Jesus, and expounded by the apostolic church in the exuberance of a transforming experience; and then to assume that it is *this* ethic which the modern Christian inherits. In fact, the Christian ethical heritage comes to us laden with the accommodations, developments, debates, disappointments, additional insights and unresolved questions, of generations of believers who have sought to apply the original vision to ever-changing situations.

There is therefore still room, and constant need, for study of the history of Christian ethics, as there is room and need for the history of Christian doctrine, not because past creeds or codes can fetter the living mind or conscience, but simply that long and wide experience shall not be wasted. Our generation is not so richly endowed with moral wisdom that it can afford to neglect the centuries of Christian thought, devotion, and experiment in discipleship, that lie behind it. Add to this somewhat utilitarian consideration any vestige of belief in historical revelation, and the case for constant re-examination of biblical ethics in the light of each new century and its needs becomes overwhelming. However contemporary we desire to be, Christianity remains a historically based and historically mediated vision of the good life, an experience of the historically revealed grace of God. The educative and stimulative ministry of the Holy Spirit within the church from generation to generation cannot be ignored; as F. R. Barry said,[7] "To understand the Christian ethic we must study it all the time in its history."

Yet neither the biblical background nor the historical development, nor both together, suffice for moral guidance today. The essence of biblical morality is not a legal system, a written code, an abstract moral philosophy, but a spirit and a loyalty, a vision and faith, incarnate in the inexhaustibly rich and varied personality of Jesus. It is this fact which has lent astonishing flexibility to Christian ethics, while ensuring that each new extension and application is kept true by being referred, at all points, to the mind and example of the Master. Though we appeal to scripture and to history, we may not forget that we follow a *living* Lord. So we seek through the record of the past the gleam of that which is timeless and unchanging. If we ask first how God in diverse manners and at sundry times spoke in the past unto our fathers, it is only that we may hear more clearly and responsively what He says now, in these last days, about our personal problems, through His ever-living Son.

It is here that the *situational* challenge of radically new moral issues find its answer in a return to first principles and the renewal of faith and vision at their original fountains. The Christian would not go naked and unprepared, with empty mind and unguided conscience, into every moral dilemma and decision-demanding circumstance thrown up by the changing mores of a society that has lost direction. He craves the whole armour of Christ.

The question which remains is whether, through all the long changes of biblical and subsequent history, and despite the emergence in our time of unprecedented problems, there has persisted a sufficient continuity of vision, ideal, moral insight, and faith, to justify our speaking of a Christian ethic after all. The answer must be, that the moral task of the modern Christian is to react in freedom to the present, ever-changing world while yet remaining loyal to the insights and ideals inherited from a long-past revelation. To *know* that heritage, and to discern what is permanent, what transitory, in its developing formulations, is a

necessary foundation for Christian ethical investigation still. To
set the student at the point where, with informed mind and
matured judgement, he may enter scripturally prepared into that
contemporary enquiry, is our immediate purpose.

1

Legacies of Earlier Hebrew Religion

CHRISTIANITY IS INDEBTED TO the long development of Hebrew religion for many elements of its outlook, faith, and worship, but nowhere more deeply than in the field of ethics. It is scarcely just to a great world religion to expound its moral teaching only in the light of what was borrowed from it: yet it is precisely because Christianity has carried forward so much from its Jewish matrix that attention must be paid to its inherited insights. It is in morals that communities are most conservative; some continuity with the past in conscience, public understanding, and social approval, is imperative if any new moral ideal is to be accepted, any moral reform is to be tolerated. A total break in matters of conduct and morality must outrage the very persons upon whose perceptiveness and sympathy moral progress depends. Because a new morality appears always to be immorality, moral change must be slow; new ideals must be seen to fulfil, not to deny, the best that has gone before. Thus Jesus freely acknowledged His debt to the faith of His fathers, and is recorded to have declared that He came not to abolish the law and the prophets but to fulfil them (Matthew 5:17).

Jesus Himself cited, interpreted, enforced and enlarged some of the ancient laws of His people, and nourished His mind upon the insights of prophecy and the devotion of the psalmists. Later, as the Christian ethic took shape in the preaching and writing of the apostolic church, it clearly derived from the Old Testament something of its authority, as rules, examples and precedents are quoted in its defence; much of its language, in terms like law, kingdom, the will of God, sacrifice, the Christian walk, true wisdom, holiness, and many more; something also of its form, as its ideals are presented as extensions of older principles, and its great commandments are quoted from the Old Testament code; and many of its basic assumptions, as the religious concept of sin, the reality of divine judgement, the social nature of religion, and much else.

Amidst this general dependence of Christianity, seven specific legacies from earlier Hebrew ethics must be described:

(1) THE THEOCRATIC APPROACH

Discussing the Old Testament's teaching concerning God, T. H. Robinson insists that "Judaism was the only religion in the world with a genuinely monotheistic basis. Nowhere else could Jesus have assumed the position which was the very foundation of all He had to say and do."[1] Luthardt long ago pointed out the essential distinction: the naturalism native to heathenism is overcome in Israel, for whom history itself mediates a personal relationship with God, who is consequently conceived as ethical personality; "In Israel, for the first time, an ethical conception of God is attained, and this not philosophically but historically; while its view of the moral life is certain of justification not only by reason but by history."[2] God is seen as the only true God, powerful, *free* – that is, not involved as a power within the world; as personal, gracious, and faithful, full of compassion, plenteous in mercy. God's holiness is demonstrated in law, in ritual, and in the sense of distance between God and His people which requires mediation; His justice is shown in promise and in judgement; His wisdom and goodness in all His covenant relations with Israel.

The other side of this conception is the obligation laid upon Israel to live as the holy people of such a God, in covenanted faithfulness to Him, an obedient response to the gracious deliverances of God experienced repeatedly in their history. That initiative of salvation on God's part is the primary motive of man's covenant to obey: the Decalogue begins, "I am the Lord your God who brought you out of the land of Egypt, out of the house of bondage"; the Law of Holiness likewise presupposes the gracious election of Israel to divine favour as the basis of the enactments laid upon her (e.g. Leviticus 18:1-4, 26:40-45).

H. W. Robinson chooses as the characteristic Old Testament word to describe God's relation to man, the frequent and inexhaustible word *hesed,* often rendered *grace, loving-kindness, mercy.* "But even the rendering *grace* does not suggest the element of loyalty, of moral obligation, of social bond, which the Hebrew word includes."[3] Later, Robinson uses "steadfastness": the covenant is on God's side unbreakable, His word unalterable, His betrothal permanent – this is His "righteousness". Hosea (2: 19, 20) recites the qualities of Yahweh's lasting engagement with His people: righteousness, justice, grace, *hesed,* fidelity. The depth of meaning in *hesed* is most dramatically revealed in contrast with the wholly unpredictable, capricious fickleness – the whims of favour or of violence – ascribed to heathen deities; they were conceived not merely as faithless but as characterless: Yahweh manifests *hesed.*

Oesterley-Robinson say that the prophets "dared to identify God with the good", insisting on His character, and on His concern with the moral and social principles which had appealed to the nomad's religious and moral instincts.[4] For the prophets, Yahweh was Lord of universal morality: wherever cruelty and injustice were found, there Yahweh's will was being defied and Yahweh sat in judgement (e.g. Amos 1, 2). However proud the oppressor, Yahweh's punishment would fall, neither arbitrary nor vindictive, but the natural, proper and inevitable consequence of wrong. Nevertheless, God's faithfulness to Israel spite of her sin, His loving-kindness and mercy and grace, leave ever open the door of repentance and the hope of redemption: "I am the Lord your God, the Holy One of Israel, your Saviour" (Isaiah 43:3, 49:26, 60:16 and *passim*).

It is impossible to exaggerate the significance of this inherited conception of the God before whose eyes the moral life has to be lived, and before whose judgement the soul must eventually pass. Three corollaries accompany this theocratic approach to ethics:

(i) Though the line between the nature-gods and the God of nature is clear, it is fine-drawn. Yahweh-Elohim's distinction from and exaltation over the natural world is explicit and emphatic, from the creation-stories to the later prophets; yet the earth is the Lord's, and the fullness thereof, the world and they that dwell therein. He is the God who rides the storm, marshals the stars, leads men through the desert with careful provision for their food, water, and clothing. His word sounds in the rolling thunder, the lightning's flash, the skipping trees, the foaming rivers, He is God of the physical world, of the family, of sex and childbirth, of health, of the flocks and the market-place, the courts of justice and the palaces of kings, of the week's work and the Sabbath rest. Religious ethics, in Israel, was never long divorced from the real world and material things: in Christianity's inherited outlook no theological basis existed for dualistic asceticism. The natural development of the doctrine of divine creation was an ethic of incarnation.

(ii) The theocratic approach binds religion and ethics indissolubly together. "The ancient world saw no necessary connection between religion and morality" says T. H. Robinson. "The gods and goddesses were magnified human beings with human virtues and vices, but without the restraints which conscience and society impose on men. There was hardly a vice or crime which could not be committed not merely with the connivance, but with the sanction and even the direct authority of one or other of the numerous deities. So complete was the divorce between religion and morality that not a few of the great souls of the ancient world discarded the gods altogether ... To them religion and righteousness were incompatible."[5]

Siddartha, Euripides, Lucretius, Socrates, perhaps Confucius, are among numerous examples. For Greece, Gilbert Murray declares that "to make the elements of a nature-religion human is inevitably to make them vicious.... The unfortunate Olympians, whose system really aimed at pure morals and condemned polygamy and polyandry, are left with a crowd of consorts that would put Solomon to shame."[6] Canaanite religion was very limited in ethical demand: human sacrifice and sacramental fornication condoned direct violation of the moral law against murder and promiscuity. Only concerning the oath did religion of this kind impose any strong moral restraint: it outlawed perjury – and that, more through fear of the gods' vengeance for taking divine names in vain, than from any high moral intuition of the value of truth. If Israel could offer no more than the syncretistic worship of Bethel, she must have perished, say Oesterley-Robinson; instead, her prophets identified religion and goodness, God and righteousness.[7]

In the words of Wheeler Robinson, "Western civilisation has come to take for granted the interfusion of morality and religion; to it, an immoral God would be a contradiction in terms, and an immoral worshipper a hypocrite. Such assumptions are historically traceable to the teaching of the Christian faith, itself drawing upon the higher religion of Israel. It was the prophetic religion that for the first time in history brought morality and religion together in a unique way."[8] Isaiah 1, Jeremiah 7:1-15, Amos 1 are typical of many relevant passages. This conjunction with religion enormously increases the weight of ethical obligation, as right and wrong have to do with divine standards and not merely with the customs of the tribe; it immeasurably lengthens the moral perspective, as expectation of divine judgement and reward reinforces social pressure as the incentive to good behaviour; and it powerfully reinforces moral strength, as God is seen to be gracious and merciful, Saviour and Redeemer, as well as Lawgiver and Judge.

(iii) The moral conception of God and the intimate connection of morality with religion carry with them the concept of moral *law*. This arises also within philosophical ethics, formulating the "sense of oughtness", the inescapable moral imperative that seems addressed to us from within and yet not by ourselves. But historically this is the controlling conception of Judaism, that of the divine Torah, making morality essentially obedience to a perceived rule or norm or requirement, imposed upon man by a personal authority that does not abide man's questioning. The significance of this appears when we compare with it the Hedonist, Utilitarian, or Idealist interpretations of morality, the Greek veneration of the sage to whom goodness is the highest wisdom, or the moral aesthete to whom goodness consists in the golden mean, the intrinsic harmony. To the Jew, goodness was not by definition a means towards happiness, welfare, or personal perfection, nor wisdom nor beauty: it was *righteousness* – the obligation to obey the divine will as the ultimate right. From that definition is but a short step to the teaching of Jesus that the good life is life under the reign of God, and to the apostolic proclamation of the Lordship of Christ.

(2) THE DECALOGUE

It is not necessary for our purpose to trace the long story of Israel's moral development, nor need we pause to evaluate accurately those lingering attitudes which became in Christianity ethical liabilities – the uncritical acceptance of militaristic precedents, the subordination of women, a persistent tendency to expect piety to bring prosperity, certain sexual inhibitions, the almost ineradicable bias of a "chosen" people towards exclusiveness and spiritual pride. But since the Old Testament is still read in Christian worship, and Old Testament ideals, personalities and principles are still living factors shaping the Christian ethos, it is necessary to look briefly at some of the peaks of Hebrew ethical thought, and to ask why certain passages and codes retain perennial value for our very different age, society, and faith.

Among such particular legacies from Judaism, the Decalogue retained prominence in traditional Christian teaching down to the beginning of the twentieth century. The Ten Commandments probably represent the standard of life which it was believed Yahweh required of His people in the nomadic period, when landed and real estate were unknown, when flocks and herds belonged to the clan rather than to individuals, when sexual morality was usually high, and when purity of blood (guarded by the law of marriage) and sanctity of life (guarded by the custom of blood-revenge, in reality a protection against peril from "unavenged" blood) were the supreme values. Moral authority lay in tradition and experience, that is in the past as represented by elders and parents, and was assumed to enshrine the inherited law of Yahweh.

We have the Decalogue now in two forms (Exodus 20:1-17, Deuteronomy 5:6-21) both ethical in content; a third, (Exodus 34:10-26) is concerned with ritual. The more familiar code is called the "Ten Words" in Deuteronomy 4:13 and 10:4, "the Testimony" (e.g. Exodus 25:16), and "the Covenant" or "the Tables of the Covenant" in Deuteronomy. The varying number, order, and translation of the Commandments show that both Jews and Christians handled the Decalogue with great freedom. Its primitive character and undoubted importance support the Jewish tradition of Mosaic origin; its form may have been elaborated – all commandments may once have been as terse as six to nine still are. The Sabbath law might seem to presuppose settlement in

Canaan, but Oesterley-Robinson think the Sabbath pre-Canaanite.[9] The failure to stress it in earlier centuries, like the toleration of images until the eighth century, may represent a lower, popular form of Yahwism while the Decalogue preserved a higher "archaic" conception. H. H. Rowley concludes a thorough examination on the side of "a highly probable Mosaic authorship."[10]

These ancient Commandments are for many Christians the ten pillars of moral wisdom, the ten foundation stones of social welfare, the unquestioned axioms of any religious morality. God is the Lawgiver and Judge, but His claim to submission rests upon His deliverance of His people from slavery – the law is based upon what God has already graciously done; the motive urged is grateful obedience. Nevertheless, "commandment" is divine language, not the tentative counsel of enlightened self-interest: "thou shalt" is in the moral world the equivalent of "Let there be ... " in Genesis 1 – the unanswerable *fiat*. Because of their age, the Ten Words require, and have received, considerable reflective adaptation and development.

The First Commandment asserts God's supremacy, against polytheism. The existence of other gods is not denied, but recognition of them is forbidden, for the gods whom you cease to worship cease to be gods to you. The commandment comes to Christians reinforced by word and promise of Jesus (Matthew 3:10, cf 4).

The Second Commandment asserts God's spirituality, against idolatry (developed later in Deuteronomy 4:15-19, Isaiah 44:9-20) Jealousy is the inevitable implicate of love – "love on the defensive" (cf Exodus 34:14). *What* we worship is morally important because we grow like the things we honour; violence, ugliness, lewdness in the idol both express and reinforce what is already in the mind of the worshipper. Moreover, an idol localises, externalises, materialises, and "fossilises" God. The tremendous influence of this Commandment may be seen in the fact that the Jews had no sculpture, and in the insistence of Jewish Christians that Jesus, alone, is the "image" of God.

The Third Commandment extends God's authority beyond the shrine to markets, courts and homes, demanding reverence for God's name. No doubt this forbids profanity, which is as Jesus said a revelation of the heart; but its first intention was to forbid perjury, the divine name constituting the oath which ensured truth and established agreements, treaties and receipts in an illiterate society. In the perfect society of the kingdom, as Jesus says again, it is enough to let one's Yea be yea.

The Fourth Commandment ("remember ... hallow") echoes Genesis 2:2 and is usually regarded as re-affirming long existing practice. In Babylon, "shabbattim" were kept every five days and every seventh day of the month for propitiating deity and abstaining from secular work. The Code of Hammurabi, five centuries before Moses, prescribed certain recurring "days of ill omen". Exodus stresses simply abstention from work by Israelites, slaves, and sojourners; Deuteronomy adds the humanitarian motive, "that they may rest." Exodus declares that God "blessed" the seventh day, and Deuteronomy recalls the deliverance of Israel from Egypt: these ideas, the religious significance of the day, the rest it confers, and the blessing granted to those who observe it, adhere to the Sabbath throughout scripture, despite the extensive and sometimes ridiculous casuistry later developed around the Sabbath rules. From the Jewish Sabbath is derived in the New Testament the "Lord's day", the first day of the week, the day of Christ's resurrection, of the giving of the Spirit, of the laying aside of gifts, of the breaking of bread, a day for being in the Spirit, hearing the divine voice and seeing the divine vision (Revelation 1:10). In principle, the Sabbath extends divine authority over all our time, as given and redeemed by Him.

The Fifth Commandment passes to the honour to be accorded to parents, as God's representatives (compare Plato: "After gods and demigods, parents should have most honour"; Aristotle: "It is proper to pay them honour such as is given to the gods"). In Exodus 21:17 to curse parents deserves death; here, the promise "that thy days may be long in the land" implies that the filial spirit nourishes the stability of society. Adequate training of the next generation is essential to social permanence, and the Hebrew home was school and church; the Hebrew parent was teacher, priest, and pastor; the child was required to learn and to submit. Later, material support for ageing parents was seen to be implied.

The Sixth Commandment declares the absolute sanctity of human life. The translation "murder" is justified, because the original undoubtedly implies violent, unauthorised killing, for profit, passion, revenge, pleasure or despair. The Old Testament certainly sanctions war, capital punishment, sacrifice, and by implication slaughter for food. Indeed, the penalty for infringing this very Commandment was death inflicted by an avenger, not by society (Exodus 21:12f); Deuteronomy forbids the purchase of immunity by wealth. The principle asserted is reverence for life as the highest value in the universe, divinely created and sustained, returning to God who gave it, always belonging to God: murder is a kind of sacrilege. Jesus extends the principle to forbid the frustrated desire to murder, in anger or vindictiveness.

The Seventh Commandment declares the sanctity of marriage. In Leviticus 20:10 the penalty for both partners to adultery is death. The Commandment says nothing of polygamy or concubinage; sexual intercourse with another's *wife* is forbidden, the principle being the sanctity of blood and family – an additional sanction lying in the rights of inheritance. The importance of the home in the stable ordering of society made adultery immoral, anti-social, and criminal, while sex and marriage are recognised as part of the Creator's design. Adultery, therefore, the sin against marriage, is again in essence sacrilege.

The Eighth Commandment asserts the right of private property. The penalty for stealing a man-slave was death (Exodus 21:16; so with Hammurabi, and at Athens); the penalty for stealing sheep or treasure was multiple restoration. In a nomadic society, private property was limited, but a minimum of possessions seems essential to personal dignity and security. Unless a man has the right to use what he makes, grows, or hunts, he is unlikely to work or to develop his skills. Civilisation could scarcely begin until the recognition of ownership through superior labour or skill, and the accumulation of food, tools, and weapons, set some individuals free from daily dependence upon war, hunting, and toil, to think, to paint, to dance and make music, and to pray. Independence is necessary to character and responsibility, while society benefits when security of ownership encourages thrift, and when the seed for next year's sowing, the accumulated wealth for the next generation's investment, are safely husbanded. Society suffers when insecurity breeds dishonesty, or wealth circulates without relation to labour done or service given. Such truisms were plain to primitive peoples: but though the security of private property was necessary to social welfare, the Jew never forgot that man is but a tenant, a steward, a pensioner, of God; luxury, avarice, oppression, and heartless selfishness, were widely condemned.

The Ninth Commandment condemns false testimony, whether as slander, false accusation, or (especially) false prosecution; the Hebrew for "bear" is "answer", a forensic word. Legal perjury was a common crime. In Deuteronomy 19:16-21 the penalty is to suffer that which the accuser sought to bring upon his victim. In primitive society, a man's reputation, his public name and honour, were a vital asset, at the mercy of lying tongues – the story of Naboth (1 Kings 21) affords dramatic illustration. Later, false accusation is seen as imperilling human justice, which God defends; in the New Testament, speaking truth with and of one's neighbour is a necessary element of love.

The Tenth Commandment, unexpectedly, forbids undisciplined desire. The first to imply a moral psychology, to assert an internal moral principle, it points straight forward to the Sermon on the Mount, and to the sin of wanting to sin, though cowardice or lack of opportunity prevent the deed. Covetousness is unlawful desire to possess something that is another's. "House" probably means the nomad's "household", the following enumeration being a later expansion. Deuteronomy understood "house" as *chattels,* and so placed the wife first. The Commandment by implication forbids every expression of covetousness – pleonexia, the desire for things because you do not have them, or because others do have them; and envy, that merely resents the prosperity of others. The law here transcends itself, overreaching its power of sanction: for the inward impulse cannot be outwardly judged, nor punished; and there is no power to inhibit the *desire* of wrong, except a power that is above and beyond the law – as Paul discovered.

Considered in this way, it is not strange that the Decalogue has held its place in the church's instruction and devotion. It defines godliness in plain and practical terms, describes a piety that begins already to manifest a social conscience, and sets the tone and direction of biblical ethics.

(3) THE BOOK OF THE COVENANT

Exodus 20:22 to 23:19 comprises a social code of *ordinances* (precedents arising from previous priestly decisions), *warnings,* and *exhortations,* making together a document described in Exodus 24:7 as the Book of the Covenant. Some claim this is the oldest existing Hebrew social legislation, derived in part from still older Canaanite sources. Most would hold that at any rate it reflects the custom-rules of the early settlement or the early monarchy, some decisions ascribed to Moses, and experience of Canaanite temptations. The Book presupposes a simple, agricultural society; its provisions are consonant with those of the Code of Hammurabi and some early Greek and Roman law, while some of its principles are said to be familiar in nomadic societies still. An apparent severity reflects these early conditions, but even this was probably an advance upon cruder customs of uncontrolled revenge; certain ritual provisions likewise point to an unsophisticated age.

At every point, the Book of the Covenant brings discrimination, justice, carefully measured responsibility, into the harsher, more vengeful impulses of primitive society. Slavery is recognised, but in the case of Israelites (who might become slaves by theft, insolvency, poverty, sale by parents, or by birth) bondage is mitigated by humane limitations. Capital offences are numerous, and reflect, in comparison with other codes, what Israel counted most serious. Thus, older Sumerian laws prescribed slavery or branding for repudiation of one's parents; Hammurabi demands the loss of hands for striking them; Plato counselled exile or death, and the Athens rule was loss of civil rights: the Book of the Covenant prescribes death for striking either father or mother. Murder, too, involves capital punishment; but the unintentional manslayer has a right of asylum at the altar – not so in Homer's laws. As in Athens, Hammurabi, and Rome, kidnapping into slavery is punishable by death, and so are sorcery, bestiality, and idolatry.

Personal injuries receive compensation, not automatically but according to circumstances, though the over-riding principle is the well-known *lex talionis* – itself a limitation upon unmeasured vindictiveness. Unlike Greece and Rome, in Israel the slave might not be killed with impunity, but enjoyed a measure of social protection; he could not plead the *lex talionis* against his master, but he was compensated by freedom. Sudden, unexpected viciousness in animals meant the animal must die, but where the animal was known to be dangerous and not restrained, the owner must die also – or redeem his life with a fine. A man responsible for leaving a pit in dangerous condition must buy any animal killed therein.

As at Athens, and Rome, and under Hammurabi, theft and burglary demand multiple restitution. To kill a burglar caught in the act and in darkness, brought no punishment. Loss of things entrusted is provided for by an oath of fidelity, taken "before God" (probably at the shrine); an oath, or decision, taken "before God" must settle disputes. Seduction requires marriage and the payment of dowry, if the girl's father agrees; if the girl was betrothed, the sin is adultery. Another group of humanitarian rules forbids oppression of the foreigner, the widow, the orphan, and the retention beyond sundown of the pledged garment of the poor. Usury upon charitable loans to the needy is firmly forbidden: commercial loans were unknown.

Reverence is demanded for God and for rulers, and the payment of religious dues. Slander, and conspiracy to pervert justice (by the oath) are expressly forbidden. Obligation is laid upon all men to give help when a neighbour's beast has strayed or has fallen under its load. The seventh day is for rest, and in the seventh year the ground lies fallow: in the Book the reasons are philanthropic; in Leviticus, for the sake of the land, and later for religious reasons; in Deuteronomy, the reason given is to facilitate the release of slaves and debtors (cf Exodus 23:10, 11 with Leviticus 25:1-7, 26:34, 35 and Deuteronomy 15:1-18).

The main principles of the Book of the Covenant are thus philanthropy and equity, reinforced by piety, a fair summary of the whole trend of Old Testament ethics. The degree of humanity and justice attained in that far-off age is impressive; even an enemy's need is to be met, and his animals succoured. Concubinage and slavery already begin to be relieved of their worst cruelties, and if the law seems harsh towards thieves and witches, it was so until very recently in Europe also. Here, as in the Decalogue, the divine control of ordinary life and affairs is asserted. God's hand is seen in the chance meeting of enemies; God avenges the cry of the oppressed; God's authority upholds the decisions of local judges; God is to be honoured with the gifts and offerings of the soil; the first-born son of each family is His; while over all Israel's life stands the divine assurance – and the warning to the heartless – "I am compassionate" (Exodus 22:27).

(4) EARLIER PROPHETIC TEACHING

Israel's prophets, it has been well said, were preachers of personal righteousness, advocates of the rights of man, and apostles of hope – a remarkable succession of men of sensitive conscience, who commented on social and national affairs in the name of the universal Lord, and whose impact upon the religion of later centuries, including Christianity, cannot be over-estimated.

Nathan's protest against David's sin (2 Samuel 12:1f) voiced the rigour of a simpler society against the sensuality and tyranny of a new order modelled on pagan luxury and despotism. Elijah likewise upheld the ethical standards enshrined in the Covenant of nomadic days, looking back (with the Rechabites and the Nazirites) to the moral "puritanism" and democracy of the desert, while his defence of "little" Naboth against the despotism of Ahab, and his opposition to the corrupting influences of Phoenician Baal-worship, were steps towards a spiritual reformation, which bore fruit in political revolution under Jehu, in moral and religious revival under Josiah, and in the unforgettable ethical insights of Amos, Hosea, Isaiah, and Micah.

For *Amos,* ethics was the basis of the Covenant between Israel and Yahweh: an amoral religion God simply despises (5:21-25). Amos rebuked the licentiousness fostered at village shrines, but his sharpest severity is reserved for those who "trample" on the needy, turn aside the poor from their right, afflict the just, accept bribes, "sell the righteous for silver and the needy for a pair of shoes" (5:11, 12, 7:16). He condemns the careless luxury that lazes upon beds of ivory amidst idle music and wine by the bowlful (6:4f). He pleads eloquently that justice might roll downward through the land as a flood, and righteousness overwhelm the nation as a mighty stream (5:24). His passionate ethical monotheism issues relentless warnings to all nations – to Damascus for intense cruelty in war; to Gaza for carrying a whole people captive; to Tyre for betraying a brotherly covenant; to Edom also for unbrotherliness, perhaps towards Israel; to Ammon for ruthless ambition and for barbarity towards women; to Moab for desecrating the dead; to Judah for rejecting God's law and following lies; and to Israel herself for oppression of the poor, maladministration of justice, incest, sacrilege, and contempt for the law of God (1, 2). Yahweh requires from all the earth righteousness rather than ritual (5:12f); special privilege does not confer immunity, it only increases responsibility (3:1f). The coming Day of the Lord will vindicate the Right – a day of calamity therefore to those who fail the righteous God! (5:18-20).

Hosea is no less sternly ethical, but he denounces more rarely, expounding instead the faithful love of God, that would discipline Israel to purity and piety of heart. Hosea's protest against the popular compromise between Yahwism and Baalism is directed mainly to religious fornication and drunkenness, a holy and home-born indignation against sexual viciousness sheltering within religion: for he sees Israel's infidelity as insult and affront to the divine love (2:2f). This concept of God as faithful love, persisting unchanged through suffering and rejection, is Hosea's special contribution to Old Testament ethics; arising from it is God's greatest demand, for *hesed* between men, for faithful love as the fount of sympathy, pity, devotion, loyalty, fidelity – at all costs, and in all circumstances (6:6, 10:12, 2:19, 20).

Isaiah of Jerusalem proclaimed the holiness of God, applying his strictly moral conception of God's will to the affairs of Judean society and to all nations as instruments of "the Lord of hosts, the Holy One of Israel." Like Amos, Isaiah surveys the world scene and finds all under condemnation for pride, idolatry, and evil-doing; while the obligation upon Israel, especially, to be a holy people is expressed in many and practical ways. For Isaiah, the root of many social evils lay in the selfish luxury of the women (3:16, 4:1), for he realised that the moral tone of society is set by the quality of its womenfolk. He demanded strict impartiality in the administration of justice (10:1-4), condemned the luxury, sensuality and selfishness of the wealthy (chapters 1-5), severely denounced in almost irreligious language a ritual that could flourish while the widow, the fatherless, the oppressed were callously ignored (1:10-17, 29:13-14), and in everything pleaded for a return to Yahweh in holiness, for the Holy One will yet keep His word to Israel. Evil must surely end in judgement (33:1).

Micah is equally fearless, equally clear, in his insistence upon the righteousness of Yahweh, especially against "those who devise evil upon their beds, who covet and take the fields and houses of the poor, who eat the flesh of the people, and pervert equity" (2:1, 2). Thousands of rams offered in sacrifice, rivers of oil poured in libation, make no atonement for social injustice. By general consent, says Wheeler Robinson, "the best epitome of prophetic teaching is to be found in Micah 6:8 ... Here, the supreme virtue of religion, as the Hebrew conceived it, is ... that humility of bearing and of conduct, 'making modest the walking' before God, which alone answers properly to man's constant dependence upon Him ... The moral virtues here named are 'justice' and 'loyal helpfulness' ".[11] *Justice* (here originally a forensic word) implies the award to every man of that which is his due: T. H. Robinson declares that one of the greatest contributions ever made to the political thought of man was that of the common brotherhood brought by Israel from her nomadic past into the conditions of a highly organised, settled community, with a strong sense of the value of human personality and an emphasis upon the rights of man as man. *Mercy,* here, is more than loving-kindness, including recognition of that social bond which requires mutual helpfulness, loyalty, a profound compassionate concern at the oppression of others. Together, justice and mercy comprise for Micah the whole duty of man towards men. In default of social justice, nothing could save the temple (3:9-12); identifying religion with mercy, and linking the righteousness of God with vindication of the oppressed, Micah became a social reformer with unexcelled religious passion and fearlessness.

Thus God appeared to Amos as justice, to Hosea as love, to Isaiah as holiness, to Micah as mercy. The resulting conception of a right relationship to God as involving – almost as consisting in – moral obedience, is fundamental to all later biblical ethics. So is the sense of corporate life, of each man's belonging to his brother, and of the responsibility of the nation as a whole, but in particular of the princes, judges, priests, and teachers, towards God. So, too, is the universal outlook nourished by such ethical monotheism. With such heroes of the religious and social conscience among its ancestors, Christianity could not fail to inherit an ethical and social vision.

(5) DEUTERONOMIC IDEALS

The Deuteronomists sought to incorporate the high morality of the eighth-century prophets in a body of laws for civil and religious reference, which could be enforced in public discipline and taught to the young, "superbly insistent upon justice, holiness, and humanity" (G. A. Smith). In a revised edition of the Book of the Covenant, with new emphasis upon humanitarian morality and inward devotion to the Giver of life (Deuteronomy 6 and 7), priests and prophets together presented to Josiah a programme for reform. The "high places", centres of amoral religion, were to be abolished. Since God is righteous, neither regarding persons nor accepting bribes, but executing justice for the fatherless and widow, and caring for the resident alien (10:17f), a similar justice and care are required of Israel – especially remembering Israel's own experience as slaves in Egypt. To the law concerning slaves is added (15:12-18) a command to give a departing slave liberal provision from flock, threshing-floor and winepress: such is the spirit of Deuteronomic legislation.

Israel's relationship to God is that of sonship, due entirely to God's grace. The holiness which this demands includes a (priestly) avoidance of all uncleanness. The two great motives appealed to are, as Wheeler Robinson remarks, love – "Thou shalt *love* the Lord thy God" (6:5, compare 20f) – and a true evangelical gratitude. From this grateful love should arise the humane treatment of the poor, the defenceless, the sojourners without civil rights. Sacred prostitution, divination, child-sacrifice, are very firmly suppressed; other humanitarian enactments include the right to glean, payment of hire before evening, a "second tithe" for widows, the fatherless, the poor; liberality is enjoined, gentleness to the infirm, reverence for the aged, friendly treatment of the stranger. Chastisement is to be carefully limited – "forty stripes, no more, lest thy brother seem vile to

thee" (25:3). Similar consideration is to be extended also to animals (22:1-4, 6f, 23:4). If love and kindness fail, divine retribution will be sure (7:9f, cf 16:20, 30:15-20).

The importance of this "second law" cannot be exaggerated. It
gathered up the best traditions of a Yahwism militant against
pagan corruption and tyranny; it summoned all Israel to a faith
and social life enriched by the prophetic movement; it emphasised in wholly new degree the tenderness and compassion with
which Hosea interpreted the will of God. It had one plain historical result: the community which went into exile possessed moral
and social standards far other than those of the previous long,
dark reign of Manasseh.

(6) LATER PROPHETIC TEACHING

Among later prophets, Jonah – or the story concerning him –
developed the universalism of Amos; Nahum emphasised again
the eternal principles of God's government; Zephaniah condemned with great moral earnestness avarice, dishonesty and corruption among court officials; Zechariah called to a national
repentance and obedience for which ritual fasting was no substitute (7:1-10). Malachi, mainly concerned with religious attitudes,
saw the cruelty of divorce, and warned that God would refine all
evil from the nation (2:13-16, 3:1-3). Jeremiah, Ezekiel and
Isaiah 40-66 contributed major insights to the ethical inheritance
into which Jesus came.

Jeremiah shared to the full the ethical ideals of the
Deuteronomists, yet he came to perceive very plainly the inadequacy of any written code of moral requirements. At first apparently lending his support to the republishing of the Covenant
(11:1-7), he lost confidence in its power truly to change the
nation (11:8-13); the external, legalist reform proved a pretence,
a self-deception (3:10). The old Covenant failed "because it had
been an external thing, written down in a book and imposed on
men by royal or ecclesiastical authority. Not so can the dealings of
men with God be rightly ordered" (T. H. Robinson[12]). Instead,
Jeremiah looked for a new Covenant, when the will of God would
be written not on papyrus but on the renewed heart of the people
(31:31-34). Equally clearly Jeremiah saw how inadequate was
any temple ritual to transform human behaviour, and he challenged the excessive reliance placed on the now centralised worship (7:1-4, 6:20, 14:12 etc). Only the new heart, the new disposition, uniting imposed command with inward inclination, would
make the legal code practicable, the cultus acceptable, and
rewarding.

How this inward transformation would take place is left undefined. Jeremiah appears to have thought that the humiliation and suffering of the exile, which he prophesied, would of itself achieve a change of heart. The ground of this hope may have lain in his own experience: his own intimate confessions, doubts, disappointments, and anguished prayers, introduced a wholly new note into Israel's relationship with God. Suffering so faced in the fellowship of God would surely renew the heart, and so the morality, of Israel also. This individual religion of the heart is the burden of Jeremiah's message, "his greatest contribution to the world's knowledge of God", and his most original bequest to biblical ethics, illuminating the inner motivation of the moral life and pointing straight forward to Jesus and the spiritual ideals of the redeemed man.

Ezekiel, disciple of Jeremiah and prophet of restoration, saw Israel seek refuge for her resentful pride in the dogma of collective responsibility, laying all blame upon an earlier generation. In protest he proclaimed unqualified individual responsibility (chapter 18). The "righteousness" for which the individual is held personally responsible is defined much as Deuteronomy would define it, as a fine blend of pure religion with just and generous humanity –

'If a man is righteous and does what is lawful and right – if he does not eat upon the mountains or lift up his eyes to the idols of the house of Israel, does not defile his neighbour's wife or approach a woman in her time of impurity, does not oppress anyone, but restores to the debtor his pledge, commits no robbery, gives his bread to the hungry and covers the naked with a garment, does not lend at interest or take any increase, withholds his hand from iniquity, executes true justice between man and man, walks in my statutes, and is careful to observe my ordinances – he is righteous, he shall surely live, says the Lord God' (18:5-9) –

– but Ezekiel's main concern is that each man, each generation, shall bear its own responsibility.

The individualism which for Jeremiah arose through personal struggle and the nearness of God, was reinforced for Ezekiel by powerful awareness of the transcendence of God, due partly to the profound sense of Israel's sin, partly to reaction from the surrounding heathenism of Babylon. For Ezekiel, therefore, individualism *meant* personal responsibility. In Deuteronomy, the corporate responsibility of the nomadic order still lingered: God visits the iniquity of the fathers upon the children to the third and fourth generation (5:9); in Ezekiel, neither the sins nor the merits of the fathers determine the destiny of the children – they answer for themselves. This is a milestone in biblical ethics.

At the same time, Ezekiel saw that suffering in itself could harden and embitter, instead of softening and refining. The inward regeneration which Jeremiah seems to have expected from humiliation, Ezekiel hoped would come from the resurrecting power of the divine Spirit (chapter 37, 36:16f). The wind of God, the breath of the Spirit, could raise out of national humiliation "a great army" of the Lord which should re-possess the land and win the future. Some have discerned a certain hardness, a "terrible" logic, in Ezekiel's thought about God, sin, and punishment: but the same logic implies that repentance will automatically bring forgiveness and restoration. While intensifying responsibility, Ezekiel's moral individualism opened the door for an individual to save himself from a perverse generation, by personal repentance and the quickening of the divine Spirit. That reliance upon spiritual regeneration is also a milestone. Nevertheless, Ezekiel attached importance also to the rebuilding of the temple and the re-enactment of the law: in the terrible experiences still to come, Israel might not have withstood heathen persecution without some external standard and stable institution to shelter and reinforce personal piety.

Isaiah 40-66 brings to harvest the ethical insights of the prophetic movement in the conviction that Yahweh is creator and sovereign, both of the material universe and of history. Here ethical monotheism reaches its zenith: the whole tone is of exultation and great hope. Sin remains sin: there could scarcely be a stronger condemnation of moral iniquity than is implied in 43:22-28, where Israel's sin has burdened even her God; or in 53 where sin has crushed the very Servant of the Lord. Nevertheless Yahweh's triumphant righteousness and redemptive love are gloriously described; and such redemption is morally conceived, and morally conditioned by a divine judgement which forever separates evil from good.

The earlier social humanitarianism is not forgotten: "Is not this the fast that I have chosen, to deal thy bread to the hungry and cover the naked?" (58:6, 7). And in all the majesty of "Deutero-Isaiah's" theology, tenderness and compassion vie with greatness and glory. This more "human" and tender conception of the divine greatness is reflected equally in the character ascribed to the Servant of the Lord, who shall bring salvation, justice, and light, to Israel and to the world. In personal quality he is to be modest, humble, gentle; he will not strive nor cry nor lift his voice in the streets, nor shall the bruised reed be broken in his hands. Yet his tenderness is strength: he will establish righteousness, without fail, but by the only means by which it can be made secure – by eschewing violence, and appealing to the hearts of men. He shall comfort those who mourn, liberate the oppressed, preach good news of compassion to the poor; he shall so enter into the need, suffering, and sin of Israel as to bear their iniquities, and atone by his own death for their sins (42:1-4, 61:1-3, 53:4-12).

So the righteousness which the Servant will establish will involve a real conversion of the people, an opening of their eyes to see his beauty, an inward liberation from evil. Not their own suffering (as Jeremiah thought), nor yet the invasion of the divine Spirit (as Ezekiel hoped) shall regenerate the nation, but the voluntary suffering of the offenceless, guiltless, Servant of the Lord for the guilty and undeserving. This is the very pinnacle of Old Testament *ethics:* nothing even in the New Testament surpasses it. The later prophets have understood the heart of God.

(7) THE CODE OF HOLINESS

Leviticus 17 to 26 attained special importance in later Judaism as the starting-point of the Jewish boy's education and (many would say) as the model for the apostolic training of converts. The social principles which here intersperse the ritual requirements have been held "perhaps the best representation of the ethics of ancient Israel" (G. F. Moore), and the great ethical chapter (19) has been ranked above the Decalogue, even though the demand that a man love his neighbour did not extend originally beyond Israel.

The name derives from the emphasis throughout upon holiness: the keynote is 20:26 "You shall be holy to me; for I the Lord am holy, and have separated you from the peoples, that you should be mine. Instruction and command are directly spoken by God, the divine "I" occuring nearly fifty times. The stress upon separateness, the solemn reflection of Ezekiel's teaching upon transcendence, the assumption of theocracy and the centralisation of worship, have suggested a date around the exile for the Code's present form; but its occasional terseness, its reliance upon previous decisions, and much that resembles Exodus and Deuteronomy, make it probable that older material is incorporated. This may explain strange tabus in 19:19, 26-28, 31. Other survivals of early points of view include the equating of moral with ritual precepts, and chance uncleanness or bodily defects with moral crimes.[13]

Humanity, philanthropy, loyalty to fellow-members of the theocracy, and love for God, all informed with a clear perception of divine holiness, suggest high motivation. The leaving of the corners of the field unharvested, a few bunches of grapes upon the vine, resembles a primitive superstition found all over the world (appeasement, or payment, made to the genii of the soil): here (19:9-10) the custom enshrines the right of the poor and the landless stranger to a share in the community's good fortune. Ill-treatment of the afflicted, the blind, the deaf, will be avenged by God; ritual prostitution is strictly forbidden; reverence for elders is reverence toward God. Commercial honesty is especially stressed, and dishonesty is seen to be wider than mere stealing; swearing falsely in business is blasphemy, while all measures of length or quantity shall be accurate and just, as before God. Wages must be promptly paid.

This demand for honest dealing extends protection also to the resident alien, and the whole Code reaches its high point in the command, "The stranger who sojourns with you shall be to you as the native among you, and you shall love him as yourself; for you were strangers in the land of Egypt: I am the Lord your God" (19:34). That the alien in Israel is assumed to worship Yahweh (17:8) scarcely dims the breadth and generosity here shown. Where in the Book of the Covenant (Exodus 22:21, 23:9) it was required *not to harm* the stranger, now something nearer to sympathy and love are explicitly enjoined. And the measure of that love is elaborated (19:17f): "You shall not hate your brother in your heart, but you shall reason with your neighbour, lest you bear sin because of him. You shall not take vengeance or bear any grudge against the sons of your own people, but you shall love your neighbour as yourself: I am the Lord." Add the words of 34 "the stranger who sojourns with you shall be to you as the native among you" and we stand plainly in sight of the Christian law.

So cursory a review cannot pretend to do justice to the depth, or to the breadth, of Israel's ethical maturing, but it leaves no question of Christianity's debt to lawgiver, priest and prophet who were schoolmasters unto Christ.

2

Legacies of Later Judaism

TO ISOLATE PURELY ETHICAL developments amidst what
has been called the extraordinary complexity of Jewish religion in the post-exilic period is to risk serious distortion, since
changes at all levels are closely inter-related. The varying political
fortunes of Judah, her manifold reactions to the changing cultural
scene, her internal divisiveness, and her immense fertility of
thought, literature, and faith, all contribute to that ferment of
ideas, sects and institutions which meets us in the opening pages
of the New Testament. Among major ethical trends, attention
must be given to the profound piety reflected in the psalms, to the
moral teaching of the influential Wisdom school, to the extension
of moral perspectives arising with increasing hope of an after-life,
and to the emergence of the priestly Torah, while just before the
Christian era dawned, important ascetic and eschatological
developments in "unorthodox" Judaism help also to fashion the
climate in which the Christian ethic came to birth.

(1) THE PIETY OF THE PSALTER

The psalms fully reflect the complexity of the period, covering
as they do a thousand years of reflection and worship, from David
to the Maccabean age, and every mood of the human soul. A. B.
D. Alexander rightly reminds that poetry is not systematic, and it
is not safe to deduce particular moral principles from passages
that glow with intensity of feeling; nevertheless a nation's character is revealed in its songs, and underlying all true poetry there is a
philosophy of life.[1] The fundamental faith of the Psalmists is
(mainly) that of the prophets before them: the nation's past history is interpreted in covenantal and redemptive terms; God is
faithful and righteous in all His ways, and His righteous triumph
at the end of history is the Psalmists' hope of vindication and
reward. Deep delight in knowing and doing the law of God
inspires Psalms 1 and 119. The divine requirement is not sacrifice,
simply, but obedience; Oesterley remarks that while many Psalms

assume the sacrificial cultus, there is also the deeper insight that looks beyond it, and a few Psalms repudiate it.[2] The joy of God's presence is everywhere celebrated as the highest good or longed for as the only relief from the burden of distress or sin. The strong and steadfast "love" *(hesed)* of God is full, illimitable, enduring for ever (86:15, 103:8, 11, 136: passim, 145:8, 9): "better than life is Thy love" (63:3). The Psalter as a whole sets beside the God of righteousness, law, and judgement, the God of grace, faithfulness, and love.

Thus fellowship with God illumines every aspect of experience in the Psalms, but the ethical conditions for being Yahweh's "guest" are stringent. They are set out clearly in Psalm 24:3-6, and Psalm 15 (cf 51:6, 66:18, 118:20, 141:2-4 etc.), those in Psalm 24 gaining added significance from the tradition that this Psalm was appointed for use as the Jew returned after Sabbath worship to market, workshop, and fields for another week's work. If he wished next Sabbath to ascend again the hill of the Lord and stand in the Holy Place, he must throughout the week maintain clean hands and a pure heart, not lifting his soul in worship of vain things (possibly in business compromise with idolatry, or perhaps in worship of wealth), but keeping scrupulously his sworn bargains and dealing in truth with all men. The close relation of worship and social righteousness is as clear here as in Amos.

Psalm 15 is almost a commentary on the earlier codes. In liturgical form, enquiry is addressed to Yahweh concerning fitness to enter the sanctuary. The answer describes those acceptable: they possess personal integrity – walking uprightly, working righteousness, speaking truth, and avoiding slander; and they are essentially good neighbours – they do no harm to their neighbours, speak no ill of them, honour the God-fearing and oppose the reprobate among them, and keep their word to their neighbours though suffering thereby. Growing awareness of the special temptations that beset an increasingly commercialised society may inspire the two added provisions: "he seeks no usury, he accepts no bribe." This again is moral religion in plain terms. Such a man will be accepted, his life established, his soul secure – "He shall never be moved" – because his life is right.

On the other hand, consideration of the precise nature of sin, and the distinction between righteous man and sinner, is in the Psalter complicated by uncertainties affecting individual, congregational, or national confessions and protestations. When the Psalmist voices his conviction of innocence, righteousness, guiltlessness, he is sometimes asserting simply his membership of the chosen people; sometimes, his inner health and sincerity of devotion to Yahweh; and sometimes his innocence of any outward act of sin. Sin, likewise, was sometimes an inner quality of weakness, dullness, crookedness; often, again, some reprehensible act or behaviour; and sometimes a state of being out of favour before God. Of the cause of that loss of favour the "sinner" may be ignorant (19:12, 69:4d–6); it may lie in unconscious violation of a ritual tabu, or be due to the curse of an enemy. But the effect is obvious – made visible in illness, distress, calamity, since a just God could not punish without good cause (see 51:4).[3]

The Psalms also reveal, however, much deeper conceptions of sin, as an inward defilement, an evil quality of imagination and desire (51:6, 10); as innate from birth (51:5); as impossible to hide from God (69:5), but banishing from God's presence (51:11). Only God can purge or forgive sin (51:7, 4), since it is directed against God (51:4). So none can stand before God or be justified in His sight (130:3, 143:2) unless God shows His matchless favour and measureless mercy (103:8 – 12). Such cleansing and acceptance require however a deep and true repentance (51:16, 17). Psalm 51 endorses all that the most perceptive of the prophets could say about the inwardness of sin and penitence, the need of regeneration, the contrast of man's sin and God's holiness, the moralisation of the idea of sacrifice and of the Levitical lustrations (16f, 7). This is precisely such a confession as Jeremiah might have composed for David: repentance is wholly moral, the appeal is to mercy and not to merit, the new rule of a better life must be written on the inner heart. If in all this sin is described subjectively, from its inward attitude, disposition, and cost, rather than in its objective, concrete, social expression as evil actions and wrongful behaviour, doubtless that is to be expected in devotional songs, in contrast with the social protest of prophetic poetry.

The moral world of the Psalmists, generally, was one of jarring conflict and open enmity between two opposing parties set in constant moral antagonism. The "good, righteous, upright, perfect, holy" ones – not as claiming moral perfection, for they often confess their sin and plead for mercy, but as protesting their honesty of purpose and sincerity of devotion – are on the side of the Lord who loveth righteousness, His beloved, and faithful, people. Yet they are also the meek of the earth, the weak, broken in heart sometimes, who go mourning because of oppression; grief consumes them; they have no rest, and pine away. Opposed at all points are the "wicked, sinners, foolish, proud, stiffnecked, scornful, boasters" who are rich, strong, ruthless, holding reins of power in the world, never in trouble as other men, who plot against the just, slandering the innocent and perverting justice. In this unending opposition of good and evil, the godly must keep ever watchful, trusting in God for strength to resist, and for refuge when the conflict grows too fierce.[4]

Clear identification of these hostile parties is difficult. Beside the familiar usage of such language, as describing the persecution of the righteous by the wicked in envy and self-justification, and to portray the cost of innocence in a sinful world, a secondary and derived usage emerges. Oesterley argues that in considering this opposition of good and evil something must be allowed for the bitter strife of later years between the "Hasidim" (the saints), loyal to Yahweh and the law, and the "Resaim" (wicked ones), who betray the inherited ideals; and for the resulting rift within society and nation, thus polarised into two sects, two policies, of resistance and compromise – the backsliding majority and the faithful remnant.[5] Mowinckel thinks that this second usage of the language of conflict may be valid for the understanding of some Psalms, as 1, 37, 73, and some others; but that yet a third usage applies the terms to national antagonism between Israel, the righteous nation, the people of Yahweh, in right relation with Him and within His Covenant, and the successive pagan powers who ruled her (for example, in Psalms 125, 58, 82; cf 28:3 etc.) In these instances, the conflict described was mainly political, though maintained for deeply moral and religious reasons.[6]

On either interpretation of particular Psalms, however, the notion of a spiritual warfare is clearly present, and with it is introduced a sect-type morality, the contention of the few godly against the surrounding evil world, and the acceptance of the lonely and costly loyalty to principle, faith, and conscience, which the good life may demand in a perverse generation. *That is a new ethical concept,* and it is handed on directly by the Psalter to become a prominent element in Christian moral experience.

In a few Psalms there are less admirable features, which Christianity necessarily left behind; but we may readily agree with Alexander that "men who could give utterance to a faith so clear, to a penitence so deep, to longings so lofty and spiritual as these Psalms contain, are not the least among the heralds of the kingdom of Christ."[7]

(2) MORAL WISDOM

The Wisdom School represents in Judaism the "humanism" that turns from temple and tradition to seek a way of life and thought which shall preserve ethical values while professing agnosticism, or something very like deism, on religious matters. Some borrowing of language and ideas from foreign intellectual circles is evident in the wisdom literature (Job, Proverbs, some Psalms, Ecclesiastes, the Wisdom of Solomon, Sirach, and a few less-known books), together with wide education, acute observation, and considerable reflection. The comparative lack of priestly and prophetic requirements, the absence of the usual religious terminology, the determination to bring down ethical vision from the peak to the plain, and out from the shrine to the market-place, prompt the comparison with humanism; but wisdom remains a gift of the Lord, its first lesson is reverence for the God seen in the world about us (Psalm 111), and the fear of the Lord is the fount of wisdom. Characteristic terms of this school are discipline, prudence, discretion, learning, practical wisdom: but these are qualities to be exercised in a world that is God's, and under His rule. Both the thought, and the literature, of this very influential group of teachers helped to shape the ethical message of the New Testament.

The wise master instructs his pupil ("my son") in the art of living. The counsel given may be mere prudence –

If a mighty man invite thee, be retiring,
And so much the more will he invite thee.

(Sirach 13:9)

or plain social morality –

Remove not the ancient landmark,
  which thy fathers have set.

(Proverbs 22:28)

or social morality sanctioned by religion –

Remove not the ancient landmark
Nor enter into the fields of the fatherless
For their redeemer is strong
He shall plead their cause against thee

(Proverbs 23:10, 11)

or plain religious warning –

Every way of a man is right in his own eyes,
But the weigher of hearts is Yahweh.

(Proverbs 21:2)

This is the ethic of pious commonsense, more practical, realist, and shrewd, than lofty; more prudent than devout; but yet not bare utilitarianism, for there is a finer strain in (for example) Job's disinterested loyalty to God. "The idea of the Hebrew sage," it has been said, "is that he who lives with reverent acknowledgement of God as lawgiver will have within his soul a permanent and efficient moral guide."[8] The spirit of man is the candle of the Lord, and the enlightened conscience is the voice of the Most High. Wisdom is at one with prophecy in holding obedience and sincerity above ceremonial, and in seeing in morality and social righteousness a man's essential duty to his God.

Proverbs preserves in neat aphorisms a practical and earthy wisdom, sensible counsel in forcible language, expressing generally a high moral tone without religious depth. Virtue is good because it is safe, and brings reward: a sane, if unenthusiastic, reverence for Yahweh is the foundation – and the height – of sensible living. Hatred and calumny are ill-advised; self-discipline and moderation are the best policy; temptation is a danger to be foreseen and avoided. The fruit of such careful planning of life will be material security, the sign of continuing favour with Yahweh.

> If your enemy is hungry, give him bread to eat;
> and if he is thirsty, give him water to drink;
> for you will heap coals of fire on his head,
> and the Lord will reward you
>
> (Proverbs 25:21, 22)

is noble advice offered for sardonic prudential reasons – though Paul can repeat it in a Christian epistle!

Ecclesiasticus, ascribed to ben Sirach and dated around 180 BC, is "a digest of lectures" seeking to impart the wisdom of the ancients that pupils might live "according to the law." "His advice ranges from points of etiquette to the life of communion with God ... behaviour at table, bringing up children, self-control, helping the poor, greed, the worship of mammon, true piety and much more besides."[9] This is "wisdom", the guidance for life of the Most High, the Almighty, acknowledged in almost deistic fashion; the fear of the Lord is here a discipline that prolongs one's days. Probably the best known passage is 44:1 to 50:24, in praise of famous men, where the grounds for praise are ethically significant – wisdom, counsel, leadership, art, mercy, and righteous deeds. There follows a biographical history of Israel, in which the good and wise are seen as vital to the ongoing life of society and the onward-moving purpose of God.

Ecclesiastes "has lost the vitality of belief in a personal God ... and takes its stand on a somewhat colourless monotheism."[10] The Preacher believes in the Deity but cannot understand Him (8:17, 3:11). God's work – the course of nature – appears in the form of an endless cycle, events and phenomena being brought upon the stage of life and banished, recalled and banished again (1:4-11, 3:15). All effort is thus paralysed, since no amount of labour can produce anything new or alter the chain of facts (1:15, 3:1-9, 14, 7:13): everything is futile, and fret of spirit (1:2, 2:17 and passim). What is ethically significant about this mixture of deism and determinism is the persistence of prophetic principles in a very different religious climate. Reverence and realism keep the Preacher's feet firmly upon the ground; he returns again and again to what is for him the only sane expectation, to enjoy life's good things in moderation, and to find satisfaction in one's work (2:24, 3:13, 22, 5:18 etc., 7:15). Yet, illogically, he assesses things in terms of good and evil, the righteous and the sinner, love and hate; it is worth while to be generous (11:1f); he rages like a prophet against injustice and oppression (3:16f, 4:1f) and is certain that the highest Authority will work retribution (5:8f). Moral evil is powerful (9:17) and widespread – there is none wholly righteous (7:20, 9:3), yet the Preacher is certain of final judgement upon it:

Though a sinner does evil a hundred times and prolongs his life, yet I know that it will be well with those who fear God, because they fear before him; but it will not be well with the wicked, neither will he prolong his days like a shadow, because he does not fear before God (8:12f).

Significant, too, in this so-called utilitarian literature, is the Preacher's conviction that material goods bring no lasting satisfaction (5:10, 6:1f, 7:1f). This realisation is an advance on parts of Proverbs, and together with the fundamentally illogical moral earnestness it testifies to the Preacher's deepest truth, that God has put eternity into man's mind (3:11).

The end of the matter; all has been heard. Fear God, and keep his commandments; for this is the whole duty of man. For God will bring every deed into judgement, with every secret thing, whether good or evil (12:13f).

The universe is moral, after all! In the *Wisdom of Solomon,* a mainly theoretic work, this persistent moralism rises to the point of representing righteousness as the way to wisdom.

Job, one of the great books of the world, finally broke with the utilitarian conception of a piety that pays, though some think that the book's present epilogue misses this point and so spoils the whole argument. The poet's intention is to contradict the jibe of the Satan, that Job serves God only for what he gets out of it, and to demonstrate the intrinsic value of godliness. Until his friends began to comfort him, the loss of everything was no problem to Job; the final vision of God silenced their contentions and his own questionings, more than satisfied the sufferer's heart. The Preacher had not understood God, and it brought him near to pessimism; Job does not understand God either, but it leads him to faith – "Though he slay me, yet will I trust him." To live rightly, in innocence and good-neighbourliness, is to be sure in the end of divine vindication, whatever the pain meanwhile: the good man knows that God is good – that is enough.

The great chapter 31 in which this truth is asserted is acclaimed for its nobility, its delicacy of feeling, its searching inwardness and demanding idealism. Oesterley-Robinson comment, "This is, many will feel, the highest point reached by the practical ethics of the Old Testament, in its justice, purity, and humanity transcending anything that we find in the law."[11] H. H. Rowley quotes with approval R. H. Strahan for the view that the picture Job presents is "extraordinarily like that of the citizen of God's kingdom, as etched by Christ in the sermon on the mount" adding that "He goes behind act to thought, and beneath conduct to the heart."[12]

Verses 1-4 affirm a personal purity in which the ever-present temptation of the owner of female slaves is restrained by the knowledge that nothing is hid from God, who rewards unrighteousness with calamity – whereas Job hopes for God's favour.

Verses 5-8 affirm a personal rectitude that despises deceit and every departure from straight dealing at the behest of covetousness (7b). Honesty must be meticulous: "If any spot" of evil (? or, of anything that is not my own) "has stuck to my hands" – then Job asks that his own trade and labour shall be profitless, and he himself be weighed in the faultless balances of God (cf Amos 7:4f). Commercial morality is part of Old Testament ethics from the Decalogue onwards.

Verses 38-40 (probably misplaced) affirm a yet deeper honesty of ownership: the unwillingness to benefit from land held by deceit (39a – the removal of landmarks, for example), or by robbery and murder (39b, cf Genesis 4:10 (Abel), 1 Kings 21 (Naboth)). The punishment is expected to fit the crime.

Verses 9-12 eschew adultery, invoking the sharpest retribution in kind, by the degradation of his own wife to slavery and rape. The heinousness of adultery, and its consuming ruin, even to Sheol, are graphically asserted: no reason is given – for this writer, none is required.

Verses 13-15(18) turn to social relationships, first to that between master and slave: the humanitarianism of the older codes here rises to the astonishing admission that master and servant are alike creatures of one God, and stand equal before Him (15). Since slaves are persons, not chattels, the master answers for them to God (14). (If 18 should follow 15, the slave is brother, also).

Verses 16-23 similarly intensifies the older humaneness towards the poor, the widowed, the fatherless, the naked. Job prays that any callousness he has shown towards them, any aloofness and withdrawal (17), any oppression of them (obtaining verdicts against the weak through his rich friends among the judges at the gate, 21) may again be punished in kind – the offending limb that struck in anger, or voted against the innocent, dropping from its socket. As in Deuteronomy, the sanction most feared is God's own vindication of the oppressed.

Verses 24-34 assert purity of heart in four distinct directions, pride, paganism, vindictiveness, hypocrisy. *24-25* reprobates the wealthy man's temptation to complacent confidence in his riches; *26-27* repudiates any secret worship of the sun, or throwing kisses to the moon, both capital offences as ungrateful treachery towards God; *29-34* breathes a spirit in attractive contrast with much in the Old Testament (even in the Psalter) of vengefulness and imprecation. Job asserts his innocence of secret spite, of finding joy in the downfall of his enemies, of privately cursing those who oppose him, or of any want of hospitality to friend or stranger, of any hypocrisy or craven fear of what men might say against him ... and the sense of how precious was his own integrity makes him break off his protestations to appeal for a plain, fair hearing in the court of God.

Here indeed is the ideal of the Wisdom School, "the crown of all the ethical development of the Old Testament" (Duhm). It demands nothing of ritual, festival, 'Sabbath-keeping, or sacrifices. It is very conscious of the danger of self-deception; it has a fine sense of justice, and an appeal to impartial judgement; it approaches very near to love in social relationships; it reveals a deep inwardness in understanding the defilement of lust, the heart's idolatries, mere pride of possession, the intrinsic depravity of adultery, callousness, disloyalty; while behind all is a reverence for God, a fear of His disapproval, and the unquestioned assumption that a clear conscience is essential to divine favour. Such a portrait is no mean forerunner of the Christian disciple.

Hebrew moral wisdom has looked on life with shrewdness and candour. It has discerned certain underlying principles of soberness, honesty, thrift, industry, and respect for authority, which make for social stability and happiness. It has learned that the long view is ever the true view; that the outcome of things, not immediate gratification, is the measure of their worth. It has discovered that much of the secret of life's success and joy lies in right relationships – brawling, rancour, hatred, spite, bad companionship, are sheer folly. And it has realised, while remaining aloof from the cultus, that life is always "under God", lived in His sight, subject at last to His judgement. The ungodly are therefore fools, whether simply ignorant, obstinately stupid, or arrogantly scornful. The ethics of Wisdom may not be the highest man may reach, but in an age when religion is dead and formal, it is a serviceable substitute for more passionate conviction and ardour.

(3) THE LENGTHENED PERSPECTIVE

The emergence of the hope of immortality affected ethical thought in several ways. Magnifying the importance of the individual soul, it added to the individualism that had arisen with Jeremiah and Ezekiel an urgent concern about one's own eternal fate. Since a timeless destiny now depended upon character, all moral decisions became supremely important. The new perspective also spiritualised, and greatly extended, concepts of reward and punishment, and transferred the divine vindication of right and judgement of wrong from this world, and material affairs, to spiritual consequences in the next. It is significant, too, that it was precisely the ethical demand for a just outcome of human striving, a fair compensation for undeserved suffering, that prompted the leap of faith towards immortality. Without another life, the present is morally unintelligible.

T. H. Robinson says that the truer conception of immortality as communion with God seems to have arisen through the slow development of belief in the *righteousness* of Yahweh.[13] Oesterley-Robinson think that Job (in 19:25f) already makes this "leap of faith: there must be still, beyond the grave, the possibility that God will see true justice done, and Job himself will know it".[14] Wheeler Robinson thinks that this solution of the problem of suffering is not found in the Old Testament;[15] D. S. Russell thinks the passage at best a glimmering of hope,[16] H. H. Rowley thinks that though here "there is no full grasping of a belief in a worth-while Afterlife with God, this passage is a notable landmark in the progress toward such a belief" – Job being assured that his Vindicator will arise, meaning probably God, and probably after Job's death, though how Job will be aware of vindication is obscure.[17]

Ezekiel 37 and Isaiah 26:19 use the idea of human resurrection as an intelligible literary figure, but offer no reason for the hope; Daniel 12:2 shows a clearer conception of the resurrection of good and bad. In 164 BC 1 Enoch opposes the Sadducean view that there is no difference between the lot of the righteous and the lot of the wicked after death (102:6-8, 11); all goodness, joy and glory are prepared for the souls of the righteous (102:3); they shall live and rejoice, and their spirits shall not perish (103:4). The Book of Jubilees (150 BC) says the righteous pass at once into the blessedness of immortality: "Their bones shall rest in the earth and their spirits shall have much joy" (23:31).[18] In the first century BC the Wisdom of Solomon (3:1-9) argues that another world will put right the wrongs of this, and full retribution will vindicate the ways of God; and 2 Maccabees 7 assumes the rewarding resurrection of the martyrs.

All this is clear ethical advance upon the older Hebrew doctrine of Sheol, the changeless torpor of the Shades beyond God's jurisdiction (Psalms 30:9f, 115:17), beyond return (2 Samuel 12:23, Job 7:9), without thought, wisdom, knowledge, or reward (Ecclesiastes 9:2, 5, 10), where "one fate comes to all, to the righteous and the wicked" (Ecclesiastes 9:2).

Thus in writings of the inter-testamental period, "the blessing of the righteous and the punishment of the wicked, based on moral judgements, are fully accomplished at the time of the Final Judgement, but even beforehand in Sheol there is a preliminary distribution of awards ... In 1 Enoch 22, for example, three compartments are visualised in Sheol, graded according to moral judgements already evident in the souls of the departed."[19] According to the Testament of Abraham (11, also 2nd century BC): "This narrow gate is that of the just, which leads into life, and these that enter through it enter into Paradise. For the broad gate is that of sinners, which leads to destruction and ever-lasting punishment" – a picture plainly recalled in Matthew 7:13, 14. Some cleansing of souls in Sheol, some moral improvement through the prayers of the righteous, is contemplated in a few passages (e.g. 2 Maccabees 12:39-45, circa 1st century BC), but generally "Sheol becomes a place of petrified moralities and suspended graces".[20] By 1st century AD, 2 Baruch can say, "There shall not be there again ... change of ways nor place for prayer nor sending of petitions nor receiving of knowledge nor giving of love nor place for repentance for the soul nor supplication for offences nor intercession of the fathers nor prayer of the prophets nor help of the righteous" (85:12). With this relentlessness goes an intensification of individual moral responsibility that explicitly refuses intercession of fathers for children, brothers for brothers, friends for their dearest, on the day of judgement. In this way the whole arena of the ethical life is enlarged and prolonged beyond anything that the Decalogue, the Book of the Covenant, or Deuteronomy envisaged.

(4) THE DEVELOPMENT OF LEGALISM

Equally far-reaching in its effect upon ethical thought was the development of the sacred Torah, expressing the whole duty of man in minute regulations of many kinds; the emergence of a sect of devoted religious enthusiasts to promote it, the Hasidim, from among whom arose the later Pharisees; the creation of an equally devoted, highly trained professional class to expound it – the scribes; and the establishment of synagogue-type worship to propagate it. The written law was completed about 400 BC; by 200 BC the oral law also was being defended as deriving from Moses. The law is the light that lighteth every man, according to the Testaments of the Twelve Patriarchs; the study of the law is the doctrine of life (Psalm 1, and Sirach); Abraham was said to have kept the whole law by anticipation. All else was subordinated to Torah: Wisdom was interpreted as the fulfilling of the law (Sirach 19:20); prophecy became subject to law (see Zechariah 13:3); prophecy and hagiography would cease because there is nothing in them not already suggested in the law – whereas the law would exist for ever. Even the Messianic expectation assumed that Israel's title to the kingdom was punctilious observance of the law: "If Israel only kept one Sabbath according to the Commandment, Messiah would immediately come."[21]

Thus completely did the law dominate later Judaism, which became absorbed with fulfilment of imposed terms and adherence to prescribed conditions of blessing. All rests on the individual's obedience to his God in detailed and specific ways. The ethical, now narrowed and formalised, dominates: the intimacy and joy of fellowship with God are largely lost in the obligation of unflinching obedience. Earlier, indeed, the law had been delight and sustenance (Psalm 19:7-11, Psalm 119), while in Deuteronomy and Ezekiel law and prophecy had co-operated. But exilic stress on the need for self-preserving Jewish distinctness led to new emphasis upon Sabbath, circumcision, festivals, and separateness. Meanwhile, priests unable to devote their energies to the cultus developed the elaborate "priestly" code of multifarious regulations and an elaborate casuistry. Already in Nehemiah, Ezra, Malachi, and Tobit the growing legalism may be seen; in Isaiah 56-66 self-righteousness, and a doctrine of merit, begin to contaminate the gracious gospel which "Deutero-Isaiah" had proclaimed. Sirach defends the oral tradition of interpretation growing up around the law (45:5, 8:9) and can speak of almsgiving as atoning for sin (3:30). Tobit, too, says that even a little almsgiving lays up treasure and delivers from death, and shall purge away all sin (4:8-10, 12:9).

D. S. Russell finds the religious outlook of the Jews summarised in Baruch 4:1: "This is the book of the commandments of God, and the law that endureth for ever. All they that hold it fast are destined for life, but such as leave it shall die."[22] The stubborn Maccabean uprising opposed all compromise with Hellenism, seeking to rescue the law by force out of the hands of the gentiles. From this movement came the inner strength of Pharisaism, determined to apply the law to every detail of daily life and "building a hedge about the law", consisting of still more severe restrictions and demands, to keep men safely within the bounds of obedience.

The standard set by Judaism was high. Against sexual aberrations and infanticide the law was stern; if less so on divorce, it was yet more austere than among surrounding peoples. Justice, pity, kindness, almsgiving, prayer and fasting were enjoined; the sharp need to overcome the innate "evil impulse" was clearly recognised – to that extent, even legalism retained something of prophetic inwardness. Undoubtedly, the law nourished in many people a true piety, and a service of others reminiscent of the spirit of the prophets. Definite precepts demand care of the sick, of widows and orphans, of the helpless; small means must not inhibit generosity. The Testaments of the Twelve Patriarchs give prominence to love for God, and for the neighbour; to forgiveness, purity of heart, and right intention: "Love ye one another from the heart; and if a man sin against thee, speak peaceably to him, and in thy soul hold it not guile: and if he repent and confess, forgive him." Again, "I loved the Lord, likewise every man with all my heart" (Testament of Gad 6:3, of Issachar 7:6). Christ may well have read this work, according to Hastings Rashdall[23] who comments that while there is much in Rabbinic teaching which is fine, there is much also that is poor; Christ shows His superior insight in sifting this teaching as well as in transcending it.

Not only was the standard generally high, it must be remembered, too, as D. S. Russell well says, that to its devotees "the Torah was much more than a survival from the glorious past, with only an archaic value; it was a living oracle, through which the word of God could come to generation after generation. Its word was not static but dynamic, capable of fresh interpretations for each succeeding age and capable of renewed application to every aspect of human life."[24] This conception was confirmed by increasing emphasis on the oral Torah, giving a contemporary relevance and elasticity to what otherwise must soon have been outgrown.

Reverence for Torah preserved Judaism from destructive compromise during centuries of foreign domination. It changed Judaism into a book-religion, and crystallised the prophetic inspiration into the moralism of Rabbinic scholarship. It prepared for the future by gradually replacing temple and priest by synagogue and scribe. Variations in interpreting the law, as those dividing the great Rabbinic leaders Hillel the tolerant and Shammai the strict, between whom Jesus was sometimes invited to adjudicate, did not affect the strong basic loyalty to written and oral law, as a means of perpetual revelation and a way of life, which underlay the intense devotion of Judaism to the will of God. This, again, helped to form the matrix within which Christian ethical attitudes were inevitably moulded, whether by acceptance or reaction.

(5) SECTS ZEALOUS FOR THE LAW

Nevertheless, those variant interpretations of Torah intensified the deep divisions generated by political oppression, pagan influences, and spiritual ferment, and produced ardent and tenacious pressure-groups, each contending for its own truth and policy. With the political compromise of the Sadducean group, the political resistance of the Zealots, we are not concerned. The sect of *Pharisees,* on the other hand, represents the orthodox Jewish foil to the whole teaching and aim of Jesus, and their ideals and interpretations confront us constantly in the unfolding of Christ's ethical meaning. Stemming (as we saw) from the resistance to encroaching heathen culture which focused in the Maccabean rising, and inheriting the outlook of the heroic Hasidim, the Pharisees grew in influence from the middle of the second century BC to become the effective religious leaders and teachers of the common people. They applied the written Torah, illumined and extended by the equally authoritative oral law, to everyday affairs in a system of education, counsel, and casuistry, for which synagogue-worship and school was the powerful vehicle. Despite the faults to which a legalist ethic is ever prone, Pharisaism nourished a profound piety, great strength of character, a sense of personal moral responsibility, and an evangelising zeal, which contributed much not only to the character of Christian leaders like Paul, but to Christian ethical thinking generally.

From the same historic background and tradition emerged also the *Essenes,* members of a movement comprising both a

monastic-type village settlement near the Dead Sea, and others –
perhaps "associates" – who retained their homes and livelihood
among the populace. The Essenes' devotion to Torah was yet
more strict than that of the Pharisees. Sympathy towards Hellenism shown by the aristocratic priesthood prejudiced the Essenes
against temple and cultus, and on the assumption of the high
priesthood by the Hasmoneans, prejudice hardened into outright
opposition. This, together with their dominant purpose of complete separation from all that defiled, pushed the Essenes by the
end of the first century BC into isolation and asceticism.

The stricter Essenes appear to have abjured private property,
and marriage (to secure entire attention to Torah); the Law of
Holiness was minutely observed – the mere touch even of a
lower-ranking Essene was defiling – and the name of Moses was
held next in honour to that of God. According to Philo, the
Essenes preferred agricultural to urban life, abhorred slavery, and
cared for the sick. "They exhibit a variety of virtues, summed up
by love of God, love of virtue, and love of man, and among other
observances they avoid oaths, and display an inexpressible friendship for each other ... They open their houses to others, have
common meals, and share the products of their toil" (R. P. Hanson[25]). Writing of somewhat later Essenes, Josephus says that
they forbade marriage but bring up others' children of tender age.
He adds that they "practise mutual love more than others", a
tribute confirmed by Philo: "their sect does not exist on the basis
of race, but is motivated by zeal for virtue and a passion for the
love of men".[26] Simplicity of clothing, avoidance of trade with
each other, intense study of the sacred literature, often in group
discussion, and a high value placed upon silence, also marked
their life.

Whether the monastic community which lived for a century and
a half, up to about AD 68, at Qumran on the northwest shores of
the Dead Sea are to be identified with the Essenes, or regarded as
only a closely related group, is still undecided.

D. S. Russell[27] thinks that the coincidence of site, customs, rites, and
beliefs, points to their being a branch of the Essenes. G. Vermes[28] claims
that most scholars think them "probably identical". Raymond E.
Brown[29] says the identification of the sectaries who composed the Dead
Sea scrolls with the Essenes approaches certainty. J. H. Charlesworth,
after discussing other possibilities, says the identification is generally
accepted by almost all scholars.[30]

Like the Pharisees, the *Qumran Covenanters* defined the will of
God in ethical terms, but were more strictly ascetic, regarded
themselves as the true Israel, enforced strict rules of probation,
admission, and discipline, and practised sharing of property,
communal meals, ardent and constant study of the scriptures,

repeated ritual washings as a symbol of moral cleansing. Amid much that awaits clarification, it is evident that the Covenanters made a threefold contribution to the milieu within which Christian ethics was fashioned:

(i) An Exacting Standard

The Covenanters carried devotion to the sacred Torah even further than Pharisees did, while yet remaining independent in interpretation and avoiding much of the self-righteousness that infected Pharisaism. They led a hard, pure life. The initiate took "a binding oath" to return with all his heart "to every commandment of the law of Moses in accordance with all that has been revealed to the sons of Zadok, the Keepers of the Covenant and Seekers of His will"[31]; he then submitted to the Guardian for further instruction, preferment depending upon more training and ever stricter discipline. Transgression of the law of Moses, whether deliberate or negligent, brought immediate expulsion and ostracism, though minor offences against the discipline were punished by penance varying from ten days to two years – the latter for *inadvertent* sin against a Mosaic precept. The increased severity attached to Moses by the sect's interpretations may be seen in the tightening and extending of the "prohibited degrees" in marriage, and in the insistence upon monogamy. The interpretation, moreover, was held to be infallible, no such discussion of meanings and applications as the Pharisees delighted in being allowed. Rigorous separation from the world of the wicked, and meticulous personal holiness, with a strictly planned discipline of worship, were insisted upon. Temple worship and sacrifice being disregarded, the Community became the sanctuary; virtue and suffering were accorded sacrificial value; a holy life had expiatory power, and "perfection of way" was the remedy for sin.

The ethical qualities valued or condemned by the Covenanters are set out explicitly in a parallel description in the "Community Rule".[32] The children of righteousness walk in the ways of light, showing all humility, patience, abundant charity, goodness, understanding, wisdom which trusts in God, discernment, zeal for just laws, holy intent and steadfastness, great charity towards all the sons of truth, purity from all unclean idols, and humble conduct; they receive blessing, peace, and joy, in life without end. The ways of the spirit of falsehood include greed, slackness in the search for righteousness, wickedness, pride, lies, falseness, cruelty, ill-temper, and folly, insolence, lust, lewdness, blasphemy, blindness, recalcitrance, darkness and guile; their end is everlasting damnation.

As with all Essenes, great emphasis is laid upon love:[33]

Penalties are set out against failures in brotherly-love, unjust accusation, arrogance, unjust anger, vengeance, slander, and complaint. Love of one's neighbour is a chief duty: "all will be in true unity, in good humility, with merciful love and with righteous purposes, each one towards his neighbour ... to practise the truth in common and righteous humility, justice, and merciful love; they must correct each other in truth, humility, and merciful love ... to walk humbly each with his neighbour ... for each one to care for the wretched, the poor, and the stranger, and for each one to seek the well-being of his brother ..."

Charity, too, was firmly organised: two days' income each month was handed over for the benefit of widows, orphans, sick, and aged, within the Community.[34] The standard of personal relationship is plainly excellent, even if it be qualified somewhat by confinement to members of the sect, and by hostility toward those in darkness and untruth.

With all this emphasis upon law and moral obligation, the Covenanter never forgot that his election as a "son of light" was a gracious act of divine favour, affording no least ground for self-righteousness. A conviction of divine predestination merely deepened the wonder at God's goodness and grace which filled his heart. All moral goodness and truth, all correct observance of the Community Rule, all knowledge of God, were alike free, unmerited gifts, as the Qumran hymns frequently emphasise: "no note of self-righteousness sounds in the Qumran writings" – "By intention, they were a company of poor and humble men constantly attentive to the word of God and grateful for His favours."[35]

(ii) A Sect Morality

The contention of the few godly against the surrounding evil world, and the notion of a sect (or remnant) engaged in spiritual warfare against the pressures of the majority, which first emerged in the Psalter, is developed by the Covenanters into an institutionalised assertion of dissent. The highly organised, self-sufficient, and strictly disciplined "assemblies of the camps" had a fairly elaborate "monastic" pattern of common life and a firmly differentiated hierarchy of administration. Lesser "men of the Covenant" lived, apparently, in "assemblies of the towns", separated less rigorously from their fellow-Jews (though forbidden to give to them, or receive from them, except upon commercial terms). Nevertheless they shared the convictions, ideals, and protest, of the "men of the Council of the Community", and were sure of their calling to be the True Israel of God.

Those who ultimately became members of the Community Council practised a religious (and voluntary) communism. Lying about possessions incurred severe penalties. Whether they were also celibate is much discussed. Hanson argues (spite of skeletons of women and children at Qumran) that the Community forbade marriage; he thinks that the Damascus document, which allows it together with slave-ownership, oath-taking, property, and trade, gives an earlier picture of the Community, before discipline and rules were sharpened into those of the Manual.[36] Allegro, however, says that women and children had a recognised place in the Community, and that counsel was given concerning marriage.[37] Vermes says that several documents refer to married members and none (of those yet available) allude to celibacy. Yet the Essenes were noted for the practice, although Josephus says *some* were married. Vermes concludes that most ("the men of the Covenant") were married, but that the absence of all mention of women in the Community Rule suggests that those seeking perfection ("the men of the Council") accepted celibacy as "more appropriate".[38]

Of course, this sect-type morality has a narrow, esoteric tendency towards exclusiveness: on the other hand it cultivates strong loyalty, shelters the weak, and enriches the character of the individualist with shared ideals and endeavour. The idea of unity lay very close to the heart of the sect, "for everything shall be held in common, truth and fair humility and faithful love, and just consideration for one's fellows in the Holy Council."[39] From this it is not very far to the apostolic ideal of *koinonia,* and the Pauline insistence upon mutual edification within the one body of Christ.

(iii) A Dualistic Outlook

The emphasis laid by Covenanters upon the sharp opposition of light and darkness, truth and falsehood, and the constant reiteration of the mutually exclusive "camps" of the "sons of light ... of truth ... of Zadok" and the "sons of darkness ... of perversity ... of the Pit" leave no question that the basic thought of the Qumran literature is dualistic, as original Hebrew thought had never been.[40] Nor can there be any doubt that this pre-Christian dualism influenced profoundly both Judaism and Christianity. It is less certain how Covenanting dualism is to be understood.

Whatever its sources, the dualism of the Qumran documents is not, like that of much Greek (or gnostic) thought, or that of Persia, an absolute and unalterable division of the universe into light and darkness, good and evil, matter and spirit. Qumran's is a relative, modified, and temporary dualism. The Covenanters were convinced monotheists, believing implicitly in God's creation of all things:

"From the God of knowledge comes all that is and shall be. Before ever they existed He established their whole design, and when, as ordained for them, they come into being, it is in accord with His glorious design that they accomplish their task without change. The laws of all things are in His hand ... He has created man to govern the world and has

appointed for him two spirits in which to walk until the time of his visitation ... It is He who created the spirits of light and darkness, and
founded every action upon them ... God has ordained an end for
falsehood, and at the time of the visitation He will destroy it for ever ...
(The sons of darkness will be annihilated) until they be exterminated
without remnant" (1QS 3:17-19, 25; 4:19, and 14).[41] For God as sole,
supreme, Creator, cf 1QH 1:7f, 13f, 19f.[42]

Certainly this relative dualism was *ethical* in nature and effect:
its "most conspicuous feature" is the pattern of light-darkness,
truth-falsehood, true righteousness-perversity – which are ethical
distinctions. "Light represents life, truth, knowledge, and eternal
life" says Charlesworth,[43] "darkness tends to represent death,
falsehood, ignorance, extinction ... Light is often used inter-
changeably for righteousness, and darkness is frequently applied
alternatively for perversity." Some correspondence seems
implied between "the spirit of light and the spirit of darkness"
and the two *"yetsers"* within man – a good impulse and an evil
impulse – of which the Rabbis spoke:

"The nature of all the children of men is ruled by these (two spirits) and
during their life all the hosts of men have a portion in their divisions and
walk in (both) their ways. And the whole reward for their deeds shall be
for everlasting ages, according to whether each man's portion in their
two divisions is great or small ... Truth abhors the works of falsehood,
and falsehood hates all the ways of truth; and their struggle is fierce
..." (1QS 4:15f).[44]

This suggests each person is engaged in a struggle between good
and evil and will be judged eventually a "son of light" or "of
darkness" according to the degree in which one or the other
triumphs within him. Similarly, the descriptions already noted in
1QS 4:2-11 of the virtuous ways of the children of righteousness
and the vicious ways of the children of perversity, clearly characterise the Qumran dualism in ethical terms.

Yet this is not its whole meaning, for behind the ethical struggle
within man lies a cosmic struggle between superhuman forces:

"(The God of knowledge) has created man to govern the world and has
appointed him two spirits in which to walk until the time of his visitation,
the spirits of truth and falsehood. Those born of truth spring from a
fountain of light, but those born of falsehood spring from a source of
darkness. All the children of righteousness are ruled by the Prince of
Light and walk in the ways of light, but all the children of falsehood are
ruled by the Angel of Darkness and walk in the ways of darkness. The
Angel of Darkness leads all the children of righteousness astray, and
until his end, all their sin, iniquities, wickedness, and all their unlawful
deeds are caused by his dominion, in accordance with the mysteries of
God. Every one of their chastisements, and every one of the seasons of
their distress, shall be brought about by the rule of his persecution; for
all his allotted spirits seek the overthrow of the sons of light. But the

God of Israel and His Angel of Truth will succour all the sons of light. For He it is who created the spirits of Light and Darkness ..." (1QS 3:18f).[45]

This goes beyond psychological or ethical dualism to find the ultimate origin of the conflict between good and evil in the way that God "in accordance with His mysteries" has created all things and has "established the whole design". The Angel or Prince of Light, the spirit of Truth, and the Angel of Darkness, the spirit of perversity (later, in 1QM 13:9-11 for example, called Belial) are not *only* within man but rule man, have "dominion", and succour or persecute man. Charlesworth concludes "The consensus of scholarly opinion has been that 1QS 3:13 – 4:26 reveals a cosmic dualism between two warring spirits who are locked in titanic warfare ... The world is ripped into two realms by two warring cosmic spirits".[46] But this is only "in God's design", and "until his time, the time of visitation"; and it is not, moreover, unrelated to the struggle within each man. Charlesworth quotes approvingly U Simon – "The struggle in the heart of man is inseparable from the cosmic array of powers".[47]

The ultimate origin of evil is not, strictly, an ethical question, though where ethics and theology are closely inter-related, it is not wholly irrelevant. The Covenanters' explanation, that all evil is due to the evil spirit of darkness, falsehood, perversity, is only one of several current in later Judaism. In 1 Enoch 6:1f, 7:1f, Jubilees 5:1f, evil is due to the fallen angels' corruption of their freedom; in Apocalypse of Abraham 26, sin originated with Adam's rejection of God's will; in the Mishnah, evil is caused by the evil inclination in man *(yetser ha'ra)* which man fails to overcome; in 4 Ezra 4:4-11, evil is simply inexplicable. The Qumran view also leaves evil ultimately a mystery – "in accordance with the mysteries of God" occurs more than once after the statement that God created the Angel of Darkness.

In a document designed to regulate the life of the Community, the ethical aspect of this dualism naturally predominates, although the human struggle for truth and virtue is only part of the "cosmic warfare ordained by the Creator and finally resolved not by men but God" (J. L. Price).[48] The purification of the "sons of light" was not yet complete: they must be alert to the seductions of the spirit of evil; only by active obedience to Torah as interpreted in the Community would those who believed themselves to be, by God's favour, "sons of light" be sanctified and made secure. In the end, in a visitation of God, men will be judged according to their obedience to the divine will, and the triumph of the spirit of light and truth within them.

The Covenanters' interpretation of the ethical situation is plainly far removed from that of the lawgivers and prophets of Israel, and very near indeed to that of the first Christian leaders.

For them, too, "we wrestle not against flesh and blood, but against spiritual wickedness in high places ... the spirit now ruling in the children of disobedience ... the prince of this world ... knowing that we must test the spirits, but confident that greater is He that is in us than he that is in the world" (cf Ephesians 6:12f, 2:2, John 14:30, 1 John 4:1, 4). The ethical conflict is seen as a local battle in a cosmic warfare, by some of the New Testament writers no less clearly than by the writers of the Scrolls: and an immeasurable dimension, and solemnity, is added to all moral issues and loyalties in consequence.

(6) THE RE-AWAKENING OF PROPHECY

It is evident that in the years before the birth of Christ a widespread, non-conformist, even "puritan" movement was on foot in Jewry, forming together with the more orthodox Pharisees and the temple establishment the confused religious background for yet another new development – the sounding again in Israel, after centuries of silence, of the voice of pure prophecy. The precise relation of John the Baptist to the wider separatist and radical movement is not clear. The Essenes, for example, sufficiently resemble John to raise the question whether he had belonged to their number; the place of his ministry, and the manner of his baptism, form links with the Qumran Covenanters. John shared, too, Qumran's rejection of the official establishment and cultus – at least as providing any sufficient preparation for Messiah; he shared their moral austerity, and their conception of a faithful community or sect within a nation needing renewal through repentance.

Nevertheless, whatever his immediate background, John's place is probably with the prophets rather than the Covenanters. His dress and his wilderness milieu deliberately placed him in the succession of that older nomadic strain to which Amos, Micah, and the patriarchs had belonged; he comes like Elijah from outside the official religious caste and institutions. The application to him repeatedly of prophecies like Isaiah 40:3f, and Jesus' own estimate of him as "a prophet, and more than a prophet" (Matthew 11:9), emphasise how very closely John stood to all that was characteristic of the prophetic movement in Israel. He shared fully their demand for moral reformation as the supreme prerequisite for salvation, their independence and criticism of religious traditions and institutions, their direct appeal to the authority of conscience in God's name, and their warning of divine judgement.

As T. W. Manson expresses it, the coming of Messiah was an idea which "indicated immediate moral imperatives to which men must bend, or perish". This is the authentic note of prophetism: John's spirit and power are Elijah's, but his message more closely resembles that of Amos, the imminence of the Day of the Lord, when the Mighty One will appear in judgement, with the consequent demand for repentance and amendment of life in preparation for that ordeal. Like Amos (e.g. 5:18, 3:2), John insisted that that Day would find Jews, no less than others, exposed to divine wrath – to be children of Abraham bestowed responsibility, not immunity. The axe of the "worthier", the "mightier" One is already in His hand; He will purify Israel by the spirit and fire of judgement. For the Messiah, as God's Viceregent, is the agent of God's righteousness, the moral imperative personified and crowned. Jesus well summarised John's message as "the way of righteousness" (Matthew 21:32).

The amendment John demanded involved total moral and religious redirection. He set an example of austerity – "John came neither eating nor drinking"; he taught his disciples to fast and to pray (Matthew 11:18, Mark 2:18, Luke 11:1). But austerity is not asceticism, and while John like others doubtless reacted against luxury and corruption, there is no evidence that he called for abandonment of the common life of the world and of the family. There appears to have been nothing "monastic" about the loosely-associated Messianic community – "John's disciples" – which he created: those he baptised returned to their daily life a "remnant" of the penitent, the would-be righteous, waiting for the rule of God.

John's conception of righteousness is broken down into detailed counsel adapted to different classes of hearers (Luke 3:10-14). The "fruits of repentance" required of common folk who asked for more explicit direction included readiness to share food and clothing with the needy – an echo of that social concern which runs through prophetic morality. Of the tax-collectors, whose official position offered opportunity for exploitation, he demanded complete honesty. Of the soldiers, similarly, he required the strictest discipline upon their special power to plunder and oppress the civil community, together with truthfulness (since their word carried most weight with the military authority), justice, and the restraint of avarice. These are evidently recorded as but examples of the kind of ethical instruction John offered to his followers: they recall the realism, directness, and practical relevance, which marked all the ministry of the prophets.

The Baptist is so plainly the herald of Christ that we tend to forget that he is also the latest feature of that Jewish heritage into which Jesus stepped. On all other counts, to treat John as summarising the past would be grossly inadequate: but ethically he had little new to say, though the forcefulness with which he said it, and the context in which he placed it, were unique. The moralism of the prophets, imbued with social concern, and strengthened by a vivid sense of accountability to God, is wedded in John to the apocalyptic hope of a new Age under divine rule, which shall convey to all willing to accept them, forgiveness and purification; and to the obdurate, judgement. In ethics, as in eschatology, John faithfully prepared the way of the Lord, and made straight in the desert of legalism the path of the gospel of Christ.

3

Jesus and His Jewish Inheritance

TO ABSTRACT THE ETHICAL teaching of Jesus from the sum total of His message, even if it were possible, would distort that teaching from the outset. For Him, ethical and religious experience are the same event viewed from different standpoints: the most we can do, to limit the field of study, is to approach the Master's thought asking moral questions rather than theological ones, but not trying to draw distinctions where He made none. Similarly, it would distort His teaching, ˄nd be untrue, to represent all Jesus said as a wholly new and original revelation, unrelated to all that man had received or discovered before. To hold that Jesus appeared "in the fullness of time" implies that His coming and His teaching answered to a process of preparation which embraced man's ethical development no less than his religious maturing. Jesus stands, consciously and explicitly, at the peak of His nation's spiritual progress, inheriting, interpreting, fulfilling, and transforming all the past. To understand Him, therefore, we must begin with His attitude towards the Judaism of His time.

(1) JESUS AND JOHN

Among all the trends and tendencies of His time Jesus stood closest to the Baptist movement. He began with the same announcement – "The kingdom of God is at hand". He upheld John's prophetic authority, submitted to John's baptism as part of the total righteousness which God required, rebuked the leaders of Jewry for not heeding John's message, adopted some of John's disciples among the most intimate of His own circle, and was made sorrowful – and to judge by His later attitude to Herod, was made intensely angry – by John's martyrdom.

Yet in two important respects, both ethically significant, Jesus differed from John. He rejected John's picture of the Messiah with threshing-shovel, flail, axe and fire, bringing judgement. So unexpected was this break with apocalyptic tradition that even

John began to doubt, and sent to Jesus the question, "Art thou he that should come, or must we yet look for another?" Jesus sent back the reply, "Tell John what you see, how the blind see, the lame walk, the lepers are cleansed, the dead are raised, and to the poor the gospel is preached: and blessed is he that shall not stumble over me" (cf Matthew 11:4f) – implying a total reinterpretation of the role of Messiah and the nature of the messianic kingdom.

Similarly, Jesus rejected John's austerity, and to this extent the prevailing outlook of the Essenes and of Qumran also. The question brought to Jesus about fasting, comparing the habits of His disciples with those of John's disciples, and the charge that, compared with John, Jesus was a glutton and a winebibber, are deeply significant of the different social attitudes of the two men. John was not likely to be accused of being the friend of taxgatherers and sinners: but the sociable, uncondemning, positive, approachable Christ, to whom even children came with pleasure, is a part of the matchless portrait, and a measure of the difference between two conceptions of life under God's rule.

Turning to Jesus' reactions to the more orthodox attitudes of Judaism, we must note first what Jesus borrowed, echoed, and approved, and then what He criticised and rejected.

(2) POSITIVE REACTIONS TO JUDAISM

(i) It is often convenient to expound Christ's teaching only by what is distinctive, but the result is partial, even superficial: Jesus fully shared so many Jewish assumptions. Ethical monotheism, the concept of moral law as enshrining the divine will, the sense of an historic purpose fulfilling a divine design, the urgency of social righteousness, the basic concept of *hesed* – of mercy, loving-kindness, faithfulness – and conceptions like sacrifice, individual responsibility, guilt, forgiveness, the relation of morals and religion, a whole history of ethical illustrations and examples, confidence in the omnipresent Holy Spirit of God, – all are ideas so fundamental and so familiar that we scarcely notice that Jesus adopted these insights of Judaism as the moral axioms of His own thought.

(ii) Christ's gospel is presented not only as the fulfilment of Jewish prophecies but as the flowering and fruit of Jewish piety. According to Matthew, Jesus insisted that He had not come to destroy the law but to fulfil it:

Think not that I have come to abolish the law and the prophets; I have not come to abolish them but to fulfil them. For truly I say to you, till heaven and earth pass away, not an iota, not a dot, will pass from the law until all is accomplished. Whoever then relaxes one of the least of these commandments and teaches men so, shall be called least in the kingdom of heaven; but he who does them and teaches them shall be called great in the kingdom of heaven. For I tell you, unless your righteousness exceeds that of the scribes and Pharisees, you will never enter the kingdom of heaven (Matthew 5:17-20).

So Jesus told the "rich young ruler" that the commandments were the way to eternal life (Mark 10:17, 19). He himself defended the principles of the legal code against the casuistical tradition which whittled them down. He said that all the commandments were concentrated in two precepts, one from Deuteronomy and one from Leviticus, and these He forcefully re-enacted as absolutely binding upon all His followers (Matthew 22:34-40). Himself a child of the law, He never broke with it; His enemies, says Scott, were continually trying to detect in Him violations of the law, but at most they could only accuse Him of trivial offences against the sabbath regulations. He observed the set ordinances, enjoined reverence for those who sat in Moses' seat, criticised scribes and Pharisees for frustrating the word of God by their evasive traditions, demanded a truer, because inward, obedience. For all that, He made the breach with legalism inevitable. Scott continues: "His enemies were unable to bring any direct charge against Him, but in their main contention they were right; the 'fulfilment' which He gave to the law involved in the long run its dissolution."[1]

Thus the whole tenor of Christ's teaching justifies Paul's declaration that: "We do not frustrate the law of God, yea we establish the law" (see Romans 3:31). The deepest insights of Judaism were to be realised, not superseded; if the gospel's method is new, the goal still remains that ideal of righteousness to which in their different ways commandments, prophets, Wisdom, and priests had made their contribution. The weightier matters of the law remained weighty – and remained the divine law.

(iii) Jesus brought to the Old Testament scriptures His own ethical discrimination. When the precedent of Elias' calling down fire from heaven upon opponents is quoted as a guide to His own conduct, Jesus regally sets the argument aside; when Moses' rule of divorce is cited, He appeals beyond Moses to the original divine intention concerning marriage; He offers His own summary of the central principle upon which hang "all the law and the prophets." Yet even for this critical attitude, Jesus took His stand within the Old Testament, rather than against it: He quotes one passage to balance another, the command to honour parents to balance the obligation to keep one's oath; on the sabbath rules He quotes "what David did", as on marriage He rests on Genesis. Jesus' sympathies were plainly with the prophetic strain in Old

Testament teaching: it has been said, "Jesus understood the prophets as no-one else in His generation: He understood the prophecy of Malachi about Elijah, He understood Daniel's apocalyptic and the allegory of Jonah ..." and we might add that He shared even more clearly the prophets' moral judgements upon society and their ideal for the character of the Servant-Messiah. Nevertheless, He so excelled and complemented the ancient scriptures that we now judge them by His commentary, not Him by them.

(iv) Jesus was indebted also to later Jewish writing and teaching. *Sirach,* and *The Testaments of the Twelve Patriarchs* had manifested a fine appreciation of disinterested virtue and of forgivingness, and as a boy in the synagogue Jesus would learn much of the traditional instruction. Rabbinic exposition is often wearisome, pedantic, based on fanciful interpretation, yet its thought is also often beautiful, with flashes of genuine moral insight expressed in memorable words. As Scott points out, Jesus borrowed from rabbinic lore in form and substance perhaps more than we shall ever know: "Whatever impressed Him as true and beautiful in the current teaching He gladly made His own."[2] Klausner claimed that Jesus was almost a rabbi, declaring that "throughout the Gospels there is not one item of ethical teaching which cannot be paralleled either in the Old Testament, the Apocrypha, or in the Talmudic and Midrashic literature of the period near to the time of Jesus."[3] D. S. Russell, citing "certain sentiments and phrases" in the Gospels which have "near-parallels" in the apocryphal literature, says, "These show how close the contents of Jesus' moral teaching were at times to the moral ideals of Judaism."[4]

This raises the question of the originality of Jesus, bearing in mind (with Inge) the dictum of Fitzjames Stephen that "originality consists in thinking for ourselves, not in thinking differently from other people." Those who heard Christ declared that they had never heard teaching on this fashion; they called it a "new doctrine", and testified that Jesus taught as one having authority and not as the scribes. In the end Jesus was put to death as an innovator who attacked Moses, the law, and the Holy Place: this unquestioned fact, together with His criticisms of current attitudes, must considerably modify any claim that Jesus was wholly dependent upon Judaist insights. In part, His originality lies in His choice of priorities. Acknowledging rabbinic parallels to much of the Sermon on the Mount, Inge adds, "But how much they taught that fortunately is not to be found there!" and Scott remarks that Jesus had the instinct which enabled Him to separate the finer metal from the dross. Moreover, the character of ethical teaching depends not only upon the proportionate value assigned to various duties, but upon the dynamic energy offered for carrying them out. "The Rabbis may have taught nearly all that Jesus taught, but Paul found no power in their precepts to overcome resistance from his lower nature."[5] That the common people heard Jesus gladly, and the irreligious and the sinful listened and were transformed, is evidence enough of something truly original in His presentation of the moral ideal.

Jesus would scarcely prize novelty in ethical teaching or behaviour for its own sake. A moral principle is not any less true or binding because more than one servant of God has uttered it. "The great principles of the moral law have been apparent to earnest men in all times;" remarks Scott, "they are bound up with the facts of life, and no one has ever reflected seriously on life without catching some glimpse of them."[6]

Scott offers a valuable summary of the features of Jesus' teaching which were in the truest sense original: He imposed an inward unity and consistency upon the multitudinous moral rules and counsels then current; He made not only fear of God but a glad trust in God the active principle of all goodness; He laid new emphasis upon the value of the individual soul; the moral quality of an act is made to consist in the thought or intention that lies behind it; Jesus is always positive, as in His version of the golden rule: it is not enough simply to restrain evil and discipline human nature – "doing no harm" – for men must take active initiative in goodness, expressing a moral impulse from within, unconditioned by circumstances, unlimited in scope, independent of reward. Jesus distinguishes clearly between moral imperatives and mere ritual or custom; and in His own character and example He gave new reality to the moral ideal. Marshall assembles a series of tributes to the sublimity of Jesus' teaching, including the words of Klausner, "If ever the day should come and this ethical code be stripped of miracles and mysticism, The Book of the Ethics of Jesus will be one of the choicest treasures in the literature of Israel for all time."[7]

However much Jesus inherited, yet in His incomparable method, His inarguable authority, His redemptive grace toward the sinful, His unimpeachable example, Jesus stands alone. Others abide our question: when Jesus speaks, we know that what He says is right, and that He has every right to say it.

(3) NEGATIVE REACTIONS TO JUDAISM

There is however another side to Jesus' relation to His heritage – His sharp criticism of certain features of current Judaism. Some of these were blemishes upon Jewish practice, symptomatic of something wrong beneath the surface; others were more fundamental misjudgements.

(i) Such a blemish, to which Jesus often drew attention, was the prevalent *pride and self-righteousness* inseparable from all religious legalism. It was expressed in the aristocratic disdain which made Caiaphas say of the common folk, "This people, which knoweth not the law, are accursed", and it brought upon Jesus the open contempt of religious leaders for His friendship with the irreligious and the sinful. Jesus mercilessly caricatured this attitude in His parable of the Pharisee and the tax-gatherer, satirised it in His portrait of the elder brother, castigated it unsparingly in the house of Simon the Pharisee, and made it publicly ridiculous by describing the lengths to which such pride will go in claiming precedence, of titles, dress, and seating, on public occasions. Jesus upgraded humility as alone the mark of greatness, and the bason and towel as its supreme symbols, as no other ethical teacher has ever done. When one recalls the deep phobia about pride revealed in Paul's more than fifty references to it, it becomes clear that Jesus here touches smartingly upon a very sore spot in Pharisaism.

Nor did Jesus hide His anger at the *hardness of heart* that valued sabbath rules above the suffering of the afflicted, and found excuse for rescuing ox or ass while leaving the sick untended. A certain cruelty underlay the attitude of legalism toward the unfortunate: it made relief a matter of religious merit and obligation, not of compassion; it prohibited medical care for religious reasons; it banished the leper and the insane to solitude; by equating health and prosperity with divine favour, it assumed all affliction to be well-deserved – the blind man must have sinned, or his parents did, and the paralytic needs assurance of forgiveness before he can believe in cure. The compassionate spirit of Jesus was bound to collide with every expression of this religious inhumanity.

Jesus saw that for the mass of the people the law's demands were simply impracticable, economically as to cost in money and time, and because of the number and intricacy of the regulations. The legalists *"bind heavy burdens,* hard to bear, and lay them on men's shoulders; but they themselves will not move them with their finger." Much later, Peter echoed Jesus, speaking of the law as a yoke which "neither we nor our fathers were able to bear"; and Matthew records the gracious words in which the invitation to the good life as Jesus conceived it was enshrined: "Come unto me, all who labour and are heavy-laden, and I will give you rest. Take my yoke upon you, and learn from me; for I am gentle and lowly in heart, and you will find rest for your souls. For my yoke is easy, and my burden is light" (11:28-30).

Jesus did not share Judaism's *attitude towards women,* nor what Henson called "the unpleasing emphasis upon sex" – probably having in mind certain discussions in the Mishnah. Sexual morality was higher in Judaism than anywhere else in the ancient world.

The orthodox Jew acknowledged no such dualism as would make him despise sex in itself: nevertheless his attitude to women had something "oriental" about it. The superiority of the male was assumed – in *religion,* as in the heart of the synagogue liturgy the Jew thanked God that he was not made a woman; in *law,* in the rules governing inheritance and divorce; and in *social custom,* as illustrated in aloofness towards women in public places – even relatives. In Jewish society the wife and mother was highly honoured, but for many the only alternative was harlotry. In His relationship with women Jesus surprised even the disciples. His friendship and gentleness, His conversation with the woman of Samaria, with Mary and Martha, and the various cameos of Luke's Gospel, all prepare for Paul's dictum: "There is neither ... male nor female for you are all one in Christ Jesus" (Galatians 3:28).

(ii) Beneath these blemishes lay more serious inadequacies. Despite foregleams in the Old Testament of a wider vision, Judaism had become increasingly *nationalistic* and exclusive. Postexilic emphasis upon separateness, while helping to preserve Jewish culture, drove the Jew so far in upon himself as to cultivate fanatical insistence upon the uniqueness of Judaism and a pride of election and privilege which Jesus forcibly rejected. His own attitude to Romans, Samaritans, Greeks, the Syro-Phenician, brought Him into collision with prevailing assumptions. His words at Nazareth about God's interest in other nations, His selection of a Samaritan to illustrate how men of any nation may fulfil the divine law of neighbourly love, His parables about men coming to the messianic banquet from north and south, east and west, and all nations being gathered before the King, show how sharply Jesus differed from Judaism's self-limited view. Marshall quotes Windisch: "The Torah, even in its purely ethical aspects, was regarded as having reference only to the Jewish people, for them alone the promises and the commands were valid, thus the Torah was concerned with national life. This connection with the Jewish people Jesus ignored, and addressed his ethical demands to man as man."[8]

A second principle upon which Jesus collided with prevailing assumptions was that of the *reward* justly due to obedience, and the doctrine of merit which derived from it. Jesus retained the idea of moral reward, but denied any human claim upon God, any assertion of individual merit. The desire to gain public recognition for almsgiving, fasting, and prayer, is sharply satirised in Matthew 6; the parable of the labourers in the vineyard asserts the unchallengeable right of God to apportion rewards as He will, without claim or explanation. The words about unprofitable servants are also relevant, and the ironic reply to Peter's "Lord, we have left all ... what shall we have?" – that God is no man's debtor, and

anyhow the first shall be last and the last first – show how strongly
Jesus opposed the cold logic of Jewish legalism, "God says what
He wants, man gives it and gets paid." This notion made man's
fellowship with God a right, based upon man's righteousness: but
for conscientious hearts such righteousness is never complete, and
so man can never be sure of God's favour. Christ's gospel of
unconditional grace based upon the divine character alone broke
with liberating gladness, not only upon the heart of a Pharisee like
Paul, but upon the common people too, and especially upon those
aware that they merited only judgement.

A third significant distinction between Jesus and Judaism concerned *the weightier matters* of the law – justice, mercy, faith – and
merely ritual, ceremonial, traditional, even literalist obligations
like tithing the small herbs at the garden's edge. An elaborate
casuistry about the precise texts upon which sabbath concessions
might be based; about exactly what forms of oath were binding
(whether swearing by the altar or by the sacrifice upon it, was the
more solemn, for example); whether an oath flung out during a
family quarrel should be held irrevocable, though it meant poverty for one's parents; the exact point on the arm up to which it
was necessary to wash one's hands after contact with common
things; precisely what meats rendered the eater unclean in God's
sight – and countless similar minutiae, obscured the plain directions of conscience, lost sight of the significant in the trifling, and
confused all moral perspectives. As T. R. Glover pointed out,
Jesus mercilessly ridicules the result: a careful straining of the
smallest "unclean" gnat from the surface of one's drink with the
broad fringe of one's praying-robe, while swallowing whole,
without noticing, a full-sized camel, head, horns, long hairy neck,
one hump, two humps, knobbly knees and all.[9]

Whenever ritual and ethical ordinances are placed on the same
level and enforced with the same degree of authority, the moral
sense becomes confused between the really important and the
plainly trivial; ritualist reasons can be given for moral barbarities
(like stoning for adultery); and religious explanations can be
offered for evading the clearest moral duties, as priest and levite
ignore the stricken traveller by the roadside. In all such issues,
Jesus stated the plain deliverance of the enlightened conscience:
the sabbath was made for man; compassion must rule one's
actions on the sabbath as on every day; what comes out of a man's
heart defiles him, but not what goes into his stomach; loyalty to
needy parents is far more important than scruples about ill-
tempered vows. The effect was far-reaching. Scott remarks that
by the words about what defiles a man, Jesus "pronounced the
doom of the old conception of religion".[10] So with the reduction
of the law to two commandments: "it never occurred to any rabbi
to challenge the necessity of the thousand other requirements

because they could be epitomised in two. Jesus boldly took the view that since the law was comprised in these primary injunctions all the rest might be left aside. Nothing was necessary but to hold fast to what was essential."

From the Pharisees' point of view, the difficulty about saying that all uncleanness proceeds from within is that no-one can assess, in any legally satisfactory way, what is within a man, whereas you can count how many times he washes his hands. Law can deal only with *externals* – with what law can measure, observe, forbid, and punish; it can only cleanse the outside of the platter and the cup. The heart behind the deed, the motive, intention, regret, are beyond the law's range, and so is the restraint, or cure, of hidden evil. As we saw, the need for a deeper inward goodness was glimpsed in the tenth Commandment, recognised in Deuteronomy, in the great words attributed to Micah, in Jeremiah's new covenant, in Psalm 51, in the doctrine of the evil impulse as the real problem of morality. Paul, in Romans 7, shows as clear a perception of the psychological inadequacy of legalism as anyone has ever done. Yet with all this awareness of the need, law could do nothing to regenerate the inner life, or even to restrain it.

This is the reason for Christ's emphasis upon the evil that lies in attitudes of the heart – in lust, hatred, contempt, vengefulness, and not only in their outward expression; and likewise upon the way that good acts, like almsgiving, fasting, prayer, may be vitiated by self-regarding motives. Not conduct alone, but character, the person behind the public performance, is the concern of ethics.

One reason for our Lord's severity upon Jewish externalism was its inconsistency. A man appeared to be generous and compassionate, when in fact he was parading his piety for public approval of his alms; a man might oppress with heavy mortgage interest the widow who must raise money on her home to bury her husband – yet he will prolong his public prayers as a pious example to his neighbours. Both patterns of behaviour are, according to the law, outwardly correct – yet inwardly despicable. One meaning of Christ's word "hypocrite" makes precisely this point: it is a stage-word, describing an actor who plays an outward part that bears no real relation to his own inward feelings and motives. A second reason for Christ's severity upon externalism was His realisation of the effect of circumstances upon conduct. Lust may never be expressed in action, but for no better reason than cowardice, or lack of opportunity, though all its sinfulness remains. The practical contribution to the temple treasury of "two mites, which make a farthing" was negligible – a mere nuisance to the temple accountants; but the *amount* was an accident of domestic economics, the *motive* – "she gave all that she had" – was superb.

From this difference between Jesus and Judaism followed

inevitably the ultimate divergence of the two faiths. Once outward actions are evaluated by inward attitudes, the social coercion of law fails, and external restraint must be supplemented by
internal impulse, a constraint within the soul. The tree must first
be made sound, if the fruit is to be good: the corrupt tree *cannot*
bring forth good fruit. Men must be changed, must become innocent and humble as children again, before their behaviour will
attain to Christ's ideal. To effect that change, and sustain the
acceptable inner life from which the acceptable outward living
will flow, demands a right relationship with God, who sees in
secret and knows what a man is within himself.

So Jesus' final criticism of Judaism concerns the inadequacy of
its *religious basis*. That is why to separate the ethics of Jesus from
the rest of His teaching would contradict His central position. For
Jesus does not so much combine ethics and religion, still less
deduce ethics from religion: for Him, a religious faith and experience *are* faith in the God of goodness and truth, and experience of
God as everlasting right.

Scott argues this well from (i) the religious assumptions of Christ's ethic
– not a philosophical conception of man's nature, or of social obligation,
but the love of the Father, and the value which the Father sets upon the
individual; the norm for men is to act as God acts. (ii) Christ's demand
always for a new will, rightly oriented towards God and men – a regeneration from within that sets men in harmony with the will of God. (iii)
Jesus' conception of fellowship with the God of love, righteousness and
holiness, as essentially moral obedience: metaphysical, or mystical,
union with God is not His thought; being one with God means having in
ourselves the will of God, and sharing in the divine nature. "In every act
of justice and compassion we become for that moment one with God,
and by constant obedience to His will we live the divine life. As men
behold our good works they glorify our heavenly Father, for He is
himself thinking and acting through us."
Marshall, too, lists the religious premises of the ethics of Jesus: the
reality of the spiritual world, an eternal moral order behind the temporal, physical order, giving moral experience its meaning and its future;
the reality of God, Creator, Providence, the Friend behind phenomena,
who is both moral norm and moral resource; the spiritual value of all
men as God's creatures, potential members of God's kingdom, capable
of becoming His children by sharing in His likeness. So Jesus insists that
true religion leads, inevitably and naturally, to a high ethic: "the right
and the good are for Jesus aspects of the will of God." At the same time,
trust in the love and help of God provides the motive and dynamic that
can make – and keep – men good.

It was not, of course, in insisting upon the intimate connection
of ethics with religion that Jesus differed from Judaism. That was
common ground. His new emphasis fell upon the depth and freedom, the assurance and joy, of the religious experience which
Jesus invited men to share; upon the supreme confidence men

may have in divine favour already freely shown, not to be earned or begged; upon the personal realisation of God's inexhaustible love. To Him, God was not simply the originator of the law, nor simply the judge of man's obedience, nor even – simply – the king whose will was best for man: He was the kingly Father, the royal Friend, whom to know was to trust, to trust was to love, and to love was to obey with gladness from a full heart. Of this, in Christ's time, Judaism knew little.

Thus, if Jesus inherited much, He altered all that He received, and rejected much that in Judaism went with it. It was because Judaism refused to follow the path of its own refinement and fulfilment in Christ, that the break between Christianity and its parent faith was ultimately unavoidable.

4

The Family of God and the Life of Sonship

URNING FROM OUR LORD'S reactions towards prevailing
moral views to His own positive instruction, we confront the
difficulty that Jesus formulated no system, and offered no
comprehensive summary of principles which we can arrange in
easily memorised patterns. His teaching was occasional, spontaneous, expressed in conversations, parables, epigrams, and invitations, in challenging exaggerations that startle attention, in provocative paradoxes, comments upon current topics and events,
answers to criticisms, replies to questions, discursive observations, and one or two longer discourses. The great set speeches in
Matthew, and to a lesser extent in the other Gospels, are compila-
tions by the writers assembling sayings uttered on separate occasions; though Jesus did sometimes address crowds at greater
length, and it has been suggested that the brief, weighty sentences
we know so well may be the texts, or summaries, of such addresses.

Moreover, we possess only a selection of the sayings of Jesus,
sifted through the memories, the contemporary interests and
practical concerns of first-generation Christians. Those who, at
first orally and then in writing, preserved for us the teaching they
loved, while careful not to invent or falsify, could not help group-
ing, sharpening, underlining, as their own experience proved the
value of this or that saying to their own situation and perplexities.

From the form in which Christ's teaching has reached us, it follows that
literalism, legalism, and archaism, are precluded from our interpretation. We have to make allowance for the paradox, the exaggeration,
poetry and parable, which mark Jesus' popular utterance. We cannot
always take Jesus literally, though we must always take Him seriously.
No one imagines we are to forgive a man four hundred and ninety times
but no more; or that we should sell our shirts to buy swords. But even
where the literal expression startles, and occasionally baffles, the intention is clear, and inescapable; an outlook, a manner of thinking, a standard of values, shine through, and we are rarely left in doubt what He
would approve.

It is clear too that by His impromptu method Jesus deliberately avoids the legislating habit of Judaism, with its attempt to prescribe for all possible cases, its evasive casuistry. "His aim was to mark out the great principles of the moral life, leaving men free to apply them, in each particular case, as the occasion required."[1] Every attempt in the history of the church to erect Christ's occasional sayings into a legal code, has misrepresented His meaning and must defeat His purpose.

Because His teaching has this unsystematised form, concentrating upon illustrating principles and not issuing legal pronouncements, it is living, flexible, adjustable, and relevant to every age. Some analysis is essential to exposition; some patterning is necessary to aid memory, but we hinder understanding if we forget that we are introducing system where Jesus left ideas to ferment, we are theorising what He left concrete, forceful, suggestive, inexhaustible – and haunting.

The form of Christ's teaching was determined, at the deepest level, by its basis. In Israel, from Decalogue to Torah the basis of morality had been law. The prophetic movement had challenged this, appealing beyond "the false pen of the scribes" (Jeremiah 8:8) to self-evident moral truth: "God hath shewed thee, O man, what is good ..." is typical of the prophets' appeal to intuitive moral understanding. In the same tradition, the Baptist invoked no document or inherited rules, but the innate authority of God's spoken word over the conscience of those who truly hear.

Jesus did the same. Insisting upon the original meaning and intention of the law, sifting tradition and re-interpreting the documents, Jesus addressed all the time the common moral sense of His hearers. Here authority must justify itself. "Why judge ye not, even of your own selves, what is right? ... What think ye? ... What man of you would ...? ... Which of you that is a father ... would ...? ... If a man have an hundred sheep, will he not go ...? Do you not see ...?" – Jesus continually asks questions to which the moral judgement of His listeners must provide the answers. When He used some more definite form of statement, the same appeal followed in the final exhortation, "He that hath ears to hear, let him hear!" The parables, likewise, sometimes become dialogues, as Jesus puts the central question to His hearers, or the listening crowd interrupts – "Lord, he has ten pounds!" (Luke 19:25).

All the time, Jesus appealed to the consenting conscience. He believed in the capacity of the general popular moral judgement to discern truth *when presented with it.* He solemnly warns against judging by appearances, urging that men "judge righteous judgement" (John 7:24). He exclaims "if the light that is in thee be darkness, how great is that darkness". He rebukes those whose wisdom can read the weather signs, but not the moral signs of the time in which they live. He thanks the Father that the truth is revealed to "babes" – simple, unsophisticated, straight-seeing people – though the self-styled wise and prudent miss it. He can

say of the clear-eyed children, "Of such is the kingdom." Herein
lies the seriousness of pretending that right is wrong and wrong
right; of saying "Evil, be thou my good"; of reaching the point
where hostility to truth makes a man say Christ is working by the
power of Satan. For that is a moral darkness, a wilful blindness, a
kind of spiritual insanity, against which even truth is helpless. It is
blasphemy against the light, against the Holy Spirit, and it cuts off
the soul from the possibility of finding forgiveness.

Thus Christ does not argue, remonstrate, or demonstrate truth
by logical analysis and consistency: the basis of His ethical position is the appeal that moral truth makes to the heart of man – if
he be but *willing* to believe. The form of His teaching is therefore
spontaneous, immediate, directed to conscience as occasion
demands. Nevertheless, some order is essential to clarity, and the
isolation of main themes helps to keep proportion and emphasis
correct. Says Inge: "At the root of Christian ethics lies what
Harnack has called a transvaluation of all values in the light of our
divine sonship and heavenly citizenship"[2]; to those two regulative
ideas should be added that of following Christ as the ideal incarnate. We shall arrange our examination of Christ's teaching under
these three themes, fully acknowledging that this pattern is no
more than a convenience of exposition.

(1) THE FAMILY OF GOD

Sonship is the fundamental presupposition and pattern of the
good life as Jesus describes it. God is the kingly Father, Christ the
beloved and only Son; prayer is family conversation addressed to
our Father in the confidence of sons who know that if they ask
bread they will not be given stones. The family is entered by birth,
by becoming as little children: its members are "children" of God
as to nature and relationship, "sons" as to status, assurance, freedom, and inheritance. Fellow-disciples are "brethren", and relationships are governed by the family law of love. The "sinner" is a
wayward son whose enjoyment of sonship has been forfeited by
rebellious departure to a far country, where he is "lost" and
"dead" to the Father's love. The rule of the son's life is the
Father's will; its aim is the Father's good pleasure; its hope is the
Father's kingdom; its under-girding confidence is that the Father
knows that he has need; its final reward is a welcome to the
Father's house. So central, and inclusive, is the truth of the divine
family, with which Jesus illumines the way men ought to live.

But men do not by nature enjoy the life of sonship, or accept its
obligations. Jesus describes unsparingly the miseries of the prodigal son, announces repeatedly that His mission is to seek and
save the lost, dispenses forgiveness as the necessary preliminary

to trust and joy in the Father, and calls sinners to repentance. The invitation to sonship is for all men, because all men need it.

Deeds, not words, declare true sonship, and by this test many are nearer to the divine family than they would claim to be. The moving parable of the Two Sons (Matthew 21:28-32) suggests that some who make no religious profession, who even say No! to religion as they conceive it, nevertheless in their actions and attitudes fulfil the will of the Father, after all. This clearly reflects the experience of Jesus among the many "irreligious" who flocked to hear him while the "religious" stood aloof. The key to the parable is the moral significance of repentance, for the family of God is a family of changed, forgiven men and women. The parable of the Pharisee and the Tax-gatherer states this even more sharply: for the penitent returns to his house "justified" *rather than* the boastful, self-righteous Pharisee. The basis of forgiveness is divine grace, free, unpurchasable, undeserved – and it must be so accepted. The story of the Two Debtors shows that in fact the much-forgiven are more likely to love God intensely and without measure than are those so sure of their own righteousness as to feel little need of pardon.

When Jesus defends His friendship for the irreligious in the parables of the lost sheep and the lost coin, the divine initiative towards man's salvation rests upon the value – for God – of what is lost, so that heaven rejoices at the finding. But in the parable of the lost son the idea of value is transcended: a "worthless" son is loved for his own sake – there can be no reason. Here, the human sonship is broken by wilfulness and folly, but the divine fatherhood remains unchanged, unaffected except by grief. When the son, coming to himself in repentance, makes his way home, the Father's welcome overwhelms his shame. Sharing the spotlight in the story, however, is the elder brother, one of the harshest of all Christ's portraits of men. He is the Pharisee, criticising the Father's leniency towards sinners. In all logic and justice, the elder brother is right: the ungracious rascal who ran from home does not deserve restoration to the family. Jesus offers no reply to his argument: just look at him, says Jesus, listen to him! That is Judaism, leaving no hope or opportunity for sinners to return to sonship.

For Jesus, as for the Baptist, the repentance which reestablishes sonship is essentially a change of mind. In Matthew's record this involves becoming as a little child, "turning" from self-righteous independence to the humility of mind which is willing to receive a place in the divine family as the undeserved gift of the Father. In Johannine terms this rebirth is represented as the beginning of new life, with a new nature of "spirit" and not of "flesh", originating in birth of the water of repentance (in John's baptism) and of the Spirit, from above. For John therefore as for Matthew, the invitation to return as son into the divine family implies an ethical transformation, a change of heart as well as of privilege and status. In the words of Marshall, "When a man recognises evil as evil, dislikes it because it is evil, and disowns it not because of its consequences but because of its character, then his repentance is complete, a permanent new attitude towards God and man."[3]

Such repentance may be awakened by reflection upon tragic events (as Luke 13:1f), by experience of the consequences of sin in the far country, by attraction to the better life exhibited in others, or by response to the invitation to take one's place in the family of God – the invitation enshrined in Christ's presence among men as Son and Saviour. Accordingly, it may be accompanied by remorse and grief, by confession and surrender, by inward struggle towards self-amendment, by the glad discovery of relief and peace, by the deep satisfaction of fulfilling all previous training and spiritual experience. Whatever the emotional accompaniments, repentance will always include redirection of life, a "conversion" or turning in one's tracks to face new goals. By reaching out for divine help to rise to new standards, and by resting on divine forgiveness to make this possible, repentance passes almost imperceptibly into faith, as moral vision and desire are focused upon the new ideal in Christ, and the life of sonship is admired, appropriated as possible in the mercy of God, and resolved upon. In such repentance and faith the new moral life is born. So faith, in turn, passes almost imperceptibly into obedience, the surrender of the self to the Christ-ideal, to Christ-control, and to increasing approximation to Him as moral strength develops and faith matures. So sinners are made sons, by the gracious action of God in Christ responded to by repentant faith; and this new moral orientation and relationship are the prerequisites of life in the family of God.

(2) THE PRIVILEGES OF SONSHIP

The obligations of sonship are made practicable by its privileges, among which is *implicit trust in the goodness of the Father,* a confidence which releases the soul from all anxious care about material provision and personal safety to seek primarily the will of God. God's providence extends to just and unjust alike, operates for man "much more" than for the grass, the fowls of the air, or the lilies of the field, and particularises to the numbering of the hairs of the head. Scott shows that prudence, forethought, and preparation, are extolled in the parables of the Talents, the Unjust Steward, and the Ten Bridesmaids, to which we may add Christ's insistence that men look ahead and count the cost of discipleship. Jesus offers no excuse for thriftlessness, or imprudence. But in place of the anxious, fretful concern that can dissipate attention from life's more central purposes, and foster envious discontent, Jesus urges a quiet faith in the wisdom, goodness, and guidance of the Father.

One of Christ's arguments is that anxiety and fretfulness accomplish nothing; another is a wryly humorous proverb to the effect that it is foolish to worry about future problems when "sufficient for each day is the evil it brings"; but His deeper reason for this carefree trust on the part of sons is the sure confidence that "the Father knows", and is faithful, and generous.

This is the Father's world: men going out to do His work in the world need only staff and shoes, for God will count the labourer worthy of his hire. For the children of the Father, life is not a struggle for existence but a serenity of trust – the unknown is in God's hands, and the universe is friendly. For men sharing that confidence, Christ's ideal becomes practicable and the good life is not burdensome but blessed.

Sonship implies too the *experience of prayer,* not only as an act of piety but as an unlimited resource for moral renewal: "Men ought always to pray, and not faint." Beside prayer for daily bread, and for help in peril ("pray that your flight be not in winter"), Jesus counsels prayer for daily forgiveness, and against temptation; for all good things, including the Holy Spirit; for vindication of the elect, and for the cause of God in the world ("more labourers in God's harvest-fields"); and for power to do God's service ("this kind goes not out but by prayer"). Prayer is also part of the service we owe to others, including those who persecute us, and those being sifted by trial and temptation. In prayer Jesus Himself repeatedly found spiritual reassurance, mental re-orientation, emotional restfulness, radiance of spirit and peace of heart – a spiritual "transfiguration" which, whatever more it implies, leaves no possible doubt of the moral value of prayer.

Yet with Jesus prayer is always morally conditioned. "God heareth not sinners" – prayer is the best guardian of a good conscience, and to watch and pray is the only way to handle situations where the flesh is weak. Certain praying is not so much unanswered as unanswerable: wrong in motive (as the prayer offered to be seen of men), or in attitude (as the vain repetitions that seek to coerce God by incantation), or in spirit (as the suggestion to call down fire upon an inhospitable village). Prayer offered in self-righteousness (as that of the Pharisee in the temple), or in disobedience (as the long prayers offered by those who devour widows' houses) can expect no answer: and with prayer that is sublimated selfishness Jesus could have no patience – the Lord's Prayer is relentlessly plural. Nor with prayers that seek to evade the Father's will: Jesus refused to pray for rescuing angels, or to be saved from the hour of crisis, or that the cup of death should pass from Him; nor would He pray that Simon be protected from Satan's sifting, or the disciple band be taken out of the evil world.

Nor, again, does Jesus counsel prayer for things that can be ours only upon conditions, as forgiveness depends upon forgivingness, fruitfulness upon abiding in Christ. Such moral conditions against prayer's misuse do not lessen its importance: they guard its value. And for encouragement to pray, Jesus points to the fatherliness of God, to the effect of importunity (even upon a conscienceless judge or a reluctant neighbour – and God is neither), and to the certainty that prayer which persists from asking to seeking to knocking will surely be answered.

Jesus appears to offer an almost unlimited assurance as to prayer: "If ye ask anything of the Father he will give it you in my name ... If ye abide in me and my words abide in you, ye shall ask what ye will and it shall be done unto you." Yet the promise is not quite unconditional, and from the ethical point of view the qualifications are deeply significant. As we mature out of the childhood of impulsive prayer, through the pain and perplexity of unanswered prayer, into the joy and power of prevailing prayer, it is not merely our prayers that change but ourselves. As God draws us nearer to Himself, and schools our hearts to love what He loves and will what He wills, so we learn to ask what He can freely grant. Abiding in Christ we request only what Christ would request. Therein lies the ethical significance of prayer.

Sonship implies, in the third place, *exalted motives and the expectation of reward:* "great is your reward in heaven." It has been said that here Jesus makes the good life a profitable speculation, that virtue is not loved for its own sake, and Christian motivation is not as pure as it should be. Inge admits that the idea of reward and the fear of hell have been frequently exaggerated, but he adds that it is very doubtful if this has done the harm ascribed to it. Attempts either to cajole or to frighten the irreligious are rarely successful: one has to be already religious to believe in them.

Certainly, the prospect of reward is not the main Christian motive for godliness. The privilege of sonship, gratitude for goodness, grace and forgiveness, a bracing sense of high vocation as sons and servants of the living God, are moral impulses of considerable value and power. If the brevity of life adds urgency to moral obligation – "the night cometh when no man can work" – so also does the hope of immortality confer vastly increased importance, assurance, and worth upon the moral life. The idea of immortality is far more than a promise of recompense, or a comfort to the sorrowing: it "raises the whole moral temperature of the world", giving life a new solemnity, a new significance, and a new heroism. Inge finds that Christ's chief motive was the commandment of love, the "enthusiasm" evident in the early Christians as an effective emotional drive towards moral endeavour.

Jesus insists too upon the intrinsic value of goodness: "Do good, hoping for nothing again" (Luke 6:35) is wholly characteristic, as is the warning that those who follow Him faithfully must expect a cross. His condemnation of the doctrine of merit reveals what He thought of "calculating goodness", the so-called enlightened self-interest.

All the same, men do look for some worth-while outcome from their struggles, self-discipline, and sacrifice. Could it be right to lose one's life, deliberately, without assurance that one will in some sense thereby save it? Can human nature be so disinterested as not to care whether the consequences of behaviour be good or ill? Is not Jesus more realistic when He asks, concerning certain accepted norms of conduct, "What reward have ye?" – what value is that? Says Scott: "What all is said, we cannot, in a world that is ruled by purpose and links an effect with every cause, escape from the concept of reward. Action by which nothing is gained is futile."[4] Moreover, if obedience to the Father count for nothing in the life of the world and the destiny of men, then God's sovereignty over nature and history becomes a meaningless abstraction. It is because His purpose is final, and the service of His will leads to the victory of that purpose, that obedience is worth any cost, and no temporary discouragement should induce despair. "The rewards offered to the righteous are simply the inevitable issue of righteousness in a world under the governance of God ... If we were living in a universe where virtue brought no reward and vice no punishment, we should no longer be able to believe in a living God" (Marshall).[5]

Of course, much depends upon the nature of the reward anticipated. The desire to save our souls is not unworthy, remarks Inge, quoting Gore: "We cannot separate love for God from a desire to find our own happiness in God. We must crave for ultimate satisfaction, recognition, and approval."[6] There is a true self-love. He who asked "What is a man profited if he shall gain the whole world and lose his own soul?" said also, "He that loseth his life ... shall find it." It will scarcely be denied, even by the most rigorous, that on the whole virtue *is* happier than vice, and right choices less likely to be regretted than wrong ones: it can hardly be unethical to point this out!

"He that is last shall be first ... Blessed are the poor ... the meek ... the peacemakers ... the persecuted ... for theirs is the kingdom ... They that humble themselves shall be exalted" – the promises of Jesus, says Scott, always turn upon some good that will accrue to the man himself. Jesus describes conditions of blessedness, fulfilling which leads here and now to fulness of life. Moral effort is rewarded by greater moral capacity, moral achievement by greater moral responsibility: he that is faithful in small things is made ruler over cities, and the right use of few talents is the way to possessing more. The immediate reward is always more fruit than prize, more a spiritual consequence than a compensation.

An ultimate reward remains. Fullness of life here; however rich, is incomplete, but we need not fear, for God will give us the kingdom; those who hunger and thirst after righteousness shall be filled; the suffering elect shall be vindicated, and the investment of time, money, labour and love in kind and generous deeds will be found to have laid up treasure in heaven. At the end are the Father's kingdom and the Father's house, the Master's approval and eternal life. Because goodness and right are of the nature of God's world, the moral life will be gloriously vindicated at the last.

Sonship implies, finally, an *abundant life*. The central gift of the gospel, by which a man comes to belong to the family of God, is the gift of life – abundant, eternal, victorious, and free; and the fullest possible realisation of this divine life within the soul becomes, for the individual Christian, the highest good. To this extent, the individualist Christian ethic is a prescription for self-realisation, so long as the self being realised is the self new-made in Christ. This will involve ever-increasing richness of personality as we enter into the freedom, understanding, blessing and service to which Christ calls us. It will involve expansion of personality as we "grow outwards" in love, sympathy, and responsiveness towards others: altruism and egoism are reconciled in Christianity because the individual realises his own life only as he finds himself in the service of others for Christ's sake. Self-realisation as God's sons will involve the indefinite extension of personal experience, constantly reaching forward in unfulfilled longing, always thirsting for the everlasting fullness of God. To say that such concepts belong to religion and not to ethics is again to put asunder what, for Jesus, God has indissolubly joined together.

These privileges of sonship are sometimes represented as solemn duties: we ought to trust utterly in divine providence, to explore the power of prayer, to deserve a worthy reward, to give unhindered expression to eternal life. The argument of Jesus is that men are invited to the life of sonship by the free grace and goodness of the Father: having entered upon that privileged experience, men find themselves longing, and enabled, to live as God's sons should.

(3) THE ETHICS OF SONSHIP

For sincere hearts, fulfilment of the obligations of sonship follows automatically from the enjoyment of its privileges: It is not that "because you are a son you ought ...." but "if you are a son you will ..."

Though this is the true evangelical context of ethical obligation, that obligation is no whit less weighty or imperative. Alongside the gracious

invitations, the Gospel writers set with equal clearness the moral indis-
pensables of Jesus:

> Except your righteousness exceed the righteousness of the scribes
> and Pharisees, you will never enter the kingdom of heaven;
> Except you become as little children, you will never enter the
> kingdom of heaven;
> Except a man be born again he cannot enter the kingdom of
> heaven;
> Except ye repent ye shall all likewise perish;
> Except I wash thee, thou hast no part with me;

– inescapable conditions which salvation imposes and which Jesus will
not permit to be evaded. It was not "the rich young ruler" alone whom
He allowed to go away grieved, crestfallen, and unsaved. The imperatives of the gospel are inexorable because they are inevitable: no man
can be rescued from what he has become *and* stay as he is. The true son
is he who, whatever his initial rudeness and rebelliousness, does the will
of the Father in the end, and engages in His work (Matthew 21:28f).

(i) The first, and most fundamental principle of the ethics of
sonship is the simplest family observation – "like father, like
son." Members of the divine family share a family resemblance
that provides visible proof of relationship. Jesus repeatedly
requires of sons that pattern of conduct which shall show them to
be indeed "the children of your Father which is in heaven
... merciful as your Father which is in heaven is merciful ..."
and worthy to be "called the children of God". He appeals from
the fact of the Father-child relationship to the expectation of a
Father-child similarity in moral attitude and character: to the
sons' being (in Paul's words) "imitators of God as dear children."

In all probability, beneath such expressions lies the Hebraism which uses
"child of ..." as a mode of description, a statement of resemblance,
rather than of literal fact. Within the Gospels we meet "sons of God and
of the resurrection, sons of the bride-chamber, son of peace, sons of the
kingdom, of light, of this world, of Gehenna, of the devil". "Sons of
God" likewise implies correspondence of moral character between
members of one family. Later, the author of 1 John was to find the
deepest explanation of this correspondence in the new birth through
which believers actually share the divine life ("He who loves ... who
does righteousness ... is born of God"); 2 Peter, likewise, speaks of our
becoming partakers of the divine nature. But while the germ of such
theological development may be present in Christ's words, His immediate meaning is that the divine Father and His true sons exhibit the same
moral qualities.

This concept of moral imitation of the divine is of the very
highest importance as a permanent new principle in biblical ethics, whether as the child's imitation of the Father, or, derived
therefrom, the disciple's imitation of the Christ. Though its meaning varies widely, the imitation of God in Christ is an ideal never

wholly absent from the Christian interpretation of ethics, and it
first enters Christian thought in this simple metaphor of the
mutual resemblance of members of the divine family. But already
that ideal is breath-taking: as T. R. Glover says, "When we recall
what Jesus teaches of God, when we begin to try to give to 'God'
the content He intended, we realise with amazement what He is
saying. He is holding up to men for their ideal of conduct the
standard of God's holiness, of God's love and tenderness ... We
are to love our enemies, to win them, to be pure – all on the scale
of God."[7]

(ii) Of almost equal importance is the implication, clear in the
ethics of sonship, that the Christian moral ideal can only be cor-
porately fulfilled. Sonship implies moral fellowship not only with
God but with each other. The good life, though it demands willingness to walk the narrow way with the few, does not remain an
isolated struggle. It is not the Lord's Prayer alone that is "relentlessly plural", but most of the precepts affecting life in the divine
family. "All ye are brethren" is the reason advanced why disciples
should not covet precedence one over the other in public hon-
ours, titles, and dress. The "brother's" trespass, the mote in the
"brother's" eye, the "brother" having aught against thee, the
"brother who sins" – all express this corporate basis of mutual
moral duty. Those who hear the word of God and do it, who do
the will of God (Luke 8:21, Mark 3:33) are acknowledged by
Jesus as "my mother, my brothers, my sisters," and the risen Lord
adheres to this language – "Go, tell my brethren." The effect is to
characterise the Christian ethical community as a family of "brethren" owing firm moral responsibilities one to the other, and
bound by a common relationship to the Father and to the divine
Son.

It is true that the term "brethren" was used also in pagan circles for
fellow-members of a religious community, but this does not determine
Christian usage. The central truth of the divine family, the Christian
name for God, and for Christ, and the related theological concepts of
new birth, adoption, show that more was intended. The special emphasis
upon the church in the "ecclesiastical Gospel" (Matthew), clearest in
chapters 16-18 but present throughout the book, confirms the interpretation of "sons", "brethren", as constituting a community sharing a
common moral loyalty under one Father, united in one divine Son. Of
course, the general truth of the corporateness of the Christian moral
ideal finds other expression also – in the kingdom-concept, in the law of
love, in the church and her worship, and elsewhere.

The family circle which embraces God's sons transcends
natural family ties: it may be necessary to "leave" houses,
brother, sister, father, mother, children, for Christ's sake
(Matthew 19:29). It will transcend also all social and intellectual
distinctions: the greatest in this circle, receiving highest honour, is

he who self-forgetfully serves the rest. The son in God's family is
– by definition – a man for others: he can no longer live unto
himself. Jesus gathered around Him the nucleus of the future
society who would "exemplify in their intercourse together those
higher relations which would hereafter be universal" said Scott.[8]
"It has been found ever since that His ethic can only be realised in
a society in which men are bound together in the most varied
relations; and this is the reason why monastic institutions have
always defeated their own end ... Their failure has been due to
nothing else than their exclusiveness."

Inevitably, this mutual loyalty between God's sons involves
sharp difference from life "in the world": the new type of character cannot but reveal itself in "eccentric", nonconforming
attitudes. Christian virtues flourish in lives at home in God's family, rather than shaped under social pressures and precedents. "It
shall not be so among you ..." repeatedly marks the essential
moral distinction of the life of sonship: and the result will exhibit
that quality of surprise, of paradox, which Marshall rightly discovers in the Beatitudes. The sons of God live already "as though
the new age has come", and so the poor, the persecuted, the
peaceable, the pure in heart, the meek and those who mourn, and
those who strive after the unattainable, are the truly blessed.
Their inner quality, shining through their lives, and their mutual
relationships and loyalties, are consequences of a spiritual sonship
nourished, developed, and rewarded within the shared experience
of the Father's love.

(iii) Of particular features of the divine image expected to reveal
themselves in God's sons, the foremost is *love,* which in this context means especially what Christians later called "brotherly-
love". The word occurs twice in Paul, twice in 1 Peter, once in
Hebrews and in 2 Peter, while the idea recurs throughout 1 John.
Even where sonship or brotherliness is urged as the motive, however, the love required is not *confined* within the circle of the
divine family. Jesus urges love of one's enemies, returning good
for hatred, and prayer for persecution, "that ye may be the children of your Father which is in heaven, for he maketh his sun to
rise on the evil and on the good, and sendeth rain on the just and
on the unjust ... Be ye therefore perfect" (ie, complete, all-
inclusive in your love) "even as your Father is perfect". In Luke's
version, those who do good, and lend, hoping for nothing again,
"shall be the children of the Highest, for he is kind to the
unthankful and to the evil" (Matthew 5:43-45; Luke 6:35, 36). It
is nevertheless within the family circle that such love must first be
manifested.

Among the several Greek words for love Marshall distinguishes *agape* as
an attitude determined not by emotional attraction, as in friendship or

sexual love, but by the free, self-determined act of him who loves; it desires nothing but to give, and its elements are recognition, consideration, and care. Taste, and inclination, are strictly irrelevant to moral love – though we must not say that Christian love is all principle and no emotion: "cold, religious kindness" is deadly cruelty. *Philadelphia* has the distinct overtone of family and brotherly affection. In 2 Peter, it is an intermediate step towards universal goodwill; elsewhere it is translated "brotherly affection", "love of the brethren", "brotherly love."

Among the detailed duties of such brotherly-love is mentioned the avoidance of that critical attitude which delights in judging fellow-disciples, and hastens to remove the mote from a brother's eye, oblivious of its own serious defects of vision and of character. Forbidden, too, by brotherly-love are the impatience that would insult a brother, or hurl contemptuous epithets at him; and anger, the denial of brotherly affection. Peter, again, is urged to turn his own bitter experience to good account by strengthening "his brethren". When a brother sins against us, brotherly affection requires that we "find our way to him, and tell him his fault in private", giving every opportunity for apology and explanation without loss of face: "If he listens to you, you have gained your brother" (Matthew 18:15). Brotherly concern can be stern, too: "If your brother sins, rebuke him ..." (Luke 17:3).

The "new commandment" to love one another is uttered likewise within the close circle of spiritual brethren, in the final discourse before the cross. It evokes, not an emotional or pietistic gentleness, but a strong mutual loyalty in shared danger and bitter suffering, a pledge to stand *together* against the persecuting world. A wider application of brotherly love is implied, though the family tie is still referred to, in the parable of the Sheep and Goats. There, too, the duties of social concern for the hungry, the thirsty, the stranger, the naked, the sick and the prisoner, are urged on the unanswerable ground that inasmuch as kindness is shown to one of these "my brethren", it is shown to Christ.

Especial emphasis falls also on the brotherly duty of *forgiveness*, arising directly from the son's experience of the Father's forgiveness. As we are received into the divine family only through the Father's pardoning grace, so must we bear ourselves graciously towards fellow-members of that family. "The unforgiving spirit," says Marshall, "is a flat contradiction of all that Christianity stands for."

No limit is permitted to the son's willingness to forgive his penitent brother. Reconciliation while the offence continues, is impossible: but the antecedent willingness to forgive may be the most potent factor producing repentance. It is implacability– so often, vindictiveness reinforced by self-righteousness – which Christ castigates. The irreconcilable spirit finds no forgiveness. The command to forgive gains force by being made part of the daily prayer: "forgive us . . . as we forgive" is a perilous petition, underlined by the unique comment that if we forgive not men their trespasses, neither will the Father forgive us. This truth is made unforgettable by the warning, in the parable of the Two Servants, that unforgivingness on our part will lead to God's *revoking* His forgiveness of us!

The duty to forgive is again widened into the Father-like love of *peacemaking,* an active concern to reconcile others as God in the gospel reconciles us. The form of the seventh Beatitude may suggest that peacemakers not only are, but are seen by many men to be, and are so "called", the sons of God. This obligation finds expression in many connections, both in explicit counsel and by implication.

Personally, Jesus forbids anything like vindictiveness, requiring the return of good for evil, and the turning of the other cheek to any offender. Legally, He advises agreement with one's adversary before one's case reaches court, when legal costs and loss of face will make settlement much more difficult. In cases where oppressors use legal process to defraud, He suggests we over-reach malice with generosity. Domestically, Jesus warns that a house divided against itself cannot stand, and He pillories the attitude of the elder brother whose unforgivingness would keep the prodigal in the far country. Religiously, He demands that any gift intended for God be left beside the altar while, as a matter of first priority, a quarrel with one's brother be resolved – the word "brother" underlining the truth that worship of the Father cannot co-exist with bitterness towards His other child. Politically, the same spirit of reconciliation is plain in Jesus' own attitude towards the occupying powers, His rejection of Zealot policies of revolt, His universalist vision. And in the vexed question, urgent for the early church, of the right attitude towards persecutors, Jesus urges an unembittered spirit, that seeks not judgement and revenge but blessing and grace for the persecutor – doing good to them that hate you, and praying for them that despitefully use you. In one Matthean passage, words are preserved which suggest, for quarrels within the church itself, a clear and resolute programme of reconciliation, which moves from private persuasion to shared, impartial enquiry and on to communal decision, in the effort to make peace (18:15-20). For the sons of God, the obligation to seek peace and pursue it is absolute, and universal.

To be a member within the family of God, accepted as a son, thus confers high spiritual privileges and carries far-reaching moral obligations. To be children, together, of the living God, is a glorious experience: to behave as children together of the living God is an exacting and ennobling ideal. Nevertheless, a worthy divine sonship is only one major theme of the ethical teaching of Jesus.

5

The Kingdom of God and the Life of Obedience

THE LANGUAGE OF JESUS' second great theme is, of course, that of the messianic hope, sublimated by Jesus into new and richer meanings. In so far as its basic thought is that of God as Sovereign, Lawgiver, divine King of men, Jesus is at one with the Torah; but what became for Judaism a political, apocalyptic, or purely religious hope was for Him essentially an ethical attitude within the heart that would transform society. The "kingdom" *means* the reign of God within each soul living under the divine sovereignty; wherever a life surrenders to the Father, there the kingdom has come; it is "within you" or "among you" (Luke 17:20, 21) just in the measure in which the will of God expressed in Christ is accepted and trusted. The equivalent experience in later gentile-Christian terms is believing acceptance of the Lordship of Christ.

The Greek feminine abstract *basileia* means primarily kingly rule, reign, the exercise of royal power, and only secondarily, by derivation, the realm or territory ruled over; the *reign* of God is therefore the more correct translation. Defending "the kingdom is *within* you", Marshall appeals to the context (a warning against attempting to locate the kingdom, or to watch for it, in the world about us); to the use of the crucial word in Matthew 23:26 for the "inside" of a cup; to two papyri citations where the word clearly means "within", and to later Greek usage. Moreover, Jesus always saw the inner state of soul as the key and source of the outward life, and His thought about the kingdom would certainly *begin* with the obedience of the heart to God. As Marshall well says: "In this conception religion and ethics meet ... God takes the initiative and comes to the soul of man with a transcendent moral claim. When a man recognises that claim, and voluntarily surrenders himself to it, he has come under the rule of God, and thus the kingdom of God is established within him." Henceforward, "on all the central issues of life he takes his moral cue from God."[1]

But although essentially an inward experience, and therefore initially individual, the kingdom is also for Jesus, *equally essentially,* corporate and social – partly because what is so central to a man's life must effectually influence the whole circumference of his behaviour; partly because one King reigns in all obedient hearts, controlling their relations with each other, their common aspirations, and their united goal.

(1) A RELIGIO-ETHICAL IDEAL

In the teaching of Jesus the kingdom appears as a present reality, inaugurated by His ministry, evident in the healing of the sick and the saving of the sinful, available to be received, inherited, entered, by all who consent; and also as a task and hope, for which men still pray, which they "seek first", which is growing like seed secretly to unforeseen fruitfulness, spreading through society like the ferment of leaven hidden in meal – until the whole be leavened. Yet *the kingdom is God's, not man's:* its coming is apocalyptic, not only as awaiting future consummation, but even more as depending upon divine initiative – the seed, the leaven, breaks into the world's inert soil and dough from another realm. This emphasis is important as antidote to the modern idea that men may build or establish the kingdom of God by their own effort or vision. "The kingdom, as Jesus knew it, was God's, and men could no more establish it than they could make the sun rise in heaven ... His attitude was always that of waiting upon God, of trust in a divine power and wisdom that are working on our behalf and will accomplish for us what we cannot do ourselves" (Scott).[2] Knowing this, men can throw themselves into God's service with all their heart and hope. The future consummation is assumed in the parables of the Great Supper, and the Wedding Banquet, in the promise of Mark 9:1f, in the words about the "coming" of the Son of Man in glory, and in the significant expectation of the disciples at the end that the kingdom was about to be set up. On both counts, therefore – as the inward ruling principle of the ideal life, and as the goal of all moral endeavour and hope – the kingdom is for Jesus *an essentially ethical conception,* though wholly inseparable from His religious vision and faith.

(i) The attractions of life in God's kingdom are set forth in the "advertisement" parables of the Hid Treasure, which men stumble upon by simple good fortune; the beautiful Pearl, which connoisseurs sacrifice everything to obtain; the Feasts of good things – the wedding of a royal prince, the messianic banquet with the patriarchs, the joy of marriage – and the implied tragedy of lost opportunities. No less than sixteen things are pronounced blessed, all of them marks of life as lived under divine rule: the gospel of the kingdom is a many-sided invitation to happiness. These metaphors would startle, were they not so familiar: together they set forth a state of life to be immensely enjoyed. Nevertheless, life under divine rule brings also its ethical *obligations*. The truth is aptly illustrated in the fragmentary parable of the Wedding Garment: to be invited, and welcomed, out of our poverty and need, to share the banquet of the King, is glorious grace; but there is no excuse for remaining among the King's guests in raiment that brings shame upon His house, and hospitality, and name.

(ii) To attain *entrance* to God's kingdom it is necessary to humble oneself as a little child. Such humility is, in the ultimate analysis, "pure receptivity" (Inge), the unselfconscious, and (in the literal sense) unassuming readiness of children to accept favours without considering whether they are deserved, without defending injured pride, but simply trusting in the kindness of the giver. Its opposites are self-important independence, and the self-righteous assertion of merit, so easily fostered by legalism. Christian humility constantly remembers that it possesses nothing that it has not received; that it is nothing but for the grace of God; that apart from Christ it can do nothing. The humble deeply believe that God resists the proud and gives grace to the lowly in heart; that because this is God's world, he that exalts himself will be humbled, and he that humbles himself will be exalted. Humility's prevailing emotion is a glad gratitude, that never presumes to repay all that it has received, together with a constant realisation that it has never attained the ideal, has everything still to strive for, and at the end of all achievement remains an "unprofitable servant" – inheriting the kingdom only by the favour of the King.

Such humility is far removed from that wilful self-disparagement which refuses to serve, to attempt, or to accept responsibility, under a cloak of incapacity; equally far from the borrowed, conventional descriptions of sinners as "loathsome as a toad" (Bunyan), "guilty, vile and helpless worms" – which some pretend to apply to themselves but would bitterly resent from others. There is nothing in the least like this in the Gospels. "God, be merciful to me, a sinner" is on a much more wholesome, and sincere, plane. Closely linked with this emphasis on humility is the profound truth that for Jesus the highest goodness is unconscious (Matthew 25:31f). He never counsels self-examination, or self-conscious character-building: virtue is the natural fruit of the good tree, the overflow of the true heart. The soul that loves God will do right and serve men spontaneously, without effort and without pride. That is the charm of Christlike character.

(iii) Several parables imply growth and development, so helping to explain *the delay* of the kingdom by illustrating how men's varying capacities for the truth, or their many excuses, or their spiritual unreadiness, hinder the coming of the kingdom for them. The moral change in men which the divine rule demands makes essential a human response of repentant faith, if God's will is to be done and His kingdom established. In the parables of the

Darnel and the Dragnet, the mixed results of gospel sowing and fishing are exhibited, and the need for patient confidence in the judgements of God. Any man may throw away his divinest opportunity: the kingdom *will* come, but each man's share in it depends upon his own response to the gracious initiative of the King.

(iv) Further, man's ethical *endeavour* for the kingdom is commented upon in several parables. That of the Unjust Steward highlights the need that people of the kingdom show as much energy, intelligence, and practical sense, as the rascals of the world; that of the Talents emphasises faithfulness, whatever be the circumstances or limitations in which men serve; that of the Labourers stresses that all reward for service in the kingdom is of God's free grace – envy is out of place, and we dare not ask for what we deserve!

Of this kingdom, so attractive, so to be experienced, so morally conditioned and served, much of our Lord's ethical teaching provides a detailed and searching description.

(2) THE LAWS OF THE KINGDOM

God's kingdom has but two explicit laws: "Thou shalt love the Lord thy God . . . and thy neighbour." These again might well be regarded as Godward and manward applications of the same imperative – that of love. As life in the divine *family* involves the reflection in the sons of the loving nature of the Father, so life in the divine *kingdom* involves equally obedience to the King's will – which again is love.

(i) Life under the divine yoke is easy and joyful because obedience springs spontaneously from those who *love God* with all their heart and soul and mind and strength. Jesus requires that devotion towards God be whole-hearted, single, concentrated: compromise is not merely wrong, or difficult, but impossible – "you cannot" divide loyalty between God and mammon. "Him only shalt thou serve" (Matthew 22:37, 6:24, 4:10). Jesus requires too that pious practices expressing personal devotion shall be such as flourish also in secret, lest motives of ostentation and pride should corrupt them (Matthew 6:1-6). Further, he who loves God will hallow the divine name, and reverence it in daily intercourse. The prohibition of oaths may owe something to Jesus' overhearing the swearing of bargainers in the market-place; its real purpose may be to safeguard integrity of speech. But a loving reverence for God will always remember that heaven is God's throne, earth His footstool, Jerusalem the city of the great King, and the temple the place where God dwells – and swear by neither (Matthew 5:33, 23:16-22). Similarly, he who loves God will exercise a reverent trust, and refuse to put God ever to the test.

"Thou shalt worship the Lord thy God ... the Father seeketh such to worship him" puts into words the unfailing loyalty of Jesus towards the public services of synagogue, temple, and festivals. His zeal for God's house, His love of the scriptures, His delight in seeking God in prayer, His strong defence of the divine meaning of the sabbath, His unshaken trust, His utter dedication to God's service, His exultant thanksgiving and unreserved joy in God, all illumine the meaning which He attached to the first law of the kingdom.

Above all, to the mind of Jesus love for God meant unquestioning obedience. To do the will of God is to know the truth about Him (John 7:17); it is of no use to call Jesus "Lord" if we fail to do God's will, while he who does the will of God is closer to Jesus than His own natural kinship. Moreover, such obedience must be unhesitating, uncalculating, without regret, if it is to "worthy of the kingdom" (Luke 9:57f). From His baptism to fulfil every command of God, to His final, dramatic and unforgettable surrender in Gethsemane, the life of Jesus provides running commentary on His own words: "that the world may know that I love the Father ... and as the Father gave me commandment, even so I do ... I have kept the Father's commandments, and abide in His love" (John 14:31, 15:10).

For Jesus, nothing is allowed to take precedence over the first and greatest commandment. The second is like unto it, but with Him it is never allowed to obscure, or to exhaust, the first.

(ii) So far from being, as some allege, "mere form without content", that second law, "Love thy neighbour", is illustrated with embarrassing fullness and variety, in innumerable counsels, examples, applications, and commands. Wider than "brotherly-love", to love one's neighbour as oneself – the briefer version of "whatsoever ye would that men should do to you, do ye even so to them" – is a succinct but sufficient definition of that active, sympathetic imagination, which transfers others' distress to our own hearts, and determines what is right, good, desirable, and fitting for others, not by what they actually do to us but by what we wish they did (Matthew 7:12 = 22:39, 40). That practical and realistic identification of Christian love as transferred self-love is sufficient, in almost every situation, to show what Christian duty dictates: whatever self-love prompts us to want for ourselves, that Christian love requires us to seek for our neighbours. Such love fulfils the whole divine requirement.

Leviticus 19:18 is quoted three times in Matthew's Gospel (5:43, 19:19, 22:39) as a significant instance of Jesus' "picking out the gold" in Judaist tradition. The absolute supremacy of love, and its summation of the whole law, are repeated in Romans 13:8f, 1 Corinthians 13 (cf 1 John 4:4-19).

The combination of the two commandments occurs in Testament of Issachar, of uncertain date (1st or 2nd century AD but using older, pre-Christian materials – B. M. Metzger). Luke in fact puts the utterance into the mouth of the lawyer (10:27) and possibly Matthew, too, thought of Jesus as speaking here wholly in line with the best Jewish teaching. Some take "on these hang all the law" (Matthew 22:40) – a phrase found also in the Mishnah – as defining the authority, or the basis, of the whole law, or as stating the general principles from which the rest of the law may be logically deduced. A supreme commandment, observance of which takes care of all the others, seems a likelier interpretation.

Addressing the crucial questions, the parable of the Good Samaritan defines both *love* and *neighbour*. It vividly portrays spontaneous care and kindness towards any stricken, suffering, helpless individual we happen upon in life's journeying. Christ's illustrations are all equally concrete – the cup of water where water was not always plentiful; visiting the sick, clothing the naked, feeding the under-nourished, befriending the ill-deserving prisoner; forgiving the offender, doing good, giving, lending without expectation of return; returning good for evil, prayers for cursing, gentleness for all ill-treatment. The ministry of Jesus is the enduring object-lesson in Christian love – His time, His sympathy, His unwearying service, ever at the command of the outcast, the helpless, the repulsive, the unvalued, the sinful, the blind and lame and leprous; His friendship towards sinners; His unfailing courtesy; His adaptation of His teaching to the comprehension of His hearers; His patience with the disciples; His readiness to devote all attention to "unimportant" individuals; His resolute refusal to meet His enemies with their own weapons; His unembittered, undefeated good will in severest rejection and extreme torture; His ability to love to the uttermost and to the end. And we are to love one another *as He has loved* us.

As defined in the Nazareth sermon, and in the reply sent to John (Luke 4:16-21, Matthew 11:2-6), the kingdom of God becomes a kingdom of love, where the lame walk, lepers are cleansed, the blind see, good news is proclaimed to the poor, broken hearts are bound up and prisoners set free, and the year of divine grace is announced. Since the nature of God is the law of the kingdom, and His love is limitless, unconditioned by race, or by man's deserving, our love too must acknowledge no frontiers, no enemies, but be "perfect" – complete, all comprehending – as the love of God for the world (Matthew 5:43-48). The three simple phrases, "Love ... as thyself"; "Love ... as I have loved you"; "Love as the Father hath loved ..." comprise the whole meaning, and motive, and measure, of love as Jesus expounds them.

Probably the dimension of love least understood in modern discussion is its sternness and strength. Christ's love reckons plainly with men's weakness, waywardness and wickedness. Jesus prays for Peter, but not that he may be spared temptation; He pleads with men, but abates nothing of His standards; His disciples disappoint Him, and He does not hide the fact from Himself or from them; He warns Jerusalem with tears of the perils of a wrong decision, but He presses His challenge relentlessly, nevertheless. Though after his denial Peter is gently re-won, each wayward step has to be consciously retraced (John 21:15-17). Warning, forthrightness, exposure, anger, irony, silence, rebuke – all lie within the compass of a love that is no timid mildness, effeminate, offenceless, and ineffectual.

Love must show its strength not in denying evil but in forgiveness and reconciliation. Knowing its own frailties, it will judge no man yet for all practical purposes it will discriminate characters and situations (Matthew 7:1-6). It extends hospitality knowing that goodness goes often unrequited (Luke 14:12) – and may cost all one has (Matthew 19:16). It faces rejection and persecution without surprise or bitterness, revealing its deepest strength in endurance. It will find itself often called upon to wash the feet of the unworthy, even to lay down its life for others – than which there is "no greater love" (John 13:3-11, 15:13). Christian love is not sentiment – but strength.

In the teaching of Jesus, such love is essentially a moral attitude: but it is also an art, and an adventure. It is an attitude of unlimited and undiscourageable good will; an art of personal relationship carried to the highest degree of delicacy, understanding, and cleverness in doing good; an adventure in which the soul reaches out from itself into others' lives and returns enriched beyond measure. Most significant of all, "upon these two commandments hang all the law and the prophets": no other requirement matters, save as it serves to fulfil the twofold law of the kingdom. *To love is enough.*

(3) THE KINGDOM AND SOCIETY'S ILLS

Because the kingdom is inward, present, and ethical, it must govern all the life of its subjects, set within society. Some criticism of current social standards is implied in Christ's words about the priest and the levite, the tax-gatherer and the Pharisee, during the feast at Levi's house, in the sermon at Nazareth, in the comment upon popular explanations of tragic events, and at the cleansing of the temple. His counsel to obey the scribes' teaching but not their example, His warning to beware the contagion of the Pharisees, and much beside, reveal a mind sharply aware of the world around it (Matthew 23:2-3 Mark 8:15). Christ's compassion on the multitude, leaderless and lost, is a poignant comment on the times; as is the comparison of weather-wisdom with prevailing spiritual insensibility; and His rebuke of the demand for a sign to prove what should be perceived by its own light (Matthew 9:36, 16:1-4, 12:38, 39). Teaching so relevant and practical must imply judgements about the thought and ways of His own time. On certain themes, however, Jesus speaks more positively, as on social aims and ambitions, on the presence of evil in the world, on the social significance of the family, and on wealth and its responsibilities.

(i) Our Lord's observations upon the things men strive after vary from half-humorous advice on how to behave when invited to a rich man's house (better to take the lowest place than risk being put in your place!) to the solemn warning against that ambition which would dominate the lives of others, such as earns for the princes of the gentiles high-sounding titles like "Benefactor", "the Great" – "it shall not be so among you" clearly prohibits for the men of the kingdom all such status-worship (Luke 14:7-11, 22:24-27). The Beatitudes affirm another standard of success: blessing lies elsewhere. The plain counsel of Jesus is that men shall seek first the kingdom as their supreme value, and let all else come and go as God wills. The alternative, to strive to gain the whole world and have it on your side, or at your feet, may involve losing your own soul. Here already is the germ of that sharp distinction between the ways of the kingdom and the ways of the world which was later to lead, *for good and ill,* to the doctrine of "separation". The aims and values of the kingdom of God are clearly not those of society at large.

(ii) Indeed, the people of the kingdom are inevitably confronted with opposition to the rule of God, in cunning and violent evil. In no respect does the popular conception of Jesus go further astray than in supposing Him to be ignorant of the sin of the world, or wilfully blind to it. *Jesus was a realist.* John says He would not trust himself to men because He knew what was in man; He himself said: "Beware of men" (John 2:24-25, Matthew 10:17). He estimated that only a quarter of His hearers would bear any measure of fruit to God; that some who were "caught" in the kingdom net would yet prove unwholesome. The usual reason for divorce was man's obstinacy and cruelty taking advantage of the defenceless. Few things have ever been said about the human heart more forthright than: "From within, out of the heart of man, proceed evil thoughts, adulteries, fornications, murders, thefts, covetousness, wickedness, deceit, lasciviousness, an evil eye, blasphemy, pride, foolishness – all these things come from within, and defile a man" (Mark 7:20-23). If the ugly list is an interpretative comment rather than a verbatim report of words of Jesus, it still testifies to the candid assessment of human nature which His contemporaries expected of Jesus; and it says no more than is implied in the gallery of rogues whom Jesus acutely observed and relentlessly described –

the unjust judge, needing to be plagued into doing his duty,
the churlish neighbour, impatient of a simple request,
the money-making farmer, with no thought above his barns,
the unfeeling glutton, ignoring the beggar at his door,
the ungrateful youth, rebelling against restraint,
the rascally steward, embezzling his master's capital,
the lazy servant, burying money entrusted for use,
the ruthless moneylender, mortgaging a widow's home,
the ostentatious Pharisee, parading his piety,
the flattery-loving scribe, delighting in obsequious tributes,
the inconsistent debtor, forgiven but unforgiving,
the heartless priest, unconscious of social duty,
the indifferent levite, ignoring the needy,
the crafty king, ruling by vulpine cunning,
the envious farmer, sowing tares in a neighbour's crop,
the bargain-hunting crowd, following for a feed,
the ruthless press-gang, compelling service for Rome,
the domineering foreman, beating and starving the servants,
the faithless servants, carousing in their lord's absence,
the slave-driving boss, demanding his supper at once,
the tyrant rulers, called great because over-bearing,
the treacherous disciples, who shall betray and forsake,
the shallow friends, boasting yet denying,
the slumbering spirits who miss festive opportunities,
the professional prostitute, whose sins were many,
the callous legalists, valuing ritual above suffering,
the misguided zealots, serving God by violence,
the trivial-minded, offering childish excuses,
the vacillating governor, unequal to his responsibility,
the blasphemer against light, placing himself beyond forgiveness,
the corrupter of children – better never born.

There is not much about human nature that Jesus does not know.

He saw how wealth may harden the heart against conscience and against God; how sin may blind the soul, ruin the young, warp the judgement; that the world is no safer for the wise and godly than for the foolish and wicked – the same storm beats upon each house. He pointed out plainly that faithfulness and truth may lead straight to a cross. He knew that He sent forth the disciples as lambs among wolves. He called for serpent-like wisdom in dealing with the world, and Himself "calculated the drift of dangerous questions and returned guarded answers" (Scott). He knew that the way to life is narrow and lonely, that loyalty to Himself might well divide families, that prophets must work without honour in their own country. Only pathetic ignorance of the Gospels can represent Jesus as a starry-eyed idealist blind to realities: His was a faith that blinked no facts. Given such courageous truthfulness, disappointments lose their power to hurt; to believe in God in spite of what we know is far stronger than to persuade ourselves that things are other than they are.

Within the political context of the life of Jesus, resistance to society's evils could be only upon a personal level of individual integrity and example. Jesus leaves no doubt that the men of His kingdom will themselves walk closely the unpopular way to life. Amid all social pressures they will be subject most of all to the interior constraint of the will of God, despising compromise and neutrality, and knowing well that he who is not for Christ is against Him. So the Christian in society will exercise the illuminating function of a candle set upon its stand, a city sited upon a hill and not to be hidden by night from far across the plain; the preserving and purifying function of salt, careful not to lose its savour by adulteration or dilution; and the inspiring, disturbing, fermenting function of leaven, bringing new moral standards, ideas and judgements to bear upon life around him. And he will do all this with such grace and humility that men seeing his good works will forget him and give glory to the Father. When men's reaction is hostile, the man of the kingdom will carry his resistance to evil to the point of accepting, even rejoicing in, the persecution which Jesus said is the lot of the prophets and of every man ahead of the average of his time. Such resistance to evil *by example and suffering* is the very heart of the gospel, from Isaiah 53 through Calvary down the long history of Christian heroism. It is the one form of resistance which does not descend to the level of the evil it opposes, which does not perpetuate the wrong it deplores, and which succeeds. Only theorists doubt the moral demand, the spiritual strength, or the final effectiveness, of Christ's prescription for overcoming evil with positive, costly good.

Facing the dilemma of passive tolerance of evil or active resistance by force, Marshall castigates the attitude of Tolstoi, who condemned the use of force, by saying it implies the condoning of crime and violence. He quotes K. S. Latourette for the view that "however incompatible the spirit of Jesus and armed force may be, and however unpleasant it may be to acknowledge the fact, as a plain matter of history the latter has often made it possible for the former to survive;" and Marshall adds: "Jesus Himself resisted evil, as His cleansing of the temple, His bitter and uncompromising exposure of the sins of the scribes and Pharisees, and His declaration that there were people in the world who deserved to have millstones tied about their necks and to be drowned in the depths of the sea, so clearly prove."[3]

Marshall examines the passage in which "Resist not evil" occurs (Matthew 5:38-41), and concludes that the words relate only to evil done to oneself: the maintenance of public law and order is not here in view. Non-resistance to evil is Christ's alternative to the *lex talionis* – Jesus would abolish altogether the restraint which law imposed upon unlimited revenge by forbidding all revenge. Whatever the personal injury, the man of the kingdom must offer no vindictive resistance. But Christ says more: when you turn the other cheek, give to a man what he is trying to steal, go a second mile when he forces you to go the first, you remain a free agent, and overcome evil with good – a high doctrine amply illustrated in Christ's own attitude to the inhospitable Samaritans, in His mildness towards Judas in the garden, His silence at His trial, and His intercession at the crucifixion.

Scott shows how this principle of non-retaliation to personal injuries brings to sharpest focus the demand for kindness towards enemies: injury received confers no right to injure in return, nor does it cancel the obligation of universal love. The principle expresses too the judgement of Jesus on the futility of evil: Satan cannot cast out Satan, nor a second evil heal a first. The return of good for evil constitutes already a moral victory, a breaking of the vicious circle of wrong, a positive reaction of self-discipline and moral dignity, and a significant step towards the ultimate triumph of love.

This does not touch the wider question of the Christian reaction to evil in society, as it bears upon *other* individuals and infects the common life. The memorable warning that they who take the sword shall perish by the sword summarises Christ's refusal to use force to propagate or to defend His ideals (Matthew 26:47-54). His response to the temptation to build His kingdom in the devil's own way, His attitude to the Zealots, and His words to Pilate, all confirm that in His view the submission of men's hearts to the will of God was not to be achieved in that way. But the ordinary processes of law, justice, and government, by which society is disciplined and crime restrained and punished, Jesus accepted without question. What He might have prescribed as an ideal reaction if the Samaritan had chanced along the Jericho road half-an-hour earlier, we can only guess. But there is certainly no command to turn your brother's other cheek, while the demands of compassion and self-sacrifice, and His own energetic defence of the weak and the ill-used, leave little doubt that He would not have us stnd aside until the fight was finished. The Christian's wider social responsibility concerns, however, issues broader than society's specific ills, and is better postponed for later consideration.

(4) THE KINGDOM AND THE FAMILY

The closest of all social pressures upon the individual is that of the family. Though Jewish family life was already widely envied, Jesus invested the home with still higher value and sacredness.

Tracing marriage not to human necessities (as Paul tended to do), nor to social expediency, but to a divine purpose expressed in the constitution of human nature (Matthew 19:3-9), Jesus held it to be founded and designed by the Father Himself ("God made them male and female"), authorised and ordered by divine law ("whom God hath joined together . . ."). In particular, Jesus held marriage to be *monogamous,* on the deep psychological ground that two so united become "one flesh". By defending the wife's right in marriage, Jesus implied that it was *equal* in privilege and responsibility for both partners. By His warning against dividing those whom God has joined, Jesus declares marriage to be *permanent.* It is possible to argue that the phrase "whom *God* hath joined . . ." does more than summarise the general divine purpose implied in the Genesis story, and points towards a *sacramental* association of true marriage in the mind of Jesus.

The statement that "they shall be one flesh" is crucial for the Christian view of marriage as monogamous and permanent: precise definition of its meaning is therefore important. (a) At its lowest it implies that unity of husband and wife before the law which affects questions of legal responsibility, possession, and inheritance; but from the argument based upon it the phrase evidently means more than that. (b) A complete unity of status, privilege and interest seems to be implied in the variant expression of the idea in Ephesians 5:28f: "Husbands should love their wives as their own bodies. He who loves his wife loves himself. For no man ever hates his own flesh, but nourishes it and cherishes it . . . the two shall become one." (c) A more psychological or spiritual oneness resulting from sexual union seems to underlie 1 Corinthians 6:13f: "The body is not meant for immorality but for the Lord . . . Shall I therefore take the members of Christ and make them the members of a prostitute? Never! Do you not know that he who joins himself to a prostitute becomes one body with her? For, as it is written, "The two shall become one" (Greek, 'one flesh'). This joining oneself – "uniting oneself to" – the prostitute is then contrasted with uniting oneself to the Lord as "one spirit with him", implying a oneness that makes common cause and becomes one in mind, emotion and experience with the partner. (d) The illustration which Jesus provides, and which Ephesians 5:31 repeats, suggests that the phrase means oneness of the same kind as that which unites parent and child. For a man leaves one form of socio-natural unit, in the family of father and mother, to create another socio-natural unit, a marriage – a new unit as close, as natural, and as permanently undeniable, as the one which gave him life: and so (as Christ's words show) as indissoluble. This is the immediate, and the deepest, meaning of "one flesh".

Christ's very high valuation of marriage is confirmed by His own attitude to the home at Nazareth (remaining to support the family until others were old enough to release Him), and by His insistence upon the duty of children towards parents (Mark 7:9-13). It is expressed in His unsparing picture of the prodigal son; in all His tender allusions to parents, children and marriage joys. Above all, by "associating the family with His central religious ideas – calling God Father and men His brethren – He gave to family life a new consecration" (Scott). To this general statement, however, two corollaries must be added.

(i) If Christ's valuation of marriage rests upon a religious foundation, it follows that to His mind the religious loyalty must be primary and the marriage loyalty secondary if ever the two should conflict. Chinese, Japanese, and some western critics claim that Jesus depreciated family relationships by declaring that those who do God's will stand closer to Him than His own family; by urging one who wished to bury his father before becoming a disciple to "let the dead bury their dead"; and by saying that unless a man "hate" father and mother, wife and child, brother and sister, and his own life also, he cannot be a disciple (Mark 3:31-36, Luke 9:60, 14:26).

Marshall usefully quotes Genesis 29:30-31 where, as in Malachi 1:3, "hate" plainly means "love less".

In answer to the conundrum about the woman who married seven husbands, Jesus declares that marriage, and its exclusive loyalties, are temporary – not of the eternal order (Matthew 22:30). Similarly, Jesus clearly acknowledges the conflict which His claims might create within many families, and the loss of domestic sympathy and enjoyment which loyalty to conscience and to God might involve – as His own experience demonstrated (Matthew 10:34-39). The way in which this loss is represented, as the extreme sacrifice which the kingdom might demand, itself implies the highest valuation of the family: only one harder thing could be required, "his own life also".

Jesus may well have felt that in Judaism the family circle had sometimes become an end in itself, an excessive family loyalty breeding indifference to wider responsibilities and jealousy of any interest beyond its own immediate concerns. Inge refers to the exaggerated family unity expressed in feuding, family massacre, and punishment of sons for their fathers' crimes. Several writers point out that those who criticise Jesus for setting claims of conscience above the family do not always feel the same when patriotism, professional ambition, or the demand for cheap industrial labour, invade family life.

Another example of Christ's subordination of marriage to higher interests is expressed in a strange passage (Matthew 19:10-12), now appended to teaching about divorce but perhaps originally belonging to a discourse on self-denial. Either way, the meaning is that refusal of marriage is not so exceptional as the disciples appear to think. Some are born to remain single; some are forced to it; others eschew marriage for the sake of the kingdom. This is not for all: "He who is able to receive this, let him receive it." Here, as with a man called to leave wife, family and home for the sake of the kingdom, the higher claim may totally exclude the lower. This again is no greater sacrifice than Jesus Himself made: and the warning may have relevance still where the perils of some chosen vocation, the demands of missionary service, the danger of inherited disease or insanity, (or, conceivably, of racial incompatibility) raise conscientious objections to a particular marriage. But it is no depreciation of marriage to say that higher considerations may preclude it. It is indeed a protection of marriage, to advise against it when moral conditions presage failure.

(ii) But if, in certain comparisons, Jesus held the family tie to be subordinate, He also held it to be indissoluble. That seems clear, although the subject of Jesus' attitude to divorce is beset with difficulties and uncertainties.

Judaism itself was divided. Deuteronomy 24:1 enacted that a husband's divorce of his wife, "if she found no favour in his eyes, because he hath found some unseemly thing in her," must be accompanied by a document conferring full freedom, so protecting the wife from mere temper, caprice, or future claim. R. Shammai understood "unseemly thing" to mean unchastity; R. Hillel took "find no favour" to include things like disappointing cookery; later (AD 135) R. Akiba was to include also finding another woman more beautiful.

When the question of divorce was posed to Jesus, He first set the Deuteronomic provision into perspective as a tragic concession to human cruelty, and not a permission to repudiate one's oath: "For your hardness of heart Moses allowed you to divorce your wives, but from the beginning it was not so" (Matthew 19:8). The divine intention had been that "the two shall become one" – not to be put asunder. Hence: "Whoever divorces his wife and marries another, commits adultery against her, and if she divorces her husband and marries another, she commits adultery" (Mark 10:11, 12). For those who live under God's rule, the divine will in marriage, as here laid down, is permanent, indissoluble unity.

Matthew however preserves another version of these sayings: "every one who divorces his wife, except on the ground of unchastity, makes her an adulteress; and whoever marries a divorced woman commits adultery ... Whoever divorces his wife, except for unchastity, and marries another, commits adultery" (Matthew 5:32, 19:9).

Why divorcing a wife makes her an adulteress is not clear, but it must be remembered that society provided neither career nor support for the unmarried woman. For the unprotected, divorce might well mean, beside disgrace, begging, starvation, or shame. A. H. McNeile comments, "her remarriage is assumed as certain" and W. C. Allen, D. Hill agree.[4]

This version of Christ's words allows one significant exception to permanent, indissoluble marriage –where the *wife* has committed adultery already. The so-called "matrimonial offence" follows inevitably from the nature of marriage, which is distinguished from friendship, partnership, and every other human relationship, precisely by the solemn undertaking to keep oneself sexually for the other. Plainly that is not *all* that marriage means, but that is the unique and constitutive factor: and it follows that the one offence which automatically destroys the essence of marriage is the breaking of that vow. Where sexual infidelity occurs, the constitutive basis of marriage is already desecrated – although of course forgiveness and renewal of vows may happily restore it. Alexander so explains the exception which – according to Matthew –Jesus had allowed: a divorce which merely recognises that the marriage *has been* broken is not itself a new fact, but only the public acknowledgement of what has already happened.[5]

There are serious difficulties, however, in believing that Jesus made such an exception. The chief is that Mark and Luke give the statement of the divine purpose that marriage be indissoluble *without exception*. We have no choice therefore but to accept either that Matthew is right, and Mark and Luke guilty of serious omission from Christ's words, entirely altering their import; or that Mark and Luke are right, and Matthew has added a clause, perhaps one universally assumed in Jewry, easing the implied austerity in the light of experience of its hardship – the church, through Matthew, making the same concession to human weakness as the rabbis had made. When Paul quotes "a word of the Lord" on this subject in 1 Corinthians 7:11 he makes no reference to any exception for adultery. Further, if Jesus made the same exception as the school of Shammai, neither His criticism of Jewish attitudes, nor the protest of the disciples against His austerity, seem in place. In Matthew 5, the whole context states Christ's moral demands without compromise: hatred, impurity, insincerity are in no circumstances permissible – does Jesus here descend to an exception, and for adultery?

Marshall concludes roundly that the exceptive-clause "is certainly not original". E. F. Scott, H. Rashdall, K. Kirk, W. R. Inge agree; and Inge argues that divorce here means separation with freedom to remarry, as in Deuteronomy, in rabbinic discussion, and all early Christian references to this passage. Separation without remarriage appears to be contemplated in Luke 16:18 (where it is the remarriage which constitutes adultery), in Paul, and perhaps in Matthew. This is not divorce: it recognises that a particular marriage has become intolerable, but that despite separation and unhappiness the sacredness of the marriage is still binding.

Scott thinks that divorce is the one issue upon which Jesus did enact a definite rule. Others hold that Jesus was here, as in all other issues, stating the ideal and leaving men to strive after it according to circumstances and capacity. This doubt, like Christian resistance to evil, raises the whole question whether Christ's teaching about life in the kingdom constitutes social legislation, or a statement of ideal principles. To that question we return when other examples of the issue are also before us.

(5) THE KINGDOM AND MATERIAL WEALTH

Men of the kingdom are involved in the life of society economically as well as domestically. On the subject of wealth and its distribution the teaching of Jesus seems to be criticised from all sides at once. He is said to be too other-worldly, and at the same time the greatest of all social reformers; He is said to preach slavish contentment and submission, and yet to be the great Democrat, the Working-man, encouraging all the world's under-dogs to be ambitious and get on. He is said to condemn wealth, and yet as the first socialist to be intent upon distributing it equally to all men. In so controversial a field, it is scarcely possible not to read our own meanings and assumptions into Christ's words.

Certainly, behind all that Jesus said about wealth lay His faith in divine providence, the assurance that those who seek God's kingdom will not go uncared-for (Matthew 6:25-33). It is equally clear that Jesus nowhere condemns riches or praises poverty. He had rich friends, dined in their houses, accepted their support; some of the disciples appear to have owned houses, or boats; renunciation of all possessions is never made a universal condition for entry into the kingdom. The rich fool is condemned, not for his riches but for the folly of thinking that wealth was the aim of life, and of forgetting to become rich toward God. In the Lazarus parable, the rich man is condemned, not for his riches but for his callous indifference towards the beggar at his gate. Such selfishness Jesus censured in everyone: it was more evident in the rich than in the poor, but not more wrong. The power of wealth to provide hospitality, feed the hungry, clothe the naked, do good and lend, finds frequent expression in His parables: it is always possible to consecrate the "unrighteous mammon" by the way you use it. Employment for wages, buying and selling, banking and interest, are all mentioned without comment. Jesus' main concern is with men's attitude towards wealth and with its right use. Here, unquestionably, He introduced new perspectives of compassion, service, and a golden-rule equality of need.

But Jesus emphasised also the spiritual perils of affluence. So responsible, and dangerous, was the possession of great riches that it made entry into God's kingdom infinitely harder; it might well be necessary in some cases for an applicant to strip himself of everything to make entry possible (Mark 10:21, 23). If right use could consecrate money, wrong use could betray its owner into exploitation, dishonesty, selfishness, merciless use of power. Worship of mammon excludes the worship of God. Jesus would reject the view that men's behaviour is determined by economic forces, but agree that man can allow himself to become so determined, so corrupted and decayed, by love of money.

"According to Karl Marx, the economic factor is the cardinal and decisive factor in history, and all men's ideas about law, politics, culture, religion, and philosophy are moulded and controlled by prevailing economic conditions" (Marshall); " . . . the driving force is really man's relation to matter, of which the most important part is his mode of production. In this way Marx's materialism becomes, in practice, economics" (Bertrand Russell).[6] The "realism about human nature" supposedly implied in such "economic determinism" used to be contrasted with Christianity's "airy romanticism and other-wordly nonsense". Paul Ramsey says: "Speaking in Marxian terms, all the higher reaches of human thought and culture seem the natural consequence of economic modes of production . . ." and adds neatly: "Sigmund Freud spoke of three offences against man's conception of himself. Copernicus gave the cosmic offence, Darwin the biological offence, and Freud himself the psychological offence to man's traditional high regard for the powers of man. It might be added that in the reduction of man Karl Marx provided the cultural offence."[7] To suggest that Marx meant only that "man in the whole, humanity" was economically determined, is unreal: only as applied to individual men and women is Marx's view comprehensible – abstractions like "humanity" have no motives – and so applied, his view is self-refuting, as countless heroic social reformers prove. For Jesus, economic determinism was not a ruling principle of human affairs, but a perpetual temptation and peril: at its most successful, it might cost a man his soul.

It is this spiritual danger which Jesus underlines. Wealth can be a hindrance, a temptation, a distortion of life's true aim. "A man's life does not consist in the abundance of his possessions" (Luke 12:15 RSV): life is more than food, or raiment, or investments. The heart will always gravitate towards what it counts precious, and there settle in the end; what you value will make you what you are (Matthew 6:21). Neglecting all other security, the soul may – as Jesus said – come to *trust* in riches, and that spells ultimate disaster: for if the heart's treasure be vulnerable to the moth and rust of corruption and the thieves of time and death, the soul must be bankrupt at the last (Luke 12:13-21).

It will not do, with Scott, to minimise this emphasis on the danger of wealth by suggesting that Christ's words are coloured by their apocalyptic setting, and so not of permanent validity: for every man (as Christ's parable suggests) the end is always near, with its audit of life's true values. Nor may we evade the emphasis by attributing it to Luke's bias, with a doctor's compassion for the poor: Jesus too had compassion, and knew that the poor are with us always. (We shall return to the "apocalyptic" argument).

But poverty, too, has its dangers. Significantly, the thorns which choke the good seed in the heart of the listener include both the cares of the world and the deceitfulness of riches. Covetousness can poison the rich soul with avarice, the poor soul with envy. Jesus is sometimes said to have had no interest in social justice, because He refused to adjudicate in a dispute over inheritance: yet it was obvious that the appellant desired neither adjudication nor justice, but only Christ's support for his own demand (Luke 12:13). As Marshall comments, Jesus was not interested in the transfer of property from one covetous man to another. With equal clearness, if not as frequently, Jesus warned against that besetting anxiety about food, raiment, and the future which may, as effectively as affluence, imperil spiritual understanding and woo the soul from God.

Wealth, then, is devalued by Jesus, as among the accidents and not the essentials of life; compared with life under God's rule, the true pearl of great price, all other treasure is handled with *detachment,* which neither seeks wealth nor despises it. Within God's kingdom, both rich and poor are, in inner attitude and spirit, "poor".

It is exceedingly difficult to decide the meaning of the first Beatitude. Moffatt's "Blessed are those who feel poor in spirit" is simply not true. The New English Bible's "Blessed are those who know that they are poor" is paraphrase, unpleasant, and needing explanation. Another scholar's "Blessed are those who are conscious of having nothing and being nothing" is neither true nor Christian. "Blessed are those who are aware of their spiritual need" is a substitute, not a translation. If Old Testament precedent determines the meaning, then the "poor" are the poor afflicted saints, "those who because of long economic and social distress have comfort only in God" – and, it should be added, because in times of foreign occupation, only the conscienceless prosper. (Psalm 69:28f – the 'needy' in parallel with the righteous, the afflicted, the oppressed, who seek God and are His own; Psalm 37 *passim*, 'the poor and needy' (14) in parallel with those who wait for the Lord, the meek, the righteous, who walk uprightly; Psalm 40:18 "I am poor and needy, but the Lord takes thought for me". So too 1 QS 4:3 – the humble poor who trust in God's help; and 1 QM 14:7 'the poor in spirit' (NB) in parallel with the fearful of heart, the dumb, the feeble, the trembling knee, the 'perfect of way').[8] On the other hand: Luke says plainly, "Blessed are you poor", linking with blessing on the hungry, the weeping, and woes on the full and rich. James has a close quotation, "Has not God chosen those who are poor in the world to be rich in faith and heirs of the kingdom ... ?", in context with the men with gold rings and fine clothing. While words about wealth and anxiety in the following mountain sermon harmonise with this quite literal interpretation. Because Judaism was costly in time and money, the offer of a kingdom whose privileges were open equally to rich and poor was good news indeed. Yet literal poverty is not in itself "blessed": Matthew's additional phrase "in spirit" is a pertinent reminder that it is upon one's attitude to poverty or wealth that everything depends.

Such spiritual detachment, the ability to be rich without avarice or pride, and poor without covetousness or anxiety, the mind that has been "initiated into the secret of having abundance or going hungry, yet in whatsoever state to be content" (cf Philippians 4:11, 12), is blessed indeed. Unfortunately, it is easier to be indifferent to others' poverty or wealth than to one's own: and just as one is never bidden to turn a brother's cheek so one is never allowed to be "detached" about another's want. A genuine spiritual disengagement from the relentless pursuit of material goods is serenity and security: those who can rise to it for themselves, while remaining deeply concerned for others' needs, already possess the kingdom.

(6) THE KINGDOM AND THE STATE

Our Lord ministered in occupied territory among a subject people, in a political situation at once explosive and hopeless. A dramatic example of what happens to prophets who defy tyranny was before Him in the Baptist's death: opportunity for action or agitation through democratic processes simply did not exist. Without entirely agreeing with Scott that all Christ's teaching was coloured by considerations of His own safety, and by His conviction that all political arrangements were temporary because the kingdom was imminent, we must acknowledge that His circumstances affect our interpretation of His words, and limit their relevance to the modern Christian's wider opportunities and responsibilities.

Marshall speaks of Jesus' patriotism, citing His sad remonstrance, "O Jerusalem, Jerusalem, how oft . . ." and His apparent limitation of His mission to His own people. Yet even this saying (Luke 13:34-35) foresees His nation's destruction, and the limitation was expressly partial and temporary, a practical necessity rather than a principle. That Jesus loved His nation and His people as much as He loved its literature and its history, need not be doubted; He everywhere accepts the right of the State to legislate, to levy taxes, and to be obeyed within its jurisdiction. Considering the danger, it is significant that His criticisms of the existing regime survive. In the account He gave of His own temptation, for example, the kingdoms of this world are represented as essentially satanic; to build His kingdom their way would be treason against God! He calls Herod "a fox", defies His threats, and later will say nothing to a king who had silenced a prophet.

Possibly, His ironic remark that among the gentiles those who dominate others are called "Benefactors" implies that to His mind the despotism of Rome was "arbitrary and oppressive" (Marshall).[9] Yet at His entry to Jerusalem, and in His words to Pilate, Jesus repudiated any violent attack against the authorities. According to John, Jesus defined for Pilate the theocratic idea of the divine source of all political power (19:11) – an account very significant for later Christian thought. In Galilee, Jesus took energetic steps to quell a movement to make Him king (John 6:15), and at the end the Sanhedrin only succeeded in persuading Pilate that Jesus was a danger to the State by giving to His words a meaning which they knew He did not intend.

Certainly Jesus expected a clash between the kingdom of God and the kingdoms of this world. According to Matthew, He knew that His followers would have to stand before kings, magistrates, and councils; He seems to have expected that some would die at the hands of the State (Matthew 10:17-18, Mark 8:34-38). His kingdom was not of this world, and His servants would not fight (John 19:36): but they would resist. His own passive yet unbreakable resistance before Herod and Caiaphas perfectly expresses His attitude. He too refused to fight: but He died rather than submit, or change course, when higher loyalties conflicted with the orders of the State.

This is the essence of the few positive counsels Jesus uttered on political matters. The right of the occupying forces to impress for immediate, though limited, military service was a constant humiliation to the proud Jew: our Lord's advice was to do what was demanded, and then double it, voluntarily, so preserving dignity and asserting freedom even in obeying (Matthew 5:41). "Render to Caesar the things that are Caesar's, and to God the things that are God's" was a non-committal evasion of a malicious trap. By demanding if it was right to pay tribute to Caesar, His enemies thought He must either deeply offend Rome or raise howls of derision at any messianic claim. Jesus' reply ought not, therefore, to be quoted as a final and sufficient pronouncement upon political responsibility. It is neither an assertion of the divine right of kings, nor of the secondary place of the State, nor of the absolute distinction between political and religious duty, so that statesmen need not concern themselves with Christian ethics. Jesus first exposes the hypocrisy of the question by forcing the questioners to produce the tell-tale coin by which they – not He – acknowledged Caesar's rule; then He deduced the obvious duty of loyalty towards one whose rule you profess to acknowledge – whether Caesar or God (Matthew 22:15-22).

To regard the use of Caesar's coinage as incurring obligation to pay for civic benefits, provides a valid argument for paying taxes: but Pharisees might have retorted that they would prefer to support a government of their own choice. We might infer from Jesus's words that the State has rightful, though not absolute, claims; that God, too, has claims, though these must not be made excuse for civil disobedience. But the exceptional circumstances of the saying must always be borne in mind. The maximum justifiable comment is probably Paul's: "One must be subject, not only to avoid wrath but for the sake of conscience. For the same reason you also pay taxes, for the authorities are ministers of God ..." (Romans 13:5f).

The curious story of the coin in the fish's mouth (Matthew 17:24) concerning first the payment of Temple tax and later of political tribute, seems to reflect the anxiety of the early church over all imposed taxation. The principle of doing freely whatever you are ordered to do, is applied again: "sons are free", but a spirit of conciliation will exercise its freedom by paying rather than by refusing. (How Peter obtained the money is irrelevant to our purpose, but playfully expressed advice to go and work for it seems more probable than a gratuitous, and wholly uncharacteristic, miracle.)

The relation of the kingdom of God to a State at war is a problem different from passive acceptance of wrong done to oneself; different also from one's moral responsibility when others are violently attacked. Wars of revenge, aggrandisement, exploitation seem to be excluded on general principles of the rule of God – the God of all nations. But what the duty of the man of the kingdom might be when evil policies take to arms and threaten the State, is easier to feel than to justify. The futility of armed force to achieve any spiritual, moral, or religious good seems clear: "they that take the sword shall perish by the sword ... else would my servants fight." Jesus lived amidst mutterings of armed rebellion; the Zealot movement plotted continually against Rome; Josephus speaks of innumerable tumults and disorders in Judea after the death of Herod the Great; the Siccari, and Barabbas, show that "the movement was already on foot which was to culminate a generation later in the great revolt" (Scott).[10] All this makes Christ's firm refusal to use or countenance armed force an eloquent protest against the idea that one can build or defend Christian values by violence. In this atmosphere, the entry to Jerusalem becomes almost a pacifist demonstration.

But when the alternative to war appears to be unresisting surrender to evil, it is hard to conceive what Jesus *might have* said. Marshall's references to the saying about a king calculating his probable success in a war before engaging in it, to Christ's dealing with centurions without condemning their trade, to the counsel to the disciples to "sell their garments and buy swords", are scarcely apposite: does Christ's reference to the embezzling steward – also without condemnation – condone dishonesty? Whether Jesus would approve naval power to keep the seas free from piracy; whether once war has begun, He would choose force as the lesser of two evils; whether He would insist that moral evil can never be restrained or overcome by such immoral means as war; whether He would say that atomic war is, for the man under God's rule, in all circumstances unthinkable; or whether He would urge that the good man cannot disengage himself from the struggles of his society, and that in this connection also, "greater love has no man than this, that a man lay down his life for his friends" – all such questions each Christian will decide according to *his own extension and interpretation* of Christ's principles. The responsibility for such a personal decision, in the changed circumstances of our time, cannot be evaded by appealing to some documented saying of Jesus, however earnestly we might wish that it could. On this topic again we face the question of the precise nature of Christ's social teaching.

(7) THE KINGDOM AND SOCIAL LEGISLATION

Problems affecting resistance to social evil, divorce, the distribution of wealth, and political obligation, all raise the question whether Christ prescribed rules to be invariably followed by the men of God's kingdom, laws to be enacted for society as a whole, or imprecise principles, standards and insights, to which any rules subsequently framed must approximate as closely as circumstances allow. As we saw, Scott held that Jesus laid down one binding rule only, in the matter of divorce. Others have tried to translate all Christ's words into legislative Acts, seeking to enforce the Christian sabbath, church attendance, payment of tithes for the maintenance of religion, and many expressions of Christian piety, upon all men. Still others, despairing of this Christianising legislation, have sought to withdraw from all social involvement and confine Christian ideals to an exclusive élite coterie within society – sometimes holding themselves free nevertheless to deal with the world on its own secular terms, to their great profit.

The ethic of Jesus has been criticised for ignoring the duty to reform society. Inge speaks of the blindness of early Christianity to the future welfare of humanity in this world: "In many of our social problems we cannot find the help in the gospels which we would have welcomed, because the early Christians never thought about an earthly future for the human race."[11]* The hope of the advent may possibly have foreshortened history's perspective for those who preserved the sayings of Jesus, but the social limitations of the early disciples, and of Jesus Himself, must not be forgotten. Where the political opportunity to shape events does not exist, the duty to do so does not arise – and Jesus never

*See also Chapter 6(3) (ii)

theorises. A third consideration is that the things Christ prized were not those which legal enactments can produce: no legislation can enforce love for God or men, or evoke obedience to God's will. It could be contended that reform by external coercion runs counter to Christ's essential method. Moral ideals are necessarily modified by any attempt at compulsion: celibacy, or poverty, when imposed involves violation of personal freedom; freely chosen, each constitutes a noble self-sacrifice. Unquestionably, Jesus believed that His way of living conferred welfare upon individuals and society; only by hearing and doing His word could men ensure that the house of their life would withstand the storm (Matthew 7:24-27). He expected men to see this. But until they did see it, no mere legislation would achieve the kingdom.

So, "Christ was not a legislator. He held up standards, He laid down principles, but He left nothing at all like a code behind Him" (Inge). Says Marshall, "Jesus must never be regarded as a second Moses ... To think this is to relapse into the very legalism which He condemned."[12] Thus, in the issue of divorce, Christ's principle of the indissolubility of marriage is fully applicable only to those within God's kingdom; in a world that is not yet God's kingdom, to make the ideal view of marriage compulsory would be to turn idealism into legalism. Avowed disciples of Jesus are in a different position from that of the general public, and possess different moral resources. Marshall instances the State's permission of divorce on grounds of insanity, whereas no Christian would abandon his wife because of her misfortune. Scott similarly argues that Jesus never prescribes the manner in which His inward principles must be realised: this men must decide for themselves in the special contingencies with which they have to reckon from time to time. Jesus aimed at creating the new universal good will, in virtue of which men would be able henceforth to make their own laws. Had Jesus laid down any detailed programme of social reform, it would have been out of date long ago; instead, His principles are universal and timeless, and no generation is exempt from the labour of discovering how they can best be applied to current conditions. This application of Christ's principles, moreover, must take realistic account of actual circumstances, risks, and probable consequences. Indiscriminate generosity to the thriftless may in fact be harmful; unlimited trust in an ex-criminal may only provide new temptations and provoke fresh evil; separation from the world, and doctrinaire non-violence, may leave the oppressed at the mercy of their oppressors. No prescribed rule, or unvarying example, can possibly apply to all cases.

Rashdall remarks that the difficulty of finding detailed guidance in external authority is instructive. The ideal – as in permanent, monogamous marriage – is certain: the wisest defence of it, and the choosing of the lesser of the evils which arise from violation of it, must be left to the Christian moral consciousness, and to experience. So, too, Jesus laid down the ideal of absolute veracity; but in legal proceedings the church has sanctioned the use of the oath, since in this particular realm the truth of testimony is a supreme concern in the defence of the innocent, and such a situation was not before Christ's mind. Infinitely more complicated are the judgements involved in following Christ's ideal in the circumstances of war.

The tension and uncertainty resulting from such necessary adjustments of the ideal to the situation cannot be evaded. They are the implicates of Christian freedom. Just because Jesus left us insights and principles instead of rules, we are free to follow the light we have as best we may: but this implies a solemn and sometimes heavy responsibility to exercise freedom with care, and with some anxiety lest adjustment involve betrayal. Thus obedience is ultimately individual. Only a predominantly Christian society can justly demand predominantly Christian laws. Yet the Christian community is part of society, a responsible, organised, vociferous part. The example of Jesus suggests that society and the State have a right to Christian co-operation and support in every good endeavour, while the Christian community now has the right and opportunity, in many countries, to offer counsel, criticism, and protest on public questions. But thereafter it cannot impose its will upon the non-Christian proportion of society, but only claim the same representation in forming the public will as is given to others. Meanwhile, it will always, and in all things, set its sights by its own ideals, and live above the average, never surprised when its peculiar judgements upon social affairs are rejected by the majority.

But neither may the Christian community, on its part, claim always to have complete and final solutions to society's problems. In a society ordered under God's rule, those problems would not arise; as Rashdall says, "In a society living up to Christ's principle, there would be no divorce for adultery – because there would be no adultery."[13] The same is true concerning crime, war, and all the problems which human wilfulness and selfishness create; there may be no ideal Christian solutions because Christian presuppositions are rejected from the outset, and Christians cannot advise pagans on making a success of paganism. This does not exempt Christians from social concern, involvement, and witness: but it does preclude all dogmatism and legislation, and leaves upon the Christian conscience the duty of finding the way from things as they are to the world as Jesus declared it might become, under the rule of God.

Inge cites the excellent summary from Peabody's *Jesus Christ and the Social Question*: "Such seem to be the principles of the teaching of Jesus

– the view from above, the approach from within, and the movement towards a spiritual end; wisdom, personality, idealism; a social horizon, a social power, a social aim. The supreme truth that this is God's world gave to Jesus His spirit of social optimism; the assurance that man is God's instrument gave to Jesus His method of social opportunism; the faith that in God's world God's people are to establish God's kingdom gave to Jesus His social idealism."[14]

(8) THE KINGDOM AND THE WIDER WORLD

The duty of the man of God's kingdom towards society and the State is further complicated by the need to look, with Jesus, beyond both, to the world at large. As a citizen of a wider kingdom, and a member of the divine family which embraces all nations, the Christian cannot identify himself exclusively with one country, or culture, against all others – least of all in an age when world communications have brought the races into touch, and the movement of peoples has intermingled them, as never before in history. Despite the Old Testament's wider vision of a world-wide messianic kingdom, and the daring universalism implied in books like *Ruth* and *Jonah,* Judaism in Christ's time (as we have seen) had become increasingly nationalistic and exclusive. Jesus' own attitude towards men and women of other races, His challenge to exclusiveness in the Nazareth sermon, and the references to other peoples in some of the parables, have already been noted as evidence of a collision with Judaism on the racialist issue. Just how far Jesus anticipated, during His lifetime, a world-mission by the church is debatable, but it would be difficult to believe that the apostolic church totally misread His mind about its own task and commission.

The mission of the disciples in Matthew 10 is strictly limited to "the lost sheep of the house of Israel", and Christ's replies to the centurion, and to the Syrophoenician woman echo this definition of His immediate aim. Yet the Nazareth sermon, the references to those who come from north, south, east and west to the messianic banquet, the parables of the mustard seed with its converging birds, and the vineyard given to others, the Johannine insistence that God loved the world, that there are other sheep of another fold, that the cross will gather together into one the children of God who are scattered abroad, and John's description of Christ's reaction to the enquiring Greeks, all tend to confirm that sayings like, "This gospel of the kingdom will be preached in all the world ..." (Matthew 24:14, 26:13) and, "Before him will be gathered all the nations ..." (Matthew 26:32) do not misrepresent His mind. The familiar argument that Jesus could not have commissioned the disciples to go to all nations in the explicit way which Matthew describes in 28:18f – otherwise the difficulty of the apostolic church over the mission to the gentiles is inexplicable – misses the important point that *the early church never was in doubt whether the gentiles should be evangelised.* From Peter's sermon to the end of *Acts* that is assumed. The difficulty was over the terms of that evangelisation, whether circumcision and acceptance of the law were necessary pre-requisites for all Christians, or only the traditional approach of the first (Jewish) disciples. Matthew, Luke and John agree that the commission to the apostles was world-wide. It is indeed possible that Jesus Himself, learning His Father's will step by step, realised the universal range of the kingdom in Syrophoenicia, as He learned the method of the kingdom in the wilderness, and its limitless cost in Gethsemane; but Matthew at any rate rightly reads His eventual conviction: that the gentiles must receive the gospel, not merely because the Jews refused it (as Paul would say), nor merely because the Jewish nation was doomed, but (as the Syrophoenician woman and the centurion both learned) because wherever "great faith" emerges, there salvation is assured.

It follows that for the man under the rule of the universal Father, social responsibility knows no frontiers. Alexander quotes with approval the view of Wundt, that the missionary movement of the last century and a half is the mightiest factor in modern civilisation. This movement had its origin in the simple moral necessity of sharing whatever has enriched and raised oneself. Not the Christian theology alone, but the Christian ethic demands the missionary expression of the Christian spirit – demands the hospital, leprosarium, school, orphanage, and refugee's shelter. As Hocking said, "Religion, from primitive times the protector of the stranger, the market-place, the truce, is the forerunner of international law; because it alone can create the international spirit, the international obligation, it alone can permanently sustain and ensure that spirit."[15] Albert Schweitzer's view, that the Christian west owes *atonement* to the rest of the world for the evils perpetrated by so-called 'Christian' exploitation, finds adequate basis in the whole attitude of Jesus. And urgent practical necessity reinforces the argument: any ideology or programme that holds the least hope for world peace *must* have universal scope, and be built upon spiritual foundations; must reconcile rival interests in a common concern and discipline – and where can any such impulse or vision be found, but in the gospel of the kingdom of God as Jesus preached it?

(9) THE KING'S JUDGEMENTS

The divine initiative waits upon human response before the kingdom of God is established in any individual life; but that does not mean that God is king only if we choose – that God is, so to speak, an elected Sovereign. Such a conception would be as impossible to the mind of Jesus as to any Old Testament prophet.

God *is* King: though His reign be rejected, His will is accomplished in the end and His judgement stands. Only one of Christ's five parables of judgement explicitly mentions the kingdom, but all plainly imply that God is Judge over the moral life of man.

The parable of the rich fool reveals that it is God's assessment of any man's success that matters; in that of the rich man and Lazarus, divine justice reverses human conditions and attitudes; the story of the barren tree given another chance illustrates the divine patience, but also the demand that life shall bear fruit in positive good; the parable of the vineyard declares for all time that the wilfulness which denies to God His right and to the Son His welcome, shall surely be punished; the parable of the sheep and goats, where all nations are gathered before the King's throne of judgement, sees the verdict fall according to men's treatment of each other – their obedience to the kingdom's second law.

In all such figures, as in phrases like "night cometh ... the door was shut ... outer darkness ... weeping and gnashing of teeth" the truth shines clear that men cannot in the end trifle with God: The blessings of the kingdom wait upon consent: but God's rule remains unshaken even when man refuses. God reigns: man chooses only whether that shall bring him joy or judgement.

The Fourth Gospel declares that "the Father ... has committed all judgement to the Son"; Paul says God will judge the world by that man whom He has ordained (John 5:22, Acts 17:31). So, in His attitude to wrong as in all else, Jesus makes known the mind of God, and His judgements become for us a rehearsal of the final judgement, throwing further light upon His ethical thought.

"In the Gospels sin is seldom mentioned except in connection with forgiveness" (Inge), and certainly Jesus differed widely from some current views on what constituted sin – an external uncleanness that could be washed away, the eating of proscribed meats, some technical or accidental omission of ritual, or the work of evil spirits. Christ's own diagnosis was nearer to that of some rabbis, who found "an evil impulse" in human nature to be the root of all disobedience of the law (recall ch 2: (5) (iii)).

(i) In accord with the inwardness of His whole teaching, Jesus extended the meaning of sin to include vindictive, lustful, censorious, or envious *thought and desire,* as well as overt acts. Refusing to attach much importance to ritual failures, Jesus held that sin, like goodness, was a quality of the inner self: "from within, out of the heart of man" the mouth speaks and all evil actions flow (Luke 6:45, Mark 7:21f). In part, the cause lies in an inner moral blindness: "the eye is the lamp of the body. So if your eye is sound, your whole body will be full of light; but if your eye is not sound, your whole body will be full of darkness. If then the light in you is darkness, how great is the darkness!" (Matthew 6:22f).

In part, the cause of sin is a defect of nature: "each tree is known by its own fruit. For figs are not gathered from thorns nor are grapes picked from a bramble bush ... So, every sound tree bears good fruit, but the bad tree bears evil fruit. A sound tree cannot bear evil fruit, nor can a bad tree bear good fruit" (Luke 6:44, Matthew 7:17f). And in part the cause of sin is the deliberate hoarding within the soul of evil suggestions, desires, attitudes: "the good man out of his good treasure brings forth good, and the evil man out of his evil treasure brings forth evil" (Matthew 12:35), which Luke interprets as "treasure of the heart". For Jesus, conduct is ever the overflow (or "abundance") of character. Consequently, He showed much greater friendliness than public opinion approved towards those believed to be guilty of the grosser and more external sins of passion, greed, or impiety, even declaring that harlots would enter the kingdom before Pharisees. Sexual morality was not the problem among Jews that it was in the pagan world, and Jesus doubtless felt that many of those who sternly condemned the outward act indulged the inward imagination of impurity, and had no right to cast stones.

(ii) Similarly, Jesus extended the meaning of sin to include sins of *neglect* – things left undone, opportunities for good that were never noticed. The barren tree figured more than once in His illustrations. The man who hid his talent was rebuked – for doing nothing. The priest and Levite were caricatured – for doing nothing. The goats on the King's left hand were sent to everlasting punishment for not giving the cup, the clothes, the kindness, which they might have given; and so it is with the rich man and Lazarus.[16] This is the converse of the law of love: whereas legalism was especially concerned that man should not do forbidden things, Jesus is concerned that they shall do what love requires. In His judgement, those who do not do what they ought are at least as culpable as those who do what they ought not.

Inge lists as the things Christ most condemned, hypocrisy, hardheartedness, worldliness; Glover adds, uncleanness in thought, indifference to truth, and indecisiveness; in a long list Marshall mentions inordinate self-love as the root of most sins, and adds complacency, pleonexia (the insatiable appetite for more), moral obtuseness, and religious ostentation; Scott mentions spiritual blindness, arrogance, and cruelty, especially towards the under-privileged. But the common ground in such summaries is greater than at first appears.

(iii) Jesus certainly condemned all *sins against love of others* – unbrotherliness, implacability, want of sympathy, cruelty of criticism, vengefulness; and all insensitive or selfish social attitudes whatsoever – such as were expressed in the Temple monopoly, the harsh terms exacted by money-lenders, the wide gulf between rich and poor, the rivalries that rent society. Marshall well reproduces the self-communing of the rich fool – "What am *I* to do, for *I* have no place where *I* can gather *my* fruits? This will *I* do: *I* will pull down *my* barns and greater ones will *I* build, and there will *I* collect all *my* corn and *my* goods; and *I* will say to *my* soul ... take *thine* ease ..." So Christ mocks the egoist. Such self-absorption lies behind all wrong social relationships, and for this reason self-denial is the first ethical condition of discipleship. Says Inge, trenchantly, "Want of sympathy for the troubles and weaknesses of others is a besetting temptation of all intellectualists." Religion can be intensely censorious and cruel: Christ's anger burned at the religious dogmatism which remained insensitive to the need and suffering of a maimed labourer, a paralysed woman, in its sabbatarian zeal. Similarly, Jesus was moved to intense indignation in the house of the wealthy Pharisee at the contempt shown for the fallen by those whose social privilege and security left them utterly unable to appreciate the temptation, the need, or the heart-broken penitence, of her whom they despised. In His eyes, only the merciful might hope to obtain mercy.

(iv) Certainly, too, Jesus condemned *sins against the light* of truth. Commentators vary in their interpretation of hypocrisy, but agree it ever earned Christ's severe denunciation. On the religious hypocrite's consciously playing an actor's part before his public, Jesus quotes Isaiah:

> This people honours me with their lips,
> but their heart is far from me

and sharply condemns ostentatious display of almsgiving, prayer, or fasting, as self-righteous window-dressing (Mark 7:6, Matthew 6:1-6). Even more sharply, Jesus warns against the professional hypocrisy which maintains a public posture of doctrine and example, though the true quality of life is far different – "The scribes and Pharisees sit on Moses' seat; so practise and observe whatever they tell you, but not what they do; for they preach, but do not practise." "Nothing is hidden," says Jesus, "which shall not be known": the real self will always be revealed in the end (Matthew 23:2, 10:26).

But the hypocrisy of which Jesus speaks yet more sternly is not that which deceives others but that in which we deceive ourselves – insincerity within the soul. Five times in Matthew 23:16f the "blindness" which cannot discern what is right is described and reproached – the all-too-familiar affliction through which religious people, clear-sighted about other's sins, fail to recognise the evil that lies nearer home. What Scott ascribes to loss of moral vision, and Marshall to pride, is a falsehood within the self: then indeed "the light that is in thee is darkness, and how great is that darkness!" (Matthew 6:22, 23).

An initial stage of this sin against light is an insincere response to truth, the indecision which withholds acceptance while seeking to avoid the responsibility of rejection. Says Glover. "What part or place can there be in the kingdom of heaven – in a kingdom won on Calvary – for people who cannot be relied upon, who cannot decide whether to plough or not to plough, nor, when they have made up their mind, to stick to it, Jesus cannot see."[17] Thence often arises that self-deception which entirely misconceives its own position, thinking itself religious while having no idea what it believes, or what standards it defends. Du Bose remarks that "Christ finds fault that we have not enough of the Spirit to know that we violate it, nor apprehension enough of the law to know that we transgress it; that we have not enough of holiness to want it, or of righteousness to hunger and thirst after it."[18] The final stage of this sin against light is the antagonism which deliberately confuses good and evil, Christ and Beelzebul, the fatal blasphemy against the Spirit of truth, unforgivable because inescapable (Mark 3:22-30).

The hypocrite, thus, never deceives the Father "who sees in secret", will not eventually deceive others, but may completely deceive himself. The man of the kingdom, on the other hand, is more transparent than most men – he has nothing to hide. The purity of heart that admits to the vision of God (Matthew 5:8) is mainly single-heartedness, sincerity. Glover repeatedly says of Jesus that He was the great Son of Fact; Christians likewise must face the truth about themselves, about the world they live in, and about God. In Christ's eyes, the tax-gatherers and harlots had fewer illusions than the Pharisees; they lived in the real world, and in that honesty and clear-sightedness lay the germ of a sincerity that might save them.

Jesus condemns also *sin against the love of God*, the want of trust in divine providence, of reverence for the divine Name, of dedication to the divine will, which betrays an inward attitude careless of God's claims, leaving God out of daily reckoning. Similar is that total misreading of the meaning and end of life which prizes things, goods, security, ease, above all other considerations: the worldliness which so distorts values as to make life meaningless, because purposeless, and worthless, because it prizes nothing worth the seeking (e.g. Matthew 6:25-33, 23:16-22, Luke 12:13-21, 32-34, Mark 8:35-37). From Christ's point of view, however, *all* sin is sin against the divine love, which in all its dealings with us, in blessing or in discipline, in grace or in judgement, in promise or warning, seeks ever and in every way, only our good.

It is true that in some sayings of Jesus sin is represented as sickness of soul, needing a Physician (Mark 2:17, Luke 7:50 etc, (Greek)); – as we might say, a psychiatrist. It is true also that Jesus sometimes represents sin as folly, a significant comment expressing a whole world-view. The worldling is addressed "Thou fool ..." and the disobedient are stupid in that they build their house of life in a way that must end in ruin. Yet no one ever treated sin more seriously. Jesus shows it reducing men to hypocrisy and lawlessness (Matthew 23:28), to loneliness and degradation in a far country; to an inward darkness that cuts them off from reality and destines them for "outer" darkness also. Through sin a man becomes lost, adrift, bankrupt towards God, "dead" to the Father's love, the Father's home (Luke 15:32). So serious is sin that it is better to lose hand or eye than to tolerate temptation: better never to have been born than to lead others into evil (Matthew 5:29-30, 18:6).

But judgement is not Christ's only word concerning sin: always He nourishes hope that sin may be forgiven and overcome. He himself met the treachery of Judas with a kiss and a word of friendship; according to what is almost certainly the true text, He met the cruelty of crucifixion with prayer for His crucifiers; He reasoned with Pilate until reasoning served no useful purpose. Being reviled, He reviled not again; though He suffered, He threatened not. Thus His own actions express His faith in the superior power of goodness, His hope that the strong man armed may find a Stronger come upon him and deliver his captives (Mark 3:27). "The great matter is that Jesus believed that God was willing to take the human soul and make it new and young and clean again. But the human soul did not believe it, until Jesus convinced it ... The Son of man is come to seek and to save that which was lost, and He did not come in vain" (Glover).[19] The final judgement of Jesus upon sin is that the sinner is redeemable: in this also He adumbrates the final judgement of God.

The kingdom of God is the central theme in the teaching of Jesus, and His unique contribution to ethical *thought*. The sovereignty of God, the absoluteness of divine law, the inescapable will of God, are all here related to the finality of moral obligation, the certainty that right and good will be vindicated, the faith that the King of all the earth loves man and seeks his welfare. So the gospel of the kingdom is good news for those prepared to surrender, the understanding and submissive: as it is warning for the obdurate, the loveless, the self-willed. But whether man assents or rebels, God – the God and Father of our Lord Jesus Christ – remains King for ever.

6

The Son of God and the Life of Imitation

FOR MOST CHRISTIANS, it is probably neither the theological concept of the family of God and the ethic of sonship, nor the more social concept of the kingdom of God and the life of citizenship, that holds greatest sway over impulse and affections, but a more intimate and personal admiration, faith, and love, focused upon the figure of Jesus Himself. Indeed, for every generation the Christian ideal has been personified in Christ, concretely, intelligibly, sufficiently, unforgettably; and a grateful devotion to Him as Saviour, Friend and Lord has been the most compelling of all Christian motive-forces. From this point of view, Christian ethics has sometimes been reduced to the single, oversimplified idea of the "imitation" of Christ, and though the term is open to misunderstanding, it is convenient to summarise what is unquestionably a third theme in the teaching of Jesus.

The imitation of Christ is, in truth, the nearest principle in Christianity to a moral absolute. Though the figure of Christ is limned afresh in every age after its own fashion in thought and in response to its own ethical needs; and though the precise meaning of "imitation" changes from generation to generation, yet the ideal of Christlikeness remains a constant through all changing emphases and temporary adaptations. The law of love may be held a second Christian absolute: but without the example of Jesus, the law remains an abstract form rather than a concrete ideal, while without devotion to the person of Christ the law lacks incentive and enabling moral energy. *When all allowance is made for varying interpretation, the imitation of Christ remains the heart of the Christian ethic.*

This contention has not passed unchallenged. Harnack held that "the imitation of Jesus in the strict sense of the word did not play any noteworthy role, either in the apostolic or in the old catholic period;" and Inge adds that Paul did not care to study the details of Christ's ministry as though to copy them, though he thinks Harnack's opinion too sweeping.[1] But this objection both misconceives the meaning of "imitation" and ignores one of the powerful motives that led to the writing of the Gospels. Modern investigation of the formation of the Gospel tradition allows significant place to the desire for authoritative pronouncements and precedents by which to resolve practical problems of Christian discipleship, both in the oral and the later literary decades, while a genuine interest in the person and story of Jesus for His own sake cannot be excluded. What Jesus said, about marriage, unclean meats, the sabbath, and what Jesus did, for the possessed, the leper, the sinful, and towards aliens and enemies, all had ethical significance for those who told and retold the stories and eventually composed the sources of our Gospels. It is assumed that disciples will think as the Master thought and do as the Master did.

The importance of the imitation of Christ in the apostolic ethic will appear later: we may here anticipate sufficiently to recall *Paul's* "walk in love as Christ also hath love us ... let each of us please his neighbour ... for Christ did not please himself ... forgive one another even as Christ forgave you ... conformed to the image of his Son ... till we all come to the measure of the stature of the fullness of Christ;" *John's* "Christ laid down his life for us and we ought also to lay down our lives for the brethren ... we love him because he first loved us ... walk in the light as he is in the light ... walk in the same way in which he walked ... we shall be like him;" *Peter's* "Christ also suffered for you leaving you an example that you should follow in his steps ... Since Christ suffered in the flesh arm yourselves with the same thought;" *Hebrews:* "Let us run ... looking unto Jesus the author and perfecter of our faith ... Jesus suffered outside the gate ... therefore let us go forth to him outside the camp." *Luke's* account of the death of Stephen, and of the later experience of Paul, clearly recall the trial and death of Jesus.

Within the Gospel records, the correspondence between the character and experience of the Master and those of the disciples is everywhere presupposed: "every one when he is fully taught will be like his teacher ... I have given you an example ..." (Luke 6:40, John 13:15). In Matthew, says G. Bornkamm,[2] Jesus calls the disciples to the imitation of Himself in life and suffering: the disciples share Christ's mission and experience at every point (10:1-16), are persecuted for His sake and bear His cross (10:32-39, 16:24). In 11:28-30, to come unto Christ, bear the yoke of His torah, learn of His gentleness and lowliness of heart, are the sure prescription for spiritual rest. "The following and imitation are (in Matthew) of the humiliated Christ as He is utterly obedient to the law of God" (G. Barth).[3]

In Luke, as E. Earle Ellis shows, "the fate of Jesus is the fate of his followers. If he is attested by God and rejected of men, so are they ... If he has no resting place in this world, they too are destined to wander, preaching the kingdom of God. The disciples are commanded to carry their cross after Jesus, and his persecution marks the beginning of their own ... These parallels are not to be understood merely as an existential imitation of Jesus, but as the working out of a corporate relation to Jesus. Jesus' disciples have his Spirit, proclaim his message, bear his cross and share his glory because they are, in Paul's idiom, 'the body of Christ' ".[4]

John's "I have given you an example" is echoed in "I am the way ... I am the light of the world; he who follows me will not walk in darkness but will have the light of life" (14:6, 8:12). For once the metaphors are interpreted, the meaning is clearly that the way the Christian walks, the light the Christian follows, are the Christ-example. The same correspondence between Christ's experience in the world and that of the disciples is insisted upon by John: they too will be hated, persecuted, disbelieved (15:18, 20; 13:16); while the whole future experience of the disciples is interpreted as being possessed by, and obedient to, the Spirit of Christ Himself, Who shall come to dwell in them. That points towards an interpretation of the "imitation of Christ" at a far deeper level.

But the simplest and most familiar expression of the imitation theme in the Gospels is Jesus' initial call to disciples, "Come, follow me." Here the process of salvation consists in a sharing with Jesus of thought, activity, and experience, in which, by the contagion of perfect and powerful goodness, men will be both instructed and transformed. The cell-nucleus method, familiar in the ancient world as a pedagogic device for philosophic discussion, was peculiarly effective where the whole moral personality of the pupil, or disciple, was to be educated. "It is enough for the disciple to be as his teacher" (Matthew 10:25): and Mary, choosing the "best portion" which is to sit at the Teacher's feet and feed upon His word, is a picture of the "star pupil" in the school of Christ, learning the Christian way from its Exemplar and Source.

(1) DEVOTION TO CHRIST AS MORAL INCENTIVE

The theological basis of this ethical formulation is fourfold:

(i) The sonship of Christ Himself is first declared in closest association with ethical perfection. "Thou art my beloved Son; with thee I am well pleased" (Mark 1:11) implies more than moral assessment, since "well pleased" has its background in the notion of choice, election, rather than simply in approval and satisfaction: yet the Jewish interpretation of divine sonship, as fundamentally an ethical quality and relationship and not (as in Greek thought) a metaphysical one, must be borne in mind.[5] The family likeness between the divine Father and the divine Son which –

with much more – lies in the title "Son of God" holds also for all who through the Son gain entrance into the divine family. Status, privilege, intimacy, community of life, are certainly implied: but it is *moral similarity demonstrating such relationship* which would first occur to the Jewish mind.

(ii) It is fundamental to biblical thought that all moral perfection is exhibited in the divine character, as holiness, *hesed,* loving-kindness, justice, goodness, love; and that God the Supreme Good is thus the ideal of His people – "Be ye holy, for I the Lord am holy" (Leviticus 11:44, 45 etc). The Christian doctrine of incarnation becomes in this light at least as important for ethics as it is for theology. As the incarnation of the divine truth, love, power and purpose in the human person of Christ becomes the determinative concept for all truly Christian theology, so the incarnation in the person of Christ of the character of God becomes the determinative concept – the *Summum Bonum* – for all Christian morality. Its obvious practical implicate is the moral imitation of God as known in Christ, who becomes at once humanity's pattern for all ethical endeavour, the standard for all ethical judgement, and the promise and prophecy of man's ethical goal.

(iii) The indwelling within Christians of the Spirit of Jesus Himself carries the same implication. This is clarified and emphasised in later apostolic exposition, when the Christlike character is seen as the surest proof of the possession of the Spirit: but already in the Gospel material the foundation for this development is evident in the Johannine representation of the Spirit as Christ's "other self"; in Matthew's promise that the persecuted disciples shall find that the Spirit of their Father will speak through them; and in the Lukan insistence that Jesus, who was born of the Spirit, surrounded by Spirit-filled people, endowed by the Spirit at baptism, rejoiced in the Spirit and began His ministry filled with the Spirit, would likewise baptise others with the Spirit, "the promise of the Father", the "power from on high" which had been manifest in Him and would soon "clothe" them (John 14:17, Matthew 10:20, Luke 1:35 etc, 24:49)[6]. Such "community" in the Holy Spirit between Jesus and His disciples plainly presupposes a similar community of character and ideals as its result.

(iv) Sharing of experience and likeness of character between Jesus and His disciples is as clearly implied in the pattern of Christian salvation as it is in the principles of Christian faith. The moral ideal enshrined in the person of Christ is never simply an example we have witnessed: it is a quality and an attitude which we have *experienced.* The command is not "Love ... as you have seen me love" but "Love ... as I have loved *you*" not "forgive

... as Christ forgave His enemies" but "forgive ... as Christ forgave you". "He laid down His life *for us* ... Ye should do as I have done *to you*" (John 15:12, Colossians 3:13, John 13:15). The motive for imitation constantly appealed to is not admiration or emulation but personal gratitude for what His splendid life and death achieved for ourselves. Criticism of the idea of *Christus Exemplar* often misses this point, without which, to preach Christ as example might well be superficial and over-confident. But apostolic Christians did not pride themselves upon admiring and copying Jesus: they acknowledged the obligation to be Christlike because it was to that same Christ-spirit they owed their lives, and all their hope of mercy.

Thus, behind the imitation of Christ lie the consistency of faith and the compelling motive of personal love. If Christianity's unique contribution among all the faiths and philosophies of the world is the person of Jesus Himself, its equally unique demand is that men should *love* Him. Jesus confronts men with a proposal of friendship, an invitation to trust and attachment: "I have loved you ... Lovest thou me?" "The love of Christ constrains us" replies Paul; "whom having not seen, ye love" agrees Peter; "we love him" says John. This love includes gratitude, the sense of unpayable indebtedness for redemption, so that the Christian "ought" is literally what the Christian "owes"; but it is primarily a devotion centred upon Christ Himself as worthy of unbounded admiration, unhesitating trust, keen delight, adoration mounting to worship. To love Him more than one's near relations is – to the loving heart – no more than His due; to feed the hungry, clothe the naked, visit the prisoner, for His sake, seems simply natural. The words of Thomas, "Let us go with him and die" (John 11:16) express love's utter devotion; Peter's, "Thou knowest that I love thee" expresses the penitent yet passionate love of a heart aware of weakness; Mary's anointing Christ's feet with her costliest gift expresses love's perceptiveness and deep emotional sympathy. Yet with all this, the essence of love for Christ lies not in emotion but in loyalty; its reality is tested not by feeling but by fact.

Three times, according to John, Jesus says that love for Him will prove its worth in keeping His commandments, just as His own love for the Father found its strongest expression in keeping the Father's commandments (14:15, 21, 23; compare 31 and 15:10, and 2 John 6 – "This is love, that we follow his commandments"). He whom we love is still our Lord, and not our equal. Beside love's delight in obeying stands love's longing to be worthy of the Lord – "worthy of me" (Matthew 10:37, 38). And reinforcing both is the fear of denying, repeatedly underlined in the story of Peter – and of betraying Jesus, a horror of personal disloyalty that still lingers in the records.

Imitating, following, loving – such language suggests naive

piety rather than moral theory. Yet not to estimate seriously the ethical impetus that throughout Christian history has derived from the hold which Jesus exercises over believing hearts would be to misconceive entirely the depth, quality and intensity of Christian morality.

(2) THE EXAMPLE OF CHRIST AND CHRISTIAN IDEALS

The example of Jesus is set before us in the Gospels in four specific ways: (i) In the familiar words, "A new commandment I give unto you, that ye love one another; as I have loved you, that ye also love one another ... This is my commandment, that ye love one another as I have loved you" (John 13:34, 15:12), the quality, measure, and endurance of Christ's love are made the pattern for Christian love. In this perhaps more than in any other single respect, the example of Jesus has impressed not only the church but the western world. The gentle friendliness of Christ toward the suffering, the outcast, the unloved, the sinful, is the feature in His portrait which for most moderns excludes, often *distorts,* everything else. Peaceableness to the point of unqualified pacifism; tolerance that never gives offence, even to the devil; sensitiveness that condemns nothing and no-one; selfless service that ministers to the instant happiness of all others at all times; exquisite tenderness that wept helplessly with men – all this adds up to a popular image of Jesus as a man of *feeling,* affectionate, easily hurt, predominantly feminine, one whom no-one would trouble to crucify! Such a picture, by its exaggeration, testifies to one outstanding quality in Christ's example, a tireless, unlimited, and uncalculating good will towards all men.

(ii) Jesus appeals to His own example, also, in submission to the Father's will: "I must work the works of him that sent me ... My food is to do the will of him that sent me ... If ye keep my commandments ... even as I have kept my Father's commandments" (John 9:4, 4:34, 15:10). Luke remarks Christ's obedience to authority in the home at Nazareth; John represents the cross as the commandment Christ received from the Father (John 10:18); three Gospels stress the act of painful submission which prepared Christ for death. In this trait in His portrait, the absoluteness of the moral law has gained complete ascendancy. Men with His story before them could not find renunciation, self-denial, poverty, sacrifice, even martyrdom, at all strange. All the rigour of His demands concerning the strait gate, the supreme love, the undeviating furrow, the surrender of home and wealth, the losing of life to gain it again – all become reasonable and compelling in the light of His own absolute consecration to a will that He never questioned and could never disobey.

Suffering or sacrifice self-inflicted, or welcomed, for their own sake, constitute an unhealthy inversion of spiritual life; accepted for the sake of Him whom the soul worships, as the inescapable price of loyalty and service, self-denial – and even death – become duty. The positive purpose is always the redeeming factor in every negative Christian attitude. Fullness of life, self-realisation, Christlikeness, the unhindered service of God and man, the Master's "Well done!" deserve whatever moral effort, self-discipline, or sacrifice the situation demands. Jesus was never influenced by the dualism between spirit and matter which later gave rise to monasticism; but He knew the opposition between flesh and spirit, and the clash of the human will with the divine. His call to renunciation and obedience is due to the expectation that the whole world order would shortly give place to the kingdom of God; to the conviction that spiritual interests are always paramount; and to the confidence that in rendering to the Father unquestioning obedience without reserve a man will discover his highest good, in the service which is perfect freedom.

(iii) Our Lord's unbreakable resistance to evil in a hostile world is made our example in His counsel: "Remember the word that I said unto you, the servant is not greater than his lord. If they have persecuted me, they will also persecute you; if they have kept my saying, they will keep yours also" (John 15:20). The words dramatise the astonishing strength of Jesus. He was far too dangerous to be ignored – men had either to submit to Him or destroy Him. To the unhesitating realism and candour of His mind, the uncompromising nature of His demands upon would-be disciples, His clear explanation of the cost of discipleship, must be added the constant impression of authority clothed with power. "His was a commanding personality" says Inge, "no one ever dared to take liberties with Him." He escaped from a malicious mob by simple force of personality. His anger in the synagogue, His indignation during the cleansing of the temple, quelled all immediate opposition. What Borchert called "His robust manliness and steel-tempered will-power" attracted, and held, very masculine disciples, and explains His immense reserve of physical strength, and His equally immense moral courage in reaction to danger. Jesus is never timid before threats, nor hesitant before enemies, nor defensive before accusers; He defies conventional prejudices, attacks authority, disappoints popular expectation, holds to His course when even friends misunderstand or betray. At the end He drove forward to Jerusalem amid Passover excitement in order to force the issue with Jewish leaders by provocative actions and words, though the outcome be His death. He was stern in challenge, clear in warning, fearless in denunciation, swift to expose falsehood, feared as well as loved. Yet His strength was ever under control, serving the interests of truth, and of others, but never of self; and none need fear it but those who preferred evil to good, who treated others with malice or contempt, or opposed their own wilfulness to God's will. In His strength, also, Jesus is our example – not only in His gentleness.

(iv) A fourth element in Christ's example is His washing of the disciples' feet, with the command "ye ought also ..." – action and command alike entirely characteristic of Christ's whole life and death. "Whoever would be great among you must be your servant, and whoever would be first among you must be slave of all" (Mark 10:43). The lineaments of the meek, self-emptied Servant of the Lord contribute unmistakably to the Christian ideal. Pride, self-consequence, self-assertion, can never be explicitly defended because the example of Jesus so plainly condemns them. Rashdall remarks that Aristotle's "high-souled" man, arrogant, despising others, ashamed to receive benefit from others lest it betray deficiency, haughty to those in power, condescending to those below him, revolts us: the reason is that not in the Upper Room only but in rejection, humiliation and death, Jesus stooped to wash the feet of the world. In every recurring Supper of Remembrance, the church is recalled to similar lowly service of mankind: here, again, the Christian ideal is unique.

In these explicit ways Jesus Himself was held to have spoken of His example: in much else also the church felt herself drawn to follow His steps. His unsullied purity, for example, His utter freedom from pretence, passion, or pride, shines through the traditions they preserved about Him. His truth, and entire integrity; the intense, positive holiness that prompted the burdened to confess to Him, and once drove Peter to plead that Jesus would let him alone; the sense that in His words God spoke and in His gracious presence God was near – had men not perceived that He possessed such qualities they could never have trusted Him with the faith they placed in God, nor addressed to Him their prayers, nor offered Him their worship. But knowing this, they acknowledged Him Master of their lives. This was not the presupposition but the consequence of their experience with Jesus. They came to discover that He had the words of eternal life, that He kindled within them nobler thoughts, better impulses, clearer insight into good, than they had ever known. So they *found* Him to be the incarnation of the highest good; and so He has remained: to hearts that love Him, the living exemplar of all we long to be; and to the world, increasingly, the conscience of the race.

More must be said about the "imitation" of Christ, for it can be variously understood: but it is well at once to recall the inwardness upon which Jesus insisted – that conduct flows from character. No mere outward conformity to the pattern of His words, deeds, and way of living could pass therefore for real likeness to His mind and spirit. Nor did He ever seek to mould all men after one image. Parables like the Sower and the Talents show that He expected men to respond according to different capacities, and His choice of the Twelve reveals the same delight in the diversity of human types. The imitation of Christ must not be so pursued as to inhibit the freedom of individual development. A Christlike mind and heart will show itself in multitudinous ways, as time and change, circumstances and disposition, opportunity and need, individual background and maturing experience, shape Christian lives to situations vastly different from those in which Jesus lived and died. That this is so raises the final question of the permanent validity of Christ's ethical standards; but that the example of Jesus has in fact provided guidance for generations of Christian disciples, needs no proof.

(3) THE PERMANENT VALIDITY OF CHRIST'S IDEAL

The centrality of the figure of Jesus to the Christian ethic provides at once some ground for the accusation that His ideal must be out-of-date, since He lived in another age, another sort of world; and ground also for the reply – that it is precisely because His ideal is expressed in a personal character, and not a code of law or a philosophic creed, that it has proved adaptable, illuminating, relevant, in the changing circumstances of different generations. Any formulation of ethical duty in words of command, of wisdom, or of warning, must belong to the age and thought-forms that produced it. A living spirit, expressing a personal vision, faith, attitude, quality and courage, defies exhaustive description or formulae, and for that very reason may be analysed and described afresh in each new age and culture without disloyalty to its inner truth.

(i) We have noted in passing some of the *criticisms* occasionally levelled against the teaching of Jesus – due sometimes to misapprehension, when poetic imagery, the occasional deliberate exaggeration, and precise context are ignored; or to illegitimate generalisation, when counsels for particular circumstances are elevated into social rules or prescriptions for life in a modern democracy – or when Christ's words against personal vindictiveness are misrepresented as policies of pacifist toleration towards crime and social evils. Sometimes, too, ideals presented for the committed disciple are wrongly universalised, as though equally practicable when divorced from their religious presuppositions: the counsels of Jesus offer no practicable ethic for a humanistic society. Again, nothing that Jesus said depreciates intellectual or aesthetic pleasure, though in His circumstances and to His associates, such were not often available – fine works of art or music hardly came within His purview!

More seriously, it is sometimes contended that an ethic of universal love is necessarily invalid, being self-destructive, and beyond the power of will or command. Bishop Butler argues well for that due and proper regard for *self* which underlies all morality.[7] Self-knowledge, self-reverence, self-control, are prerequisites of altruism, just as a true self-assessment, and even a controlled self-assertion, are inseparable from the carrying of responsibility and the wielding of influence. Self-respect is the beginning of self-discipline: self-contempt is the end of all morality.

This serious argument is frequently ignored in pious circles: an individual's own larger good ought not to be sacrificed to the trifling whim, the temporary advantage, or the inbred selfishness, of another simply because that other desires it. One's own debts ought to be paid before self-impoverishing generosity is shown to others. The prayer "Oh to be nothing, nothing ..." finds no justification whatsoever in the teaching of Jesus. He required love for one's neighbour not instead of oneself but as oneself – assuming that the normal man does love himself! On occasion, Jesus withdrew from the clamorous needs of one day's crowds that He might seek renewal of strength for the next day's ministry. There is nothing selfish in the measure of self-care that avoids becoming burdensome to others, and husbands one's strength to serve them better.

The truth is, so far from universal love involving destruction of the self, it is an adventure in which the soul is immeasurably elevated, expanded, and enriched in the life of others.

The contention that love cannot be commanded assumes that Christian love means personal affection founded upon personal attraction: whereas Jesus expressly insists upon a love that flows equally towards the unattractive, the enemy, the undeserving, because it is founded upon valuation, compassion, and need – the Godlike love for sinful men. Love cannot be complete, and certainly cannot be Christlike, without genuine emotional sympathy and good will: yet essentially it is not emotional, but a resolute purpose to seek in all circumstances another's good as we seek our own. Even that deliberate, moral attitude probably cannot be extended to "humanity" – a mere abstraction. Christ speaks of love for one's neighbour, literally the one near, near enough to do good to, and possessing no other attraction, claim, or distinction, than his nearness and his need. The control of affections and emotions is probably more within the individual's power than is sometimes assumed: but in any case, the final test of morality, and of feeling, is *action*. The emotional accompaniments of sympathy and true friendship are as likely to follow the deliberate choice of a good will as to precede it. Confusion between love as an intimate, tender, and absorbing relationship impossible towards strangers and toward groups, and love as the deliberate and universal sentiment of good will, is due not to anything invalid in Christian ethics, but to the poverty of language.

To speak of Jesus as a "socialist" is as anachronistic as to assert that He was not. Even if, just conceivably, it is argued that His attitude towards private wealth carries inferences which could be extrapolated in the direction of an economic theory involving universal and compulsory social ownership of the means of production, distribution, and exchange, it is quite certain that He Himself never said anything of the kind. Jesus did not justify embezzlement of a master's goods: He merely used one case as an illustration of cleverness in an unworthy cause. He did not say that a man may do what he likes with his own – only that some employers do act so. Jesus was scathing in His opposition to specific faults which by His time had obscured the earlier virtues of Pharisaism; but His attitude to Nicodemus, His eating with Simon the Pharisee, His public agreement on essentials with the young lawyer, show that He bore no undiscriminating and relentless ill will. The suggestion that He was petulant, "ill-tempered", "unjust", towards a fruitless tree that failed to feed Him out of season, really accuses Jesus of being not morally defective but mentally deficient! In fact, the withering of the barren tree at the gates of Jerusalem at the height of the Passover was an act of prophetic symbolism so charged with meaning as to help in bringing about His death.

Historically, the total impression and the general drift of the teaching of Jesus have prompted very few serious criticisms among those prepared to accept His religious and moral premises. It cannot be pretended that His words and deeds can be made acceptable to every man, upon every conceivable moral assumption. More needs to be said, however, concerning the permanence, and the finality, of Christ's ethical thought.

(ii) As to its *permanence:* it has been argued that the ethical vision of Jesus was severely restricted, in scope and application, to a so-called "interim" period between His own appearance in Galilee and His imminent parousia at the end of the age; and that such an "ethic of the interim" can have no general validity or permanence, history itself having disproved Christ's expectation. J. Weiss held that much of Christ's teaching – especially His super-human demands, His austerity towards wealth, family, and all the goods of a world soon to be destroyed, and His indifference to the world's future – is to be understood in the light of the end of the present world-order, rapidly drawing near. A. Schweitzer similarly held that Jesus was not a "world-affirmer" but a "world-denier", dissociating Himself completely from the life, hope, and culture of this world.

Rashdall examined this argument in detail, analysing the apocalyptic sayings of Jesus, on alternative liberal, conservative,

and literalist interpretations, and setting beside them other sayings of Jesus which show the kingdom to be already present
among men. He concludes that the teaching of Jesus is in fact
little affected by its apocalyptic setting, except in the subjection of
all things to the interest of the kingdom – a principle which
remains binding though the apocalyptic expectation no longer
overhangs us.[8]

Scott holds that the whole "interimsethik" theory rests upon
the false hypothesis that Jesus prescribed set rules for life in given
situations; in fact He enunciated abiding principles. "The man
who gives effect to the highest things of the coming age, as of this,
is following out, in the face of difficulties and limitations, the will
of God as it must *always* be."[9] Jesus modified and adapted the
current apocalyptic outlook, rejecting its deep pessimism, holding
that God already rules the present world, showing no interest in
the how, when, where of the coming new age, such as monopol-
ised the attention of the apocalyptists. Jesus' one concern was
with the moral government of the new order; and He so accepted,
and so profoundly changed, the apocalyptic vision as to supplant
it entirely – even as He accepted, changed, and supplanted the
Judaist law and the messianic hope. For Christ, the coming kingdom is a point of vantage from which to apprehend and set forth
the *timeless* and *absolute* moral law. The ground of His appeal is
that His ideals are *right,* as the unsophisticated moral sense of
unspoiled people could see – not that they provide a temporary
expedient in a doomed world, a makeshift morality for a passing
age.

Inge insists that the inwardness and spirituality of Christ's
teaching are manifest: eternal life is closely associated with righteousness, and the kingdom is already within or among men. The
salvation Christ offers is illustrated repeatedly by the growth of a
seed, whereas apocalyptic is essentially catastrophic. Inge quotes
Harnack: "We cannot derive the ethical ideal of Jesus from the
eschatological", and Peabody: "to find in Jesus a Hebrew
enthusiast announcing a Utopian dream is to distort the perspective of His teaching and rob it of unity and insight ... Nothing is
more unlike the teaching of Jesus than the apprehensive, excited,
nervous sense of an approaching catastrophe". Inge himself adds
"the way in which apocalypticism faded out of Christianity, the
place of the kingdom relegated to 'heaven' and the time to the
unknown and distant future, indicates that nothing essential was
being surrendered when this Palestinian dream died a natural
death."[10]

Nevertheless, the apocalyptic hope was certainly before the
mind of Jesus, and the eschatological assumption – that the
achievement of the divine will depends upon the inbreaking of
God's power, not upon unaided human effort – was native to His

thought. The effect was not to distort but to intensify His ethical demands, adding a note of "terrible earnestness" in His warning of the coming day of light and judgement. The approaching End would not change the principles by which good men live: but the duty of watchfulness, alertness, preparedness, the need for girded loins and replenished lamps, are constantly emphasised, and the ideal, the perfect order that is to be, is held in judgement over the existing, imperfect state of things. Eschatology always has ethical implications. Jesus' message is of an inaugurated divine rule, here already to be enjoyed and obeyed, though still to be established in universal and final sovereignty. The will of God is changeless, timeless, binding here and now just as it will be at the consummation of all things.

(iii) The *finality* of Christ's ethic has likewise been challenged, mainly because the form, context, and first application of His teaching belong to His time, while the morality of modern Christians has to be differently expressed and differently orientated. Yet no Christian could admit that the ethical ideal of Jesus is no longer valid. Growth and development are the evidence of truth and life, while the progressive activity of the Spirit in the exposition, application, and development of the teaching of Jesus, is a necessary complement of belief in the historic revelation of God in Christ. Apostolic teaching already exhibits such ethical development, without the least disloyalty to the Master. Later still, to take only one example, Christians came to see that Christian morality requires more than the alleviation of suffering, poverty, oppression; it requires their cure, and by an irresistible moral logic requires also their prevention, the active reorganisation of society to impede their arising.

Henson names as factors affecting such ethical development of the principles of Jesus, the influence of national and racial character, giving rise to varying versions of the Christian ideal – a Chinese, Indian, African, or western emphasis; the pressure of new situations like the rise of democracy, the barbarities of slavery, the emergence of total war; and the increase of knowledge, which Christian morality "accepts, assimilates, and absorbs" in the faith that all truth is God's.[11] The capacity for such endless unfolding of Christian morality is itself a sign of vitality and inner fruitfulness, and one of the grounds of its permanence.

Scott defends the finality of Christ's teaching by urging that Jesus dealt always with inner, changeless moral principles and only the abiding centralities of religion, deliberately leaving the temporal working out of His insights to each succeeding generation. "His ethic can lose its authority only on the one condition that love, truth and goodness should some day cease to be regarded as the highest ideals", whereas "we cannot but believe that somehow His concept of what is highest is bound up with the ultimate order of the world – that it answers, as Jesus Himself affirmed, to the will of God."[12] More than one ethical system has died through failure to touch the emotive springs of conduct: Scott's final argument is therefore important – that Christ's ideal moves men to seek it and can in a measure be fulfilled, given the dynamic of a living faith in God.

In the last analysis, however, the finality of the ethic of Jesus rests upon His person. "Where is the peer of Jesus to be found?" asks Marshall. "Jesus is the norm of personal morality, approximation to whom has constituted moral advance" asserts Henson. Says another, the founder of Buddhism is no model for normal men, the founder of Islam no model for any man; "Buddhism requires the Asiatic temperament, Islam cannot be reconciled with the higher culture, Judaism is incorrigibly nationalist: but Christianity is frankly human, matching the need of humanity always and everywhere." "The authority of Jesus is final," Henson concludes, "because He is the ideal man in whom all men can see the true version of their own manhood."

And – let it be stated quite clearly – He is the ideal in whom all women can see the true version of that moral humanity in which manhood and womanhood alike can find their goal, and have done so. When the character of Jesus is analysed in detail, and His strength and tenderness, purity and love are fully described, the unity in one character of mainly 'masculine' and mainly 'feminine' moral traits is unmistakable.

"His moral perfection lies in the unique balance of *opposite* virtues. It is the presence in one soul of seemingly contradictory qualities that gives His character its completeness; it is their perfect harmony that lends to His whole life that poise which is perfection of strength. Strength of mind and of will are so rarely wedded to gentleness; gentleness and sympathy do not always succeed in preserving the highest standards of righteousness and purity; and again righteousness and purity so rarely keep their tolerance and goodwill, especially towards the unrighteous and the impure. It seems enough if we could excel in one virtue or the other: Jesus reveals the summit of each in one symmetrical character. This is part of the meaning of that great phrase of Paul about 'the measure of the stature of the fullness of Christ'."[13]

It is also part of the explanation why Jesus has always appealed as strongly to feminine love and devotion as to masculine obedience and loyalty.

Though not entirely sympathetic to historic Christianity, Lecky can yet declare that "it was reserved for Christianity to present to the world an ideal character, which through all the changes of eighteen centuries has inspired the hearts of men with an impassioned love; has shown itself capable of acting on all ages, nations, temperaments and conditions; has been not only the highest pattern of virtue but the strongest incentive to its practice; and has exercised so deep an influence that it may be said that the simple record of three short years of active life has done more to regenerate and to soften mankind than all the disquisitions of philosophers, and all the exhortations of moralists. This has indeed been the well-spring of whatever is best and purest in the Christian life."[14] And Goethe, (quoted by Marshall) affirms: "However much intellectual culture advances, let the human mind expand as it will, beyond the sublimity and the moral culture of Christianity, as it gleams and glitters in the Gospels, it will never go."

7

Ethics in the Primitive Church

IF THE ETHICAL TEACHING of Jesus is a newly-opened
spring of moral inspiration, fresh and inexhaustible, fed from
the deep reservoirs of Israel's long experience, then apostolic
ethics represents the channelling of that renewing stream out into
farther lands, different circumstances, wider areas of application,
daily discipleship in a pagan environment. Between fountain and
stream it is hard to draw defining lines. The Gospel records are
themselves products of the apostolic church, and if the emphasis
now falls rather upon a present faith in the ever-living exalted
Christ, than upon the treasured memory of the days of His flesh,
the apostles and their converts had not the slightest doubt that it
was one Christ whom they remembered and worshipped.

Yet much had changed by the time the apostolic records were
compiled. The move out of Jewry to a wider, gentile context
demanded retranslation of basic principles into new terms, and
posed entirely new problems of conscience and behaviour. The
crucifixion of Jesus transferred the meaning and message of the
kingdom from the exciting fulfilment of prophetic hopes into an
atmosphere of hostility that was to remain the church's daily
experience, in varying degree, for over two centuries. The
emergence of the Christian society, as a sect, a movement, a
brotherhood, a propaganda-pressure-group, and finally a religious institution close-knit against persecution and heresy, itself
created a new moral situation and evoked new loyalties and
duties. Contact and conflict with ethical systems other than Judaism also affected the development of Christian moral teaching.
The experience of Pentecost added yet another dimension to
Christian living; an ardour, joy, and spiritual dynamism, for which
the current terms "Holy Spirit" and "intoxication" were not in-
appropriate, matched spiritual resources to the splendour of the
moral ideal. Meanwhile, even the passing of time brought a
changed perspective, as the advent hope receded and Christians
had to come to terms both with the need to earn a living in the
world, and with the task of converting the world. They soon discovered, if they needed to, that the message of Jesus was no

"interimsethik" but a programme for doing the will of God in the world as it is. For all this, apostolic ethics is in no sense divorced from the ethical teaching of Jesus: it is merely the beginning of that inescapable moral discipline which faces the church still – that of discovering, and doing, the mind of Christ in circumstances far different from those in which He spoke and lived.

(1) THE ORAL PERIOD

For some twenty-five years Christian faith and obedience depended upon oral traditions concerning what Jesus had said and done. Our knowledge of the first ethical interests of the church is derived from the shape which this tradition assumed, and from the marks left by the church's initial experiences on the epistles and gospels she eventually produced. The *arrangement* of this tradition by Matthew and Luke belongs to a later period, but it is possible to trace, with fair probability, the problems of conduct that perplexed the very earliest Christians from the "pronouncements" of Jesus which were treasured, repeated, and finally written into the gospels, and from linked groups of sayings which seem to have been used in the first training-classes of the church. Vincent Taylor drew attention to some twenty "pronouncement-stories" in Mark, in each of which the church found an authoritative answer to some question of practical importance to Christian living.[1]

We can, for example, almost overhear the controversies between inexperienced disciples and Judaist critics on issues like the obligation of fasting, the observance of the sabbath, the essence of the law, the Pharisaic requirement of ritual washings, and almsgiving, and on the true significance of the temple and its worship. What is striking here is the speed with which the church seems to have grasped the great radical principles which governed the thought of Jesus: fasting is right when it truly expresses a pious sorrow – not otherwise; the sabbath is a divine gift and privilege, not an obligation; all the law is in love; only what comes out of a man's heart and mind can truly defile him; not the place or the form but only the spirit and truth of worship determine its acceptance. Decisive words of the Master could be quoted against extremists who provoked official displeasure by refusing to pay temple dues or public taxes. Converts facing family rejection were reminded of His saying about His true kindred, those who unflinchingly do the will of the Father. Strict and sensitive Jewish Christians, and Jewish critics, were reminded of the friendship Jesus showed towards the irreligious. And all who wished to be contentious and unyielding over moral issues within the infant community were faced with His stern words about the unforgiving spirit. These are the memories to which a perplexed church appealed for guidance – as well as on wider issues affecting marriage, wealth, character and doctrine.

A whole group of sayings of Jesus (Mark 8:34 to 9:1) underlines the cost of discipleship and the form of "profit" which a man may expect from faithfulness: the first Christians had faithfully learned the realism of Jesus. Spiritual care of others, and of oneself, is the theme of another group (9:37-50). Yet a third (13:28-37) makes Christian vigilance and fidelity the true "ethic of eschatology", as the hope of the advent is held before young Christians to confirm their new resolves.

If the insight gained from this source is not great, it is suggestive. It reveals a church in earnest about the daily task of translating love for Christ into Christian conduct, and anxious to be loyal to His word and His example in the details of discipleship.

(2) THE LUKAN PICTURE

Luke's account of the early church's life yields a little more information about her ethical thinking, although Luke's main interests lie elsewhere. From the few characters he actually describes, we may infer the kind of people whom Luke regarded as typical products of the new faith. He makes Stephen and Barnabas singularly attractive, broad in sympathy, strong in conviction, Stephen is especially marked by courage, and by his Christlike death, praying for his tormentors; Barnabas by his gracious friendliness, his readiness to recognise good, and particularly by his loyalty to those in need of encouragement at crises in their lives – Paul, John Mark, and the Antioch church are examples. Tabitha, full of good works and acts of charity, deeply and widely lamented at her death, was also of a strongly practical quality that appealed to Luke's mind.

Of another kind is the story of Ananias and Sapphira. Stressing that the whole city was moved with awe and even with fear, Luke adds that the church, too, was grimly reminded of the severe judgement that must fall upon avarice and calculated deceit to obtain an unjustified share of the material charity of the church. The total effect of the story is that the power within the church is not such as to awaken superstitious fears, but is of a moral and cleansing quality that demands ethical respect, and a wholesome fear of the Lord. Christ's own ministry to the sick continued through the apostolic church, but in Acts it is the power at work, rather than the compassion that prompts, which is emphasised. As in his Gospel, too, Luke draws attention to a stoic manliness and courage which Christianity engenders. Beside Stephen, Peter's courage before the Sanhedrin, and Paul's bearing at

Lystra, at Philippi, at Ephesus, and especially on the doomed ship, were exactly such as would appeal to the leaders in pagan society for whom Luke writes.

In Peter's Pentecostal sermon, the call to repent for having crucified the Messiah is extended in the exhortation to "Save yourselves from this crooked generation", which implies a salvation "out of" this present wicked world, from the influence, example, and fear, of one's environment. Implicit here is the "demand to be different", the acceptance of the principle of separation from the world. This note was to be repeated later, in the Petrine epistles, in an obscure baptismal parallel with Noah, saved by water from a wicked generation, and in the Johannine doctrine that the whole world lies in the evil one. It is not surprising that, under pressure of criticism and of persecution, the disciples should early draw together in defensive unity, and the line between church and world should begin to be firmly drawn.

The only other reference Luke makes to the ethical thought of the earliest church is his description of the so-called "communist experiment" of Acts 2:43-54, 4:32-37:

Fear came upon every soul; and many wonders and signs were done through the apostles. And all who believed were together and had all things in common; and they sold their possessions and goods and distributed them to all, as any had need ... The company of those who believed were of one heart and soul, and no one said that any of the things which he possessed was his own, but they had everything in common. And with great power the apostles gave their testimony to the resurrection of the Lord Jesus, and great grace was upon them all. There was not a needy person among them, for as many as were possessors of lands or houses sold them, and brought the proceeds of what was sold and laid it at the apostles' feet; and distribution was made to each as any had need. Thus Joseph, who was surnamed by the apostles Barnabas ... sold a field which belonged to him, and brought the money and laid it at the apostles' feet.

Luke appears to tell the story with enthusiasm, as one of the many wonders and signs done through the apostles, part of the testimony given with great power, part of the evidence of the great grace upon them all. Nevertheless his next words are "But a man named Ananias ..." and he appears deliberately to set the actions of Ananias and Barnabas side by side.

There is much we would like to know about this spontaneous organising of Christian generosity. It plainly expresses something native and characteristic in Christianity, and set a model for many later "brotherhoods" and "settlements", for the enrolment of a recognised order of "widows" as objects of the church's care and servants of her cause (Acts 6:1, 8:39; compare 1 Timothy 5:3f), and for much else in Christian social effort and thought. At the same time, it had precedents in the community life and common ownership fostered at Qumran. The recording of the exceptional gift of Barnabas, and Peter's explicit reminder to Ananias (5:4), underline the spontaneous, voluntary nature of the movement: there is no suggestion that povery was the rule, or sharing one's goods the precondition, of church membership. There was, clearly, no universal and public vow of poverty or common ownership (Acts 12:12, 16:15, 24:26, 28:30) – as the repeated appeal for generous giving sufficiently shows.

It is evident that something had to be done to succour disinherited and homeless converts: this is the "need" which prompted distribution (2:45, 4:35), and which shows in its true light the offence of Ananias. Some argue that the experiment was a failure, leading swiftly to the jealousies which necessitated the election of officials to supervise the church's almsgiving, and leading also, perhaps, in the end to the poverty of the Palestinian churches which made necessary two collections among the gentiles for the poor saints at Jerusalem (Acts 11:29, 24:17, compare 2 Corinthians 8:4, 9:11-13). It certainly led to the abandonment of any attempt to make mutual subsistence the rule in church life. Others argue that this is mean and specious criticism of a splendidly generous impulse towards fellow-feeling and social concern, entirely in line with the "loving one another" which Christ requires of His friends, and all too obviously absent from the later church. What cannot be doubted is that Luke saw in the early church a serious attempt to maintain that sense of responsibility about wealth, and that concern for the unprovided and unprotected, which he makes a leading feature of his portrait of Jesus.

(3) THE PRIMITIVE CATECHESIS

Our third source of information about the primitive church's ethical insights lies half-concealed in the outlines of oral teaching given to the first converts in the earliest missions and catechumen classes, and now discernible in many allusions and echoes remaining in the existing apostolic literature. This "common storehouse of catechetical material", already known to both writers and readers of the epistles, is often referred to (Romans 6:17, 16:17, 1 Corinthians 15:1f, 11:23, 1 Thessalonians 4:1, 2, 2 Thessalonians 2:15, 3:6, Acts 23:25 and perhaps a dozen other passages). It probably followed fairly closely the pattern of education of Jewish boys in synagogue schools, using similar key-words; it developed into the full catechumenate system of the later church; and a great deal of the common instruction and exhortation in the epistles to Rome, Ephesus, Colossae, Thessalonia, and in the First Epistle of Peter, is derived from this source.[2]

(i) By the meticulous comparison of parallel passages the main outlines have been recovered of the moral training given to young Christians in the primitive church, the themes and duties mainly emphasised in preparing candidates for baptism and church membership. One pattern of instruction stresses sanctification and love, responsibility towards God and towards the newly joined Christian community, though with concern also for those who are "without":

(You received from us how you ought to walk) in sanctification and holiness; abstain from fornication, fleshly desires, living in sanctification (of the Spirit) and not in passionate desire, in (gentile) ignorance, or in cupidity. For you are not called in uncleanness but holiness, by His Holy Spirit. Concerning love of the brethren (neighbour), love one another, doing your own business, not interfering with others; have a concern for those that are without; live so as to glorify God, never returning evil for evil but seeking only good.[3]

This group of exhortations will be found in 1 Thessalonians and 1 Peter, several parts of it also in Ephesians and Colossians, with distant echoes in Romans and James. The key-word here, "Abstain ..." (four times) occurs elsewhere in the epistles only at 1 Timothy 4:3, and is rare. It appears however at Acts 15:20, 29 in the letter addressed by the Jerusalem Council to the newer churches concerning the terms upon which gentile converts might be admitted to fellowship with strict Christian Jews. Whether the decree be interpreted ritually or ethically, "abstention" from that which offends one's fellow-Christians is essential to partnership.

Here again we are very close to the daily social and ethical problems of that early church. "Abstain" is not an attractive key-word for ethics: yet clearly, some recoil from the excesses of pagan licentiousness and idolatry was imperative to young converts, both for witness and for safety. They were called to a costly dedication to a holy Lord. Some of the danger involved in such negative withdrawal from life around them would of course be countered by the new loyalty towards the community they now joined. The psychological truth here is that a man may choose the environment by which he shall allow himself to be shaped: living within the church and within the world, he decides which shall mould his character – pagan society, or the communion of saints; and decides by choosing what he shall abstain from, or embrace.

(ii) Another pattern of instruction, echoed in several epistles and supported from many parts of the New Testament, runs:

As to times and seasons, brethren, you need not that I should write to you, for you know with exactness that the Day of the Lord comes as a thief in the night; when they say Peace, suddenly cometh destruction (or, the Day). But you are not in darkness but are sons of light; therefore pray, watch, be vigilant, avoiding drunkenness, girding your loins, being sober, and hopeful, putting on God's armour, for He has appointed us to obtain salvation.[4]

This teaching reproduces the same connection of eschatology and ethics discernible in the sayings of Jesus. The Age-to-come has arrived, as the kerygma announced; the convert has stepped already out of darkness into light; he must therefore live in the light. This again is no ethic for an interim, but the ethic of inaugurated eschatology: a new moral dignity is conferred, a new moral impetus awakened, by the sense of belonging to a new Age and to the world to come. Spiritual alertness, watchfulness against temptation, sobriety, and valour in conflict, are qualities fitting the sons of the light which Jesus brought.

(iii) Perhaps the most convincing reconstruction of this pre-literary catechetical material is that which finds the following sequence of ideas reproduced in 1 Peter, James, Colossians, Ephesians, Romans, and in part in Hebrews:

Putting off, therefore, all wickedness, deceit, hypocrisy, evil speaking, falsehood, abusiveness, blasphemy, the works of darkness, filthiness, and all encumbrances – Put on (or, arm yourself) (with) the mind of Christ, the Lord Jesus Christ, the armour of God, the arms of light, the new man, a merciful (etc) spirit . . .[5]

The ('put off') motif is usually connected with disrobing for baptism, and it appears that teachers used the obvious symbolism as the occasion required, urging the convert to "put off" wickedness generally, or specific forms of untruth, sexual evil, hindrance to the heavenly race. The putting-on of garments after baptism was likewise linked with exhortations to put on the garments of the renewed soul (Colossians 3), or the armour and weapons of spiritual warfare (Romans 6:13, Ephesians 6:11f, 1 Thessalonians 5:8). Plainly, a total moral change is here associated with baptism into Christ. Renunciation is implied, and more: although the self remains identical before and after conversion and baptism, the soul confronts the world in wholly new guise, clothed with Christ, the old life behind and the new transfigured, and endued for fight.

This theme of conflict is present in the memories treasured of Jesus, both in the Temptation-story and in the Johannine portrait of Christ the Victor. The background is a relentless spiritual warfare against forces of evil, personalised in Satan, universalised in the principalities and powers of pagan demonology. But the armour and weapons are always *ethical* – a breastplate of faith and love, for a helmet the hope of salvation, "weapons of righteousness", the whole armour of truth (or integrity), righteousness, peaceableness, faith, an experience of salvation, the word of God, and prayerfulness. The spiritual battle is not to be won outside oneself: the struggle consists in opposing to an evil world an unsullied and undefeated soul.

(iv) The social ideals set before new converts are reflected in yet another sequence of thought, echoed in 1 Thessalonians, 1 Peter, and Romans:

Be at peace (of one mind); cleave to the weak; be patient, sympathetic, compassionate, sharing in necessity; not returning evil for evil but good before all men, and blessing; rejoicing, and praying; not quenching the Spirit, but fervent, and ever serving the Lord. Hold fast the good, turning from evil, considering one another with abounding love, affection, brotherliness, and humility – loving thy neighbour as thyself.[6]

Loyalty to the new Christian community is here plainly underlined. With this may also be noted a group of ideas shared also with 1 Timothy, Ephesians, and Romans:

Respect those who labour among you (rule over you), especially in the word and teaching, as prophets, or as serving just as each has received a gift (within the one body).[7]

This presupposes co-operative service within a differentiated community, with duly appointed officers, spokesmen, and authority. Thus early does church life begin to create its own duties and responsibilities, directed towards the specifically Christian group. Such church-duties were in time to become so pressing as almost to obscure all wider obligations.

(v) In this early period, however, wider social duties are already emphasised, as in the teaching-pattern, shared by seven or eight epistles,[8] of which the key-word is "subject yourselves." Here, the basic principle of Christian humility, originally conceived as a theological virtue – humility before God – then intensified by the emphasis upon love – humility before one's brethren – is worked out in a system of *social subordination,* affecting civil obedience, slaves and masters, wives and husbands, parents and children, elder and younger. Such a code has close parallels in both Jewish and pagan (Stoic) teaching, the difference being that Christian "subjection" is "in the Lord." The obedience of the Christian to social and domestic order is limited by his higher obligation to the Lordship of Christ, who is for him the supreme authority in domestic, social, civic and church matters alike.

So wives are to submit to their own husbands "as it is fit in the Lord"; husbands are to love their wives as Christ loved the church – which, as the context shows, means sacrificially; children are to obey their parents in the Lord, and parents must nurture their children in the admonition of the Lord. Christian servants obey their masters in singleness of heart, fearing God, doing all their service heartily as unto the Lord, for so they serve the Lord

Christ. Masters too must be just and fair, knowing that they have a Master in heaven.

The impression of careful and far-seeing instruction in the essential orderliness of a Christian home, society, and church, is here very plain. But much more is involved. Like "abstain", "be subject" is an unwelcome key-word, but it touches a nerve of Christian morality. Basic to the biblical concept of sin, as the Eden story typifies it, is self-will, the assertion of God-given freedom of choice against Him who gave it. "Sin is lawlessness" – disobedience of a righteous command, insubordination: that was man's fall, and is his predicament, and will be his final condemnation. Salvation, therefore, must involve submission; where disobedience brought ruin, only obedience, subjection of the will to the absolute moral law, can restore man's inner unity, security, and health. Such insights underlie the Jewish insistence on law, Christ's gospel of the kingdom – where submission to the divine rule is still basic to man's welfare – and the apostolic proclamation of the Lordship of Christ. In so far as the original surrender to Christ, from which all else flows, is a free action of the believing heart, the submission is self-determined, and no real violation of personal liberty. Yet the acceptance of divine rule, worked out at different levels of order and obedience, remains the fundamental ethical principle of conversion. The same basic attitude which, theologically, is faith, ethically is obedience, socially is subjection, is in the last analysis the essential opposite of self-will: it is outgoing, non-demanding, non-assertive *love,* to God and man – the supreme and sufficient *law* of Christ. The catechetical code of subordination merely spelled out in detail the new attitude to God and the world which the saved man had adopted in surrendering to Christ.

(vi) A final section of the early moral instruction included such ideas as:

Persecution is a ground of rejoicing, and a test of character; it was foretold, is common to all, will be sudden, indicates the nearness of judgement and deliverance. Endurance is needed, but the reward is sure. Vigilance, the girding of the loins, prayer, and a well-armed spirit, are required, that the Christian may stand firm, knowing that God is near.[9]

This sequence of thought is "borrowed" by nearly every strand of New Testament teaching, and it indicates further the clear-sightedness, and the resolution, of the first Christians, as well as the care of the church for her young converts as they faced with trembling faith the hostility of the world.

On these last-mentioned patterns, Caird makes the comment: "In several of the epistles there is a fourfold form of instruction. Each of the four divisions has its key-phrase: Put-off – put on, submit, watch, resist", and he concludes a cautious summary of the evidence for this whole reconstruction of early church teaching with the words, "This means that already at an early date the Hellenistic church had discovered a sound alternative to the legalism of the Judaists, and was regularly demanding from its converts a high ethical standard as the logical outcome of that inner change which they underwent at the time of their admission to the church."[10] Even if the reconstruction of the primitive Christian catechism he held unproved, this oft-repeated instruction remains, of course, part of the New Testament, and part of the preparation for Christian life offered by the church to her converts.

Its thoroughness is evident in the difficulty of summarising it. It assumes in each convert a spiritual crisis of transforming intensity, a passing out of one Age into another, from darkness to light, from self-will to the Lordship of Christ. The ethical results of that experience are expected to be (a) deliberate abstention from all that defiles, that identifies the soul with the passing Age and the surrounding world of unbelief – an inner sanctification appropriate to those redeemed by a holy God; (b) loyal co-operation with the new Christian community, valuing fellowship and accepting divine discipline within the present form of God's kingdom, the church; (c) the out-working of Christian obedience in social relationships of home, employment, citizenship, subject always to Christ as Lord; and (d) watchfulness, alertness, resistance and endurance – the Christian "military virtues".

The church has probably never prepared her converts more thoroughly than she did in these first years, for consistent and effectual discipleship in the Christian community and in the world.

8

Pauline Moral Theology

PAUL'S INDEBTEDNESS TO THE common ethical tradition of the church into which he was baptised is evident from his allusions to what he had himself received, his quotations from current teaching, his references to the traditions his readers had received, and the form of teaching to which they "had been delivered", and his use of words spoken by the Master.[1] Nevertheless, Paul brought his own insights, experience, training and emphasis to the interpretation of that common teaching. He was no more a systematic moralist than a systematic theologian. Even in the later chapters of Romans, where his exposition is most orderly, the thought is still presented defensively, as in Galatians it is presented polemically, and elsewhere incidentally to immediate needs of the readers. In gathering his scattered comments on related topics into some kind of pattern for purposes of exposition, we must beware of imposing a system, or assuming a consistency, which Paul himself might vigorously repudiate.

It is necessary to begin with Pauline psychology because Paul's assumptions about human nature – the flesh – are often presumed to have led him astray from the simplicity of Christ. And with Paul's presuppositions, because as in all Christian ethics, his moral teaching and his theology are inextricable, while his conversion-theology in particular is often supposed to limit his ethical relevance to Christians of similar "Damascus-road" experience.

(1) PAUL'S MORAL PSYCHOLOGY

Paul has been held responsible both for the fundamental dualism between flesh and spirit that underlies extreme asceticism, and for the doctrine of man's complete spiritual incapacity – so-called total depravity – which undermines all moral responsibility. It is therefore important to understand precisely what Paul assumed concerning man's moral nature.

(i) The "Flesh"

It is obvious, as Inge, Glover, and Marshall point out,[2] that Paul's thought stands near to the Greek idea of the pure soul imprisoned within flesh that is essentially evil, because material. Sayings like "flesh and blood cannot inherit the kingdom of God, neither can corruption inherit incorruption", and "things seen are temporal, things unseen are eternal", echo Hellenistic thought. Marshall quotes, apparently with approval, Holtzmann's, "The Pauline ethic as a whole is dominated by the metaphysical contrast between flesh and spirit", and Bousset's, "When Paul regards spirit and flesh as two forces which absolutely rule the human will, and seeks the root of the flesh in man's physical constitution, he departs from Rabbinical theology and introduces an austere Hellenistic point of view into Christianity." From this it is an easy step towards blaming Paul for the dualistic asceticism of the second and following centuries, and for the whole anti-humanist tradition which (it is said) has corrupted with Greek negations the happy and human gospel of Jesus.

In reply, at least three things must be said:
(a) As Inge shows, Paul never, like the Greeks, identified "sinful flesh" with the physical body. For Paul, "flesh" is a moral concept rather than a material one, a psychological force rather than a physical substance. In his thought, man's physical body has been dignified beyond measure by the incarnation – "God sent his son, made of a woman ... in the likeness of sinful flesh"; it is sanctified, too, as the temple of the indwelling Holy Spirit; it is capable, moreover, of being yielded to God, its members becoming instruments of righteousness, the whole a living sacrifice, holy and acceptable to God; it is destined to be raised, incorruptible, to share in final redemption. No Greek dualist could accept such a faith; nor could he say, as Paul does, either that the body may be defiled by sexual sin (in Greek thought, it could be defiled no further, being inherently evil), or that the spirit can be defiled (2 Corinthians 7:1). Plainly, Paul's view of man is very far from that of Greek dualism.
(b) H. Wheeler Robinson maintains that, despite Paul's use of some Greek terms like "inner man", "conscience", and "mind", he remains in psychology a Hebrew of the Hebrews.[3] Paul, he contended, accepts the Old Testament analysis of man's nature: heart, soul, spirit, flesh – where "flesh" means man's visible personality. Paul then associates *soul* with the life of the flesh, and *spirit* with man's higher aspirations and experiences, while he adds a new general term, *soma,* for the physical body as a whole.

The threefold division in 1 Thessalonians 5:23 "your whole spirit, soul and body" Robinson compares with "heart, soul, mind, and strength" (in the great commandment) – a mere emphasis upon the whole man.

This fourfold analysis is then (so to speak) polarised into a contrast between the inner and the outer life, intensified in the experience of moral conflict. The inner and outer man, living an inner and outer life easily becomes a "higher" and a "lower" self. The lower, supplying the energy of the higher life's foes, becomes identified with physical impulses, the so-called natural life of the outward man. This dualism is Hebrew rather than Greek, and moral rather than metaphysical – more the outcome of experience than of intellectual analysis.

(c) The very wide range of meaning with which Paul uses the term "flesh" must be scrupulously observed. In one group of references, the flesh and its life is readily associated with "the lower instincts erected into a principle of life and action" (Inge), and with "the natural impulses and instincts which, while not sinful in themselves, master us and become occasions of sin unless we master them" (Marshall).[4] Paul speaks ten times of the *desires* of the flesh, of the flesh lusting against the spirit, of our serving with the flesh the law of sin, of the flesh as somehow involved in the awakening of sin within him. So flesh is described as sinful; we are to make no provision to fulfil its lusts, in the way that gentile converts once "walked according to the flesh". Sometimes, this conception of the flesh as sensual, as the seat and vehicle of sinful desires, is connected directly with "the motions of sin in the members" and "the body of the sins of the flesh"; and its "works" include adultery, fornication, uncleanness, lasciviousness, murders, drunkenness. Such references support the association of Paul's term with the modern meaning of "carnal" as implying "sensual" and even "sexual".

But, spite of all this, in another group of references Paul as plainly uses the term in contexts where sensuality is only remotely in view. Other "works of the flesh" include idolatry, witchcraft, hatred, strife, jealousy, anger, selfishness, dissension, party-spirit, and envy. The immature "babes in Christ" at Corinth are described as "fleshly" because they exhibit qualities which befit "ordinary", unregenerate men (1 Corinthians 3:1f). Worldly wisdom is wisdom of the flesh; boasting is glorying in the flesh; human religious regulations, austerities, pride in visions, and the like are all satisfying to the flesh, and bolster confidence in the flesh rather than in God and the Spirit. To conduct Christian warfare in wrong ways and by unworthy arguments is to fight with fleshly weapons a fleshly war. Vacillating and inconsistent planning of one's life and work is "purposing according to the flesh". None of these uses, it is clear, presupposes sensuality.

In a third group of references to the flesh, no blame whatever is implied. Christian teachers share spiritual things with their hearers, and should justly receive in return "carnal", fleshly (that is material) gifts and maintenance. Paul may be present at a church meeting "in spirit", though absent "in flesh" – that is, bodily. Circumcision "in the flesh" is the outward, physical rite; knowing Christ in the flesh means knowing Him in His earthly life, or from a human point of view; living one's present life in the flesh means daily service of Christ; slaves have masters according to the flesh – in a human, secular sense. Christ was born of the seed of David according to the flesh, as was Abraham born "according to the flesh" – as to human, physical origin. And the sensitive, responsive human heart, in contrast to stone tablets, is a "heart of flesh". James Stewart says that in the majority of Pauline passages, *flesh* stands simply for human nature on its material side, for everything – impulses, thoughts, desires, and the like – which belongs to the outward man; in Calvin's phrase, whatever is "outside Christ". Flesh is simply human nature apart from God.[5]

Flesh, then, in Paul, is not to be identified with sex or with the physical body. It is closer to the Hebrew thought of the physical personality – the self including physical and psychical elements – as vehicle of the outward life and the lower levels of experience. It is man in his humanness, with all the limitations, moral weakness, vulnerability, creatureliness, and mortality, which being human implies. But for that very reason, "though not evil in itself, the flesh is that part of man's nature which gives evil its opportunity. It is the thing upon which sin impinges, to which sin attaches itself. It becomes sin's willing and obedient organ and instrument: 'with the flesh I serve the rule of sin' " (Stewart).

Of itself the flesh, without Christ, mere unregenerate humanity, cannot be justified in God's sight, nor serve God; its ways are enmity against God; in it dwells no good thing. The rule of law might have accomplished much, had it not been weak through the flesh; flesh is man's moral weakness – "the infirmity of your flesh" – even when the spirit is willing. It is the part of man's nature opposed to his mind or rational control (Romans 7:25), opposed to his spirit and religious aspiration (Romans 8:4-9, 12f). So, though not itself evil, flesh is contrary to spirit, and if the impulses of the flesh have their way unhindered (a man minding the things of the flesh) spiritual life dies. He that sows to the flesh must of the flesh reap corruption.

Nevertheless, it was in the flesh that Jesus came, suffered, and ascended, and it is in the flesh that redemption will be consummated in resurrection. The Christian has crucified the flesh, yet in the flesh he serves God through his members, now yielded to God. The life now lived in the flesh is the life which "Christ liveth in me", the very life of Jesus manifested in our mortal flesh. The body may become the temple of the Holy Spirit just as surely as it can become carnal, sold under sin, the occasion and vehicle of all manner of evil, the sure way to corruption.

Such is one side of Paul's view of human nature. Without God, man is creaturely, vulnerable, prey to all manner of pride, folly, spitefulness, and sensuality, yet not in any natural and inescapable constitution of his nature essentially evil. *The flesh is a vehicle, open to sin on the one hand and to God on the other.* At different times Paul can say, "Not I, but sin that dwelleth in me ... Not I, but Christ dwelleth in me ... Not I, but the grace of God which was with me." Man is vulnerable both to evil – and to God; he is a vehicle, a channel, a dwelling-place, a temple, a battlefield (Paul uses each metaphor) for good and evil. Which shall possess, indwell, master him, whether sin, evil, the spirit that now worketh in the children of disobedience, or Christ, the Holy Spirit, faith, grace, – it is for each man to choose.

That he *can* so choose, brings to view the other side of Paul's conception of human nature, man's conscience and the human *spirit.*

(ii) The Human Spirit

Despite disproportionate attention given to Paul's teaching on the "flesh", there is much to show that he believed equally firmly in other "higher" elements in human nature that were open to God, "our spirit" to which the Holy Spirit bears witness, "the spirit of the man which is in him" (Romans 8:16, 1 Corinthians 2:11). Paul certainly believed that man was made originally in God's image; whatever may have happened since, he had not ceased to be man. Marshall remarks that "the mere fact that Paul describes the soul of man as an arena where the forces of good and evil are striving for the mastery, and declared that man's native desire to do the right was over-powered by the flesh, makes it quite clear that he recognised that however depraved man was, the depravity was not total."[6] Paul's statements in Romans 1 and 2 concerning unregenerate man are clear and conclusive:

What can be known about God is plain to them, because God has shown it to them. Ever since the creation of the world his invisible nature, namely his eternal power and deity, has been clearly perceived in the things that have been made. So they are without excuse; for although they knew God they did not honour him as God or give thanks to him, but they became futile in their thinking and their senseless minds were darkened. Claiming to be wise, they became fools, and exhanged the glory of the immortal God for images resembling mortal men or birds or animals or reptiles. Therefore God gave them up in the lusts of their hearts to impurity ... because they exchanged the truth about God for a lie ... Since they did not see fit to acknowledge God, God gave them up to a base mind ... Though they know God's decree that those who do such things deserve to die, they not only do them but approve those who practice them ... When gentiles who have not the law do by nature what the law requires, they are a law to themselves, even though they do not have the law. They show that what the law requires is written on their hearts, while their conscience also bears witness and their conflicting thoughts accuse or perhaps excuse them on that day when ... God judges the secrets of men by Christ Jesus.

Here Paul affirms of pagans (a) a universal moral knowledge, intuitive ("written on their hearts . . . a law to themselves") and natural ("by nature") coinciding with the moral requirements of God made known to Jewry in the Mosaic legislation; (b) an active, universal conscience, which bears witness to moral truth, and awakens the conflict of accusing and excusing thoughts within the gentile soul – a reflective self-examination of feeling and intellect on moral questions and conduct; (c) a resulting universal responsibility: "although they knew God they did not honour him . . . They are without excuse . . . They exchanged the truth of God for a lie . . . They know God's decree . . ." but they disobey; (d) a real freedom of moral choice, either of repentance and obedience or of rejection and disobedience, together with responsibility and judgement inevitably involved in that choice.

Whether or not this idea of conscience owes anything to Stoic thought, the Old Testament certainly teaches it. When David's heart smote him, and Job's heart did not reproach him; when "Solomon" declares that the spirit of man is the lamp of the Lord, searching his innermost parts, and possibly when Micah proclaims that God has shown to man – all men – what is good and what He requires, the essence of Paul's thought is being formed. Just so did Jesus, as we have seen, appeal to the innate moral judgement of ordinary men and women.

W. Lillie[7] discusses whether conscience, in Paul, signifies such a faculty of moral judgement, or just the pain caused by reflection upon wrong committed. But he acknowledges that some recognition of right and wrong is involved in this pain, and in the memory of it; and that, in any case, for Paul "the pagan has some kind of law written on his heart, and the power of reading it, whether or no we call that power conscience . . ." H. Wheeler Robinson shows that in the Pauline psychology *mind* in its good sense is that which comprehends the law of God, delights in it, and approves it (Romans 7:23, 25); while *conscience* includes a sense of rectitude, the appeal to moral judgement in others and the faculty for moral judgement in oneself – though this may become defiled (1 Corinthians 8:7). Conscience is not, for Paul, a source of ethical knowledge: it exercises judgement on the moral quality of acts after they have been committed.[8] This, as we have just seen, does however imply learning from experience.

Whatever terminology we prefer, it is clear that Paul regards the knowledge of right and wrong, the capacity to choose between them, the responsibility for having chosen, the resultant pleasure or pain that arise upon reflection, and the ability to awaken similar moral judgement in others, as all part of human nature and man's original condition – before Christian conversion – no less than his physical constitution and "fleshly" vulnerability. Man, for Paul, is a *moral* creature.

But man's conscience is certainly not infallible. It can be weak, corrupted, or insensitive; it does choose only between presented courses of action that which is preferable in the light of past experience, education, and its own limitations of insight – it never presents a third, ideal possibility on its own initiative. Conscience is educable, and redeemable, but it needs enlightenment and development, by law, culture, training, or by Christ, before it can perceive the perfect will of God.

It is Paul's view that God has never left Himself without a witness, but has so made, sustained, and governed the world that men may feel after Him and find Him. That is why what can be known of God is plain to men. They know His decree (Romans 1:19, 32). Within Israel the revelation was far more clear and explicit, and the earnest mind bore witness that God's law was holy, just, good, "spiritual" (Romans 7:12, 14). In all his confession of humiliating failure, Paul offers no extenuating plea of ignorance, of misunderstanding, of God's will. Among the gentiles, the revelation of the divine decree was through the things God has made and the law written upon the heart: such knowledge was necessary to constitute "transgressions" – where there is no law, no knowledge of what God requires, there can be no transgression in the full sense of sin. Such knowledge of God's will is necessary to moral adulthood and personal responsibility (Galatians 3:19, Romans 4:15, 3:20).

Behind this doctrine that man knows God's requirements is the concept of "Natural Law", which Lillie defines as "a universal standard of conduct, morally binding upon all men, and discernible by them",[9] whether its origin be traced to reason, or to social institutions and experience. The Christian theory of natural law, according to Brunner, finds it to be "simply and solely the order of creation ... The natural man was well aware of these orders of creation, though without knowing the Creator." In all societies there are rules, tabus, customs, which protect marriage, parental authority, life, property, the safety of the social unit, the obligation of contracts, and elementary justice. As Lillie shows, there is also a natural abhorrence of certain patterns of behaviour as contrary to natural instinct. Says Kant, "Human beings feel ashamed to mention those things of which it is shameful for humanity to be capable." It is in such areas that "natural law" rises to consciousness, however variously or imprecisely it be defined.

As a Jew, Paul traced all such rudimentary natural morality to the reflection of the Creator in His creation, as remnants of what might be known of God from the things that He has made, if sinful man did not persist in holding down the truth in unrighteousness (Romans 1:18). In itself that view implies, both positively and negatively, a very exalted estimate of man's moral nature and responsibility; unlike all other creatures, man is spirit, as well as flesh.

(2) PAUL'S PRESUPPOSITIONS

To Paul's mind, all worth-while theology had ethical implications, but three themes were related more closely than others to his central positions in ethics.

(i) Universal Failure

Paul's high estimate of man's moral potential intensifies his sense of man's moral tragedy. The opening chapters of Romans argue universal failure to fulfil God's law ("all have sinned"), and to achieve God's ideal and intention ("all have come short of the glory of God"). This is proved by the moral and social decadence of the gentile world, by the evil reputation which the Jews had among gentiles (confirmed, according to C. H. Dodd, by ben Zadok, a contemporary of Paul), and by the testimony of the Jewish scriptures. Paul's conclusion is that all men, of all races, "are under the power of sin", which he frequently personifies as a force at work in the hearts of men (Romans 3:9). "Sin sprang to life; sin deceived me, slew me ... it is no more I that do it but sin that dwelleth in me." This bondage to sin is in Romans 6 described as "thraldom", a "reign of sin"; in chapter 7 it is analysed psychologically; in Ephesians 4:17-19 its close association with ignorance of God is made clear; elsewhere, its manifestation in every kind of sensual and anti-social vice is detailed (Romans 1:29f, Galatians 5:19f, Ephesians 2:1f). Its immediate consequences are hardening of conscience, darkening of mind, disintegration of personality (Romans 7:21-24); its ultimate consequence is destruction: "The wages of sin is death".

The seriousness of sin, in Paul's eyes, cannot be exaggerated. It takes possession of a man, alienates him from God, instils hostility in his soul towards God, and leaves him helpless to reform himself (Colossians 1:21, Romans 7:24). He can will what is right, but he cannot do it. When he would do good, evil is present with him; he discovers a law in his members, making him captive. This was the deepest futility of legalism: though in itself holy, wise and good, the only effect of the law on the natural man was to provoke resistance, creating desire for the thing forbidden. "I should not have known what it is to covet, if the law had not said, Thou shalt not covet ... Sin, finding opportunity in the commandment, wrought in me all kinds of covetousness ... The very commandment which promised life to me proved to be death." This is confessed, we must remember, by a Pharisee "immaculate by the standard of legal righteousness" (Philippians 3:6). But that standard was not sufficient for a heart so eager, so passionate, and perfectionist. "If there had been a law given which could have given life, verily righteousness should have come by the law." But in fact, all law was "weak through the flesh"; and what Paul had been taught by the law to long for, the law itself "could not do" (Romans 8:3).

With Paul's *explanation* of this desperate situation, ethics is not directly concerned. Would he trace universal sin, as well as universal mortality, back to Adam's transgression, or is the parallel of Adam with Christ simply an illustration? Would Paul say, with Baruch 54:19 "Every one of us has been the Adam of his own soul" – since in Romans 7, telling his own story, Paul says "sin deceived me", echoing the Genesis story of Eve? Or would Paul say with some fellow-Pharisees and 4 Ezra 3:26 "the evil heart – *yeser ha'ra* – explains Adam's sin" and men continue to do even as Adam did because they also have the wicked heart? Or would Paul trace all evil to the power of demons, as Ephesians 2:2, 6:12 might suggest? Deissmann (according to Glover) offers the guess that in Romans 7:9 – "Sin came to life and I died" – Paul reveals "a memory of the first deep consciousness of sin and failure when a child, a memory of a youth darkened by the shadow of sin falling on a gifted nature, and growing intenser with the years, till it is distress and anxiety."[10]

We do not know just how Paul would have explained the universal failure. The most we can say, and it is significant, is that Paul never for a moment seeks to excuse, by history, heredity, or demonology, the sin that dogs his life and is the tragedy of mankind. With the fullest possible acknowledgement of man's helplessness and guilt, Paul retains his hold on man's full moral responsibility.

(ii) Divine Reaction

The divine reaction to this universal failure is twice described: a revelation of righteousness and wrath (Romans 1:17f, 3:21); a destiny of wrath and of salvation (1 Thessalonians 5:9). Of the reaction of "wrath", ethics needs to notice only that divine judgement is for Paul a manifestation not of anger but of righteousness. It is the inevitable consequence of wrongdoing in a moral universe where whatsoever a man sows, that shall he surely reap. For this reason, God's judgement is represented as the divine ratification of human choices – God "gives men up" to whatever they prefer: God's justice gives free men what they want, deception for those who refuse to love the truth (2 Thessalonians 2:10f), uncleanness, vile affections, a reprobate mind, for those who preferred these to obeying God's law (so Romans 1:24-28). T. R. Glover draws out the moral consequences of such judgement in the conscience cauterised or stained, the mind darkened, the heart deadened, the soul without God and without hope. So the moral conflict of the sinner becomes steadily more hopeless: "man's nature steadily growing less and less able to sustain it, as conscience lost faculty after faculty and the will was more and more divided."[11] So men become estranged, at enmity against

God, whom they blame for their condition. But that *is* the divine judgement. "Paul was not a Jew for nothing": he believed firmly in the objectivity of moral values.

The divine reaction to human failure did not stop at the revelation of judgement: God "put forward", thrust into (Romans 3:25) this desperate situation *the gift of Christ, the cross of Christ, the Spirit of Christ,* bearing together divine salvation, and each having far-reaching ethical significance also.

(a) "God sent forth *his Son* ... in the likeness of sinful flesh ... born of a woman" and so sharing our humanity, "born under the law" and so sharing our situation. He is given to redeem them that are under the law and in the bondage of sin, to reconcile the alienated, to liberate the enslaved, to make the defeated "more than conquerors," to reveal to us and even to "commend" to us, the love of God. Part of the moral work of Christ was to deal with the situation which man's sinfulness had created for a holy, just God who cannot ignore sin and its consequences, and for the moral order of the world. He so dealt with it as to liberate men from the fascination and bondage of sin, to awaken within them a new moral impulse of gratitude, and to evoke an answering, constraining love, that constitutes a unique ethical dynamic in men and in society (Romans 8:2, 7:25, 2 Corinthians 5:14, 15). At the same time, Christ became Himself both the moral end and ideal, in conformity to whose image men would find their highest good; and the incarnate assurance of divine assistance and love, from which neither life nor death, things present nor things to come, nor spirits of the height or depth, shall ever separate Christians again (Romans 8:29, 33-39).

(b) It is especially to *Christ crucified* that Paul ascribes salvation. T. R. Glover's summary of the *ethical* significance for Paul of the death of Christ can scarcely be improved:

"Paul could not give up, and did not, the fundamental conviction of God's supreme righteousness: 'let God be true and every man a liar' (Romans 3:5). But he discovered in the cross of Christ a moral and spiritual 'more-than-equivalent' for the Judgement. The cross did something, and did it so thoroughly, that it made man's existing conceptions of God's judgement seem antiquated. It took at once that central place in history, in human outlook, in the universe, which had been held by the Great White Throne. It solved the problem of God's righteousness and man's sin.

The problem was to square moral instincts with grace. Greek and Jewish notions of God's forgiveness failed, as Plato and others saw, because they involved the simple giving-away of the very ideas of law, order, and righteousness ... It undid the universe, and yet cost nobody anything ... The cross enabled man to share God's view of the seriousness of sin, but without despair; it allowed him to hope, to trust, to live – without cheapening God, or righteousness. Repentance was a genuine sharing of God's outlook at all costs to oneself ... the cross was for Paul a revelation of God's ways and of God's nature so surprising in its inconceivable generosity that it melted his heart ... Throughout his whole life he could never speak or think of it without the element of wonder or surprise ... The cross revealed at once the brightness and warmth of God's love and the horribleness of sin: and if a man accepted the love ... he could not forget how exceedingly sinful sin had been shown to be." [12]

That keeps very close to the essential meaning of Romans 3:21f. H. Wheeler Robinson similarly stresses the ethical effect of salvation through the cross – without denying for a moment other more "theological" effects of Christ's death for us:

"The work of Christ for us and in us is a unity, which can be disting-uished as subjective and objective only by abstract thought, but was hardly so distinguished by Paul. When Christ died and rose from death, He not only brought men who were spiritually united to Him into a new sacrificial relation to God, but brought into operation spiritual forces effective in the believer through Christ's indwelling presence ..." [13]

In a single phrase, by the death of Christ, men are saved not only from sin but from sinning.

(c) Beside the presence of Christ among men and the death of Christ for men, Paul saw as God's yet more powerful saving reaction to sin, *the Spirit of Christ within men*. "God sent forth the Spirit of His Son into our hearts" (Galatians 4:6, compare 4). "The law of the Spirit of life in Christ Jesus has set me free from the law of sin and death. God has done what the law, weakened by the flesh, could not do: in order that the just requirement of the law might be fulfilled in us who walk not according to the flesh but according to the Spirit" (Romans 8:2-4). The whole Pauline doctrine of the Spirit in the moral life of man is integral to the Pauline ethic: on the one hand, Paul moralised the primitive conception of the Spirit, by transferring Christian emphasis from the more spectacular "gifts" of ecstasy, tongues-speaking, visions, to those more ethically significant, "righteousness, peace, joy, in the Holy Ghost" (Romans 14:17), preaching, edification, (1 Corinthians 14:1-5), and especially love (1 Corinthians 12:31 – 13:3). On the other hand, he transformed the Jewish-Christian conception of ethics, by seeing all moral problems in the light of the Spirit of holiness dwelling within men and producing by His own inmost operation the qualities of Christlike life (Galatians 5:22f, 2 Corinthians 3:18).

Against the rule and power of sin within weakened human nature, Paul asserts the invasive power of the Holy Spirit, the source of new incentives and new resources. The result is "a life of heightened individuality" (Glover), but also of deepened relationships both with God and with men. The effects of sin on the stained conscience and darkened mind are countered by a Spirit-enlightened understanding, a new intuition into spiritual things, the restoration of lost powers of emotion, vision, and will. "By the Spirit of God," says Marshall, "the Christian man is put into the moral sphere of God ... It is significant that all the fruits of the Spirit ... are ethical qualities."[14] Just as the external power of sin invades man's nature through the weakness of the flesh, so deliverance comes by the invasion of God's Spirit, who entrenches Himself in the "inner man". Thus the law is fulfilled by the rule of the Spirit (Romans) and the fruits of the Spirit replace the works of the flesh (Galatians). Paul, in fact, ascribes all Christian qualities, graces, worship, assurance, understanding, relationships, and service to the renewing power of the Holy Spirit.

Citing *forty-three* Pauline passages in illustration, Wheeler Robinson comments, "Paul's doctrine of the Spirit as active in the regeneration and sanctification of the believer united with Christ through faith and baptism, is his most important and characteristic contribution to Christian anthropology ... The Spirit of God comes to be for Paul the dynamic energy of God ... available for all who are in His abiding fellowship. With this great conception Paul comes to the help of the man whom the facts of moral experience have compelled to cry 'Who will deliver me from the body of this death?' "[15]

It is easy to distinguish, but it is impossible to separate these three saving agencies, either in Paul's thought or in Christian experience. It is by Christ, by the cross, and by the Spirit together that man's universal failure is to be recovered, a lost world redeemed, and the Christian ideal fulfilled.

(iii) Repentance, Faith and Salvation

The third presupposition of Pauline ethics concerns the way in which God's redemptive reaction to man's sin actually impinges upon the life and conduct of the Christian man and the Christian society. As everywhere in the New Testament, salvation is experienced through repentant faith. Writing to Christians, Paul rarely uses the word *repentance,* but the idea is prominent in his thought: "All the riches of God's kindness, forbearance, and patience, are meant to lead men to repentance ... God may perhaps grant that they will repent and come to know the truth ... Godly grief produces a repentance that leads to salvation." Significantly, the repentant spirit is not left behind with advancing Christian experience: for those who fall into sin and in spiritual pride refuse to repent, Paul can only mourn (Romans 2:4, 2 Timothy 2:25, 2 Corinthians 7:9, 10, 12:21).

The sharp break with the past which *is* repentance is dramatically described and laid as a continuing obligation upon Christian hearts: the converted man shall no longer walk as other gentiles walk, shall put off the old self and its ways, shall keep in mind not things of the flesh but things of the Spirit, shall have died with Christ, being crucified with Him, and shall reckon himself so dead, so that old things are passed away and all things become new. "Ye were once darkness, but now are ye light in the Lord." After a forbidding list of vices, Paul can say of the Corinthians: "Such were some of you: but ye are washed ... sanctified ... justified in the name of the Lord Jesus and in the Spirit of our God." Nevertheless, for Paul as for Jesus, repentance is only the negative implication of that crucial re-orientation of life by which man is redeemed. The positive aspect is faith, the outgoing of the soul in trust, longing, and commitment towards God, towards the moral ideal represented in Christ, and the moral resources made available in Him. "Believe on the Lord, Jesus Christ, and thou shalt be saved", is Paul's gospel; almost every page of his correspondence echoes it clearly: "By grace are ye saved, through faith, and that is God's gift." Exploring Paul's conception of faith, J. S. Stewart finds in it the conviction of the reality of the unseen, confidence in the promises of God, an epitome of the whole Christian religion, a conviction of the gospel facts, but especially an utter self-abandonment to the God revealed in Christ.[16] That psychological and ethical aspect of faith Wheeler Robinson further describes as primarily an attitude of trust and assured confidence, directed towards Christ, and especially towards His death and resurrection, through which Christ dwells in the heart in a union of personality so intimate and real that the consequent life is Christ's rather than the believer's.[17]

The salvation into which such faith introduces the soul consists, on its mainly *religious* side, of forgiveness or justification, access to God in reconciliation, adoption, sonship, the reception of the Spirit, and the hope of immortality. On its mainly *emotional* side, salvation includes a strong and enduring spiritual assurance, an inner peace, a confident courage and fearlessness, a buoyant joy. On its *practical* side, salvation comprises effective prayer, day-to-day guidance directing life's affairs, and dedication to the purposes of the new-found Saviour. On its *ethical* side, salvation includes a new moral dynamic released within the soul, adequate for life, for service, and for great endurance; freedom from the bondage of law and of sin, from fear of men, and of the future; a totally new sense of community which transcends individualism in the unity of Christ; and a prevailing sense of victory, of moral triumph and ascendancy, of being more than conquerors through Him that loves us. In such an experience, according to Paul, life is made entirely new.

Thus, at every point, Paul's presuppositions about man's nature and need, and about God's saving activity and man's response, imply the most radical revolution in life's ideals, direction, and resources, whether or not that revolution has the dramatic intensity and emotional accompaniments of his own Damascus-road experience. To Paul, the Christian is a *saved* man, and the Christian ethic is *the ethic implied in the process of salvation:* to be redeemed at all is to be morally transformed.

(3) REDEMPTION AS MORAL TRANSFORMATION

Salvation is for Paul emphatically a moral concept, though that view has been challenged continuously from his day until ours. From his thesis that salvation is by faith only, and not by works, the false inference has been drawn that so long as a man "believes" he may continue in sin, so that free grace may abound towards him (Romans 6:1); that as man is not saved by merit, or endeavour, Paul's gospel is the end of Christian ethics. That this is nonsense is sufficiently shown by his fourfold insistence: "Do you not know that the unrighteous will not inherit the kingdom of God? Do not be deceived, neither the immoral, nor idolators, nor adulterers, nor homosexuals, nor thieves, nor the greedy, nor drunkards, nor revilers, nor robbers will inherit the kingdom of God ... The works of the flesh are plain: immorality, impurity ... jealousy, anger ... selfishness ... and the like. I warn you, as I warned you before, that those who do such things shall not inherit the kingdom of God ... Be sure of this, that no immoral or impure man, or one who is covetous ... has any inheritance in the kingdom of Christ and of God ..." (1 Corinthians 6:9, 10, Galatians 5:19-21, Ephesians 5:5). Could anything be more explicit? Yet this emphasis is further underlined by the doctrine of the judgement that awaits all – believers and unbelievers alike:

" ... on the day when God's righteous judgement will be revealed. For he will render to every man according to his works: to those who by patience in well doing seek for glory and honour and immortality, he will give eternal life; but for those who are factious and do not obey the truth ... there will be wrath ... God shows no partiality ... We make it our aim to please him. For we must all appear before the judgement seat of Christ, so that each one may receive good or evil, according to what he has done in the body. Knowing therefore the fear of the Lord, we persuade men ..." (Romans 2:5-11, 2 Corinthians 5:9-11).

The familiar words, "Whatsoever a man sows, that shall he also reap" were written to and about Christians; so was the warning, "We shall all stand before the judgement seat of Christ ... So then every one of us shall give account of himself before God;" and the exhortation: "Of the Lord ye shall receive the reward of the inheritance ... But he that doeth wrong shall receive for the wrong which he hath done: and there is no respect of persons" (Galatians 6:7, Romans 14:10-12, Colossians 3:24-25).

There is in Paul no relaxing the ethical assessment of a man's life, and no escaping the final judgement of God.

Nor are these only ultimate insights: Paul acts upon them, exercising a stern church discipline by excluding from fellowship "any man that is called a brother" who is found guilty of persistent sin (1 Corinthians 5:11). This unvarying insistence that, though we are not saved "because of good works", yet we are saved – created in Christ Jesus – "for good works, which God prepared beforehand that we should walk in them" (Ephesians 2:8-10), finds its fullest expression however in the detailed exposition of Paul's gospel, as the fulfilment of righteousness, by the moral miracle of faith, in the life of new men who steadily advance towards the goal of redemption in Christlikeness.

(i) The Fulfilment of Righteousness

All Paul's evangelical themes are ethically qualified. (a) *Justification by faith* – the divine verdict of acquittal granted to guilty men on the ground of their faith in Christ – is given freely, yet conditioned in two ways: the faith which justifies has (as we shall see) very considerable moral significance; and in the new relation to God which results, the law hitherto broken, and dreaded, is *fulfilled*. "What the law could not do ... God did, sending his own Son ... that the righteousness of the law might be fulfilled in us who walk not after the flesh but after the Spirit ... We are made the righteousness of God in Christ" (Romans 8:3-4, 2 Corinthians 5:21). As Augustine said, "The law is given that grace may be sought; grace is given that the law may be fulfilled."[18] So, "being reckoned righteous" (being justified) is never a substitute for being righteous, but a preliminary thereto: instead of keeping the law to obtain God's favour, the believer receives God's favour to enable him to keep the law. He is bidden to think upon whatsoever things are righteous, to yield his members as weapons of righteousness, to put on the new nature created in righteousness, to wear the breastplate of righteousness, to work as a servant of righteousness, and to live in the kingdom which is righteousness as well as joy and peace. This is the "righteousness which exceeds", which Jesus said was necessary to all who would enter the kingdom.

(b) Paul likewise echoes Jesus concerning *the kingdom of God* (Acts 17:7, 20:25, 28:23, 31, Romans 14:17 etc) and we have seen how firmly he stated the moral conditions for "inheriting" the kingdom. Marshall remarks that "the ten authentic Pauline letters mention the kingdom only a dozen times, yet these reveal precisely the same polarity in Paul's thought about it as ... in the teaching of Jesus."[19] Eight references are eschatological, the rest represent the kingdom as "an internal spiritual reality experienced here and now,"as men are delivered from the dominion of darkness and transferred to the kingdom of God's dear Son. Eight of the total have ethical overtones, two introducing the thought of being *worthy* of the kingdom, one declaring that the kingdom lies not in talk but in power, and another that the kingdom does not concern itself with ritual regulations but with righteousness, peace and joy in the Holy Ghost – a remark especially close to Christ's own teaching. For Paul as for Jesus, the kingdom is an ethical concept: "the rule of God in us is our redemption" (Herrmann).

(c) Translating the originally messianic language of divine kingship into terms familiar to gentiles from the slave market, the heathen temple, Roman politics (for which Caesar was sole *Lord*), and the Greek Old Testament (in which Yahweh was Lord), Paul made *the baptismal confession of the Lordship of Christ* the ruling concept of Christian ethics (Romans 10:9, 1 Corinthians 12:3, Philippians 2:11, 2 Corinthians 4:5, Acts 16, 31 etc. Compare Mark 8:27-30). The implications of this step are endless. Phrases like the word of the Lord, the Lord's day, the Lord's Table, the Day of the Lord, we are the Lord's, the Lord's body, the Lord of glory, if the Lord will, the Lord is at hand, receive her in the Lord, labouring in the Lord, the Lord is the Spirit, Christ Jesus my Lord, may serve to illustrate the range of experience directly related to Christ's Lordship, as Paul's constant appeals to the law of Christ, the example of Christ, the teaching of Christ, the explicit words of Christ, as sufficient rule for conduct, may indicate how practical was this conception in apostolic obedience.

This conviction of the divine rule, both in its Jewish and its gentile form, is ultimately eschatological, and raises again the question how ethics is related to eschatology. According to Paul, the new age has come, one world has ended and another has been inaugurated: "You are not in darkness, brethren, for that day to surprise you like a thief. For you are all sons of light and of the day: we are not of the night or of the darkness ... Since we belong to the day let us be sober, and put on the breastplate of faith and love, and for a helmet the hope of salvation" (1 Thessalonians 5:4-8). Yet the new age is only inaugurated, full daylight is ahead: "You know what hour it is, how it is full time now for you to awake out of sleep. For salvation is nearer to us now than when we first believed. The night is far gone, the day is at hand. Let us then cast off the works of darkness and put on the armour of light ..." (Romans 13:11-12). As in the teaching of Jesus, certainty of the future reign of God, so far from making all ethical considerations merely "interim", in fact imposes moral restraint and intensifies moral obligation. The Christian must not say "Let us eat and drink, for tomorrow we die" – that is an evil slogan which corrupts good behaviour. Nevertheless, as we shall see, in some details of counsel the hope of the advent somewhat foreshortened Paul's view.

From every side of Paul's gospel, then, we confront his ethical demand. The moral redemption of man was not simply the desired consequence of being saved, it is an essential element in its *meaning*. As J. S. Stewart remarks, "the idea of a religion where the demand for absolute obedience to God was abrogated, never entered Paul's horizon."[20]

(ii) The Moral Miracle of Faith

Since Paul combines this demand for righteousness with unwavering insistence that men are saved by faith alone, we are compelled to ask, What then is faith? In Romans 1:16, which speaks of "the power of God unto salvation to every one who *believes*", faith is no passive receptiveness or intellectual assent: it appropriates the saving energies offered in the gospel. In similar active sense we read of "the work of faith", "faith working by love", "the good resolve and work of faith" (1 Thessalonians 1:3, Galatians 5:6, 2 Thessalonians 1:11). "The obedience of faith" suggests positive submission rather than passive trust: Brunner can say that faith is obedience, nothing else – literally nothing else at all; Stewart can add that faith, as Paul conceives it, is love – utter self-abandonment.[21]

Equally significant is the way Paul passes (in Romans 6) from his argument for justification by faith to certain consequences which may be drawn from *baptism*. The transition is coherent only if baptism be the outward sign and deliberate expression of justifying faith. But baptism is said to express voluntary and acknowledged *union with Christ* in His death to sin and in His rising again to newness of life. Faith in the Christ set forth as a propitiation (3:25) carries with it acceptance of Christ's death as a just judgement upon sin, and commitment to share Christ's attitude of implacable hostility towards sin, renouncing it, "dying to it", once for all. To say "I believe that Jesus died for me" is to say "He died *my* death – I am dead." I say Amen to what He did, take up His cross, am planted together with Him in the likeness of His death, crucified with Him. "For we thus judge, that if one died for all, then were all dead ... no longer to live unto themselves, but unto Him which died for them ... They that are Christ's have crucified the flesh ... their nature (is) transformed to die as He died" because He died (Romans 6:5f, 2 Corinthians 5:14, 15, Galatians 5:24, cf Philippians 3:10 (Moffatt)).

This representative and inclusive character of the death of Christ is basic to all Paul's thinking, and the implication that faith in the death of Christ involves dying with Him, is everywhere plain. "Ye are dead ... The cross, by which the world is crucified to me and I unto the world ... You were buried with Him in baptism, in which you were also raised with Him through faith

. . ." If Christ died for me *because of* sin, so that I need not die, He died also for me *to sin,* so that I die with Him. I cannot rest in one side of the truth without accepting the other. In prosaic essentials, Paul is describing the negative implicate of faith in Christ, elsewhere called repentance: Julicher well says that for Paul, faith is an activity of conscience.

The positive implicate of faith is union with Christ in life and resurrection, the personal relation to the ascended Lord which Paul everywhere calls being "in Christ". Borrowed from earlier sources, and used some one hundred and sixty-four times, the phrase affirms that mystical experience in which "Christ is the redeemed man's environment" – his world, his resources, his very life. The Christian lives "in" the risen, glorified Lord: Christ is his life, and life in Christ is the source of new moral motives, power, and aims, a new quality of existence that shows itself spontaneously in Christlike behaviour. Union with Christ is Paul's more inward "imitation of Christ".

Neither the mystical synonyms for faith, nor the public and irrevocable expression of it in baptism, explains just how faith achieves ethical transformation.

The form of baptism by immersion vividly *recalls* the death and burial of Jesus, focus of the faith being confessed; and as vividly *suggests* the death and burial of the Christian, not in the same sense but as an act of renunciation towards all that He died to. Yet faith-baptism is no mere homiletic illustration of a moral truth; nor is it sufficient to say that faith in Christ, or the baptism which expresses it *ought* to mean that the convert has died with Christ. As Cullmann and others have emphasised, baptism involves not only an imperative but an indicative. The tenses in Galatians 5:24, Colossians 2:20, 3:1, 3, and the whole argument of Romans 6, underline the fixed point of past time at which the believer died, was crucified and buried, with Christ. From this arises an abiding obligation to reckon oneself dead, but the basis of this continuing exhortation lies in what has already happened, in the decisive public act of faith-commitment to Christ.[22]

Full exploration of the rationale of faith, as the means whereby the saving energies of Christ become operative within the soul, is beyond the scope of ethics; but when Paul's faith-union with Christ is analysed (as by Sanday-Headlam) in psychological terms, it is seen to be an intense personal apprehension of Christ as Master, Redeemer, Lord, so persistent, so absorbing, so dominating, that it creates virtual identity of will with Him.[23] For Paul, saving faith *means* such moral identification with Christ, sharing His death to sin and His resurrection to newness of life. Its depth is personal devotion to Jesus as one entirely loved, admired, and trusted; its emotion is a moral passion for all that Jesus stood for, against all that He died to; its strength lies in appropriation of the power of Christ to save and to keep; its effect is to conform the believer to the image of Christ, step by step, and to liberate through him in place of sin the very life of the ascended Lord. That is the moral miracle of faith.

(iii) The New Man

That redemption includes moral transformation is clearly implied in Paul's very frequent references to the crisis of change through which his readers have passed, and to the radically new moral nature which that experience has produced in each of them. The change is repeatedly recalled, sometimes with eschatological overtones – "once you were darkness, now are ye light in the Lord" – a change from one age to another, to a new "day" and dispensation (Ephesians 5:8). Or with baptismal background – a death and resurrection with Christ, a putting-off and putting-on (Romans 6 etc, Colossians 3:5-14). Sometimes with allusion to the Genesis story of creation – "If any man be in Christ, there is a new creation" both of the man and of his total world: "old things are passed away ... all things are become new"; "It is the God who said, 'Let light shine out of darkness' who has shone in our hearts, to give the light of the knowledge of the glory of God in the face of Christ" (2 Corinthians 5:17, 4:6). And sometimes in literal statement of fact – "Such were some of you, but you were washed, sanctified, justified ... Among such we all once lived, but God ... made us alive with Christ; Remember that at one time you were separated, alienated, far-off, strangers, hopeless, without God, but now you are brought near, reconciled ... You were the slaves of sin, but now are set free ... You turned from idols to serve the living and true God" (1 Corinthians 6:11, Ephesians 2:3, 4, 12f, Romans 6:17, 18, 1 Thessalonians 1:9). Paul will not let converts forget their past.

The new moral nature resulting from such change, Paul declares to be essential to salvation ("Neither circumcision counts for anything, nor uncircumcision, but a new creation" (Galatians 6:15)), and echoes of the Genesis story occur again in the declaration that the "new man" is created after the image of its Creator, in knowledge, righteousness, and holiness (Ephesians 4.24, Colossians 3:10). Such a "new" personality is already implied in Paul's account of the meaning of repentance as a sharp break with all the past, and of the new liberty and sense of community created by the invasive energies of the Spirit. A soul thus passing under Christ's Lordship, to be "in Christ" and filled with His Spirit, must be a new self. New ideas possess the mind renewed in knowledge, transformed to know the perfect will of God, as the convert is renewed "in the spirit of the mind" (Romans 12:2, Ephesians 4:23). New motives operate upon the will, the constraint of Christ's love, the fear of Christ's judgement, the "minding" of the things of the Spirit (2 Corinthians 5:11, 14, Romans

8:5-8), and – very significantly – the eager desire to prove "worthy of God ... of our calling ... of the Lord ... of the gospel ... and of the kingdom" – all given to us in our unworthiness (1 Thessalonians 2:12, Ephesians 4:1, Colossians 1:10, Philippians 1:27, 2 Thessalonians 1:5). New resources are available for living in the grace sufficient for salvation and for suffering, in the power of the indwelling Spirit, in the life of Jesus manifested in us and in the strength continually renewed in the inner man. And a new direction integrates all life's plans and energies, as the personal drives turn from self to Christ, as affection is set on things above, and we press toward the mark, the measure of the stature of the fullness of Christ. A decisive step has been taken, the direction for new moral development has been established, and the personality is "made over" in the power of Christ.

If this emphasis upon revolutionary change owes something to Paul's apparently sudden conversion, the long and deep preparation for that event, and the slowly unfolding consequences, warn us not to exaggerate its suddenness. James Stewart argues that Christian history has shown that Paul's experience has been understood and shared by many. He quotes Denney's remark that Paul's message has proved "incomparably the greatest source of spiritual revivals", and concludes that "it is precisely the intense individuality of Paul's experience that makes his gospel universal ... Had the experience been something less than the individual, singular, distinctive thing it was, the resultant gospel would have been something less than the universal, catholic thing it is."[24] Stewart appears to mean that what is close and vital to one intensely human being, at the centre of his humanity, cannot be unintelligible to other humans: "Damascus, so far from setting Paul apart from us and keeping him away, has made him brother of us all."

From a strictly ethical viewpoint, only those whose experience approximates *in essentials* to that of Paul, as a man transfigured by invasive power and passion evoked by Christ, can ever hope to understand, or approximate to, the high ideal Paul held before his converts, and himself so eagerly pursued. From the wider viewpoint of mankind's moral hope, we may add, with Marshall, that "the heresy that human nature never changes lies like a foul barrier across the path of human progress",[25] and set against the heresy the Pauline gospel of men made new in the power of Christ.

(iv) The Goal of Redemption

However dramatic the conversion-experience, continual moral effort remains necessary, pressing toward the target set in Christ, not counting oneself to have attained, or to be already mature, but reaching forward constantly towards things beyond immediate grasp, while God works in us to accomplish His good pleasure

(Philippians 3:12-14, 2:13). Paul can say "we were saved", "you have been saved", as to status, acceptance with God, forgiveness, peace; but speak also of "us who are *being* saved" and even say "we shall be saved" (Ephesians 2:8, 1 Corinthians 1:18, Romans 5:10) when he is thinking of progressive refinement of Christian character and approximation to the Christian goal.

One description of that goal, *maturity,* implies full-grown understanding, stability ("not blown about" by every new idea and varying impulse), and social integration (being co-operative rather than quarrelsome, egotistic, as "babes in Christ"). This last evidence of maturity is emphasised frequently: only with *all* the saints can any believer comprehend the dimensions of the love of Christ; the goal is that *all* should come, in the unity conferred by a common faith, to a perfect man. In isolation, the individual remains a spiritual child – or becomes a religious crank: we grow together because only together can we grow.

Paul's definition of the goal of redemption is *Christlikeness,* "the measure of the stature of the fullness of Christ", the progressive creation of the new man in the image of its Creator,[26] the process of "beholding the glory of the Lord (and) being changed into the same image." Paul "travails" until Christ be formed again in his Galatian converts, while all Christian experience assures him that to those who love God, all things work towards the fulfilment of God's predetermined purpose, that we should be conformed to the image of His Son (Ephesians 4:13, Colossians 3:10, 2 Corinthians 3:18, Galatians 4:19, Romans 8:28f).

Once more we meet the New Testament principle of the imitation of Christ. (a) The *example of Christ* is both pattern and incentive for Christian forgiveness (Colossians 3:13); for truth-speaking in love, and growing up into Him in every way (Ephesians 4:15), including cleanness and self-discipline (Ephesians 4:20) and self-giving love (Ephesians 5:2); and for anxiety to please "not ourselves but our neighbour" for his good (Romans 15:2, 3). Where possible, (b) *words of Christ* are appealed to for settlement of practical questions of behaviour: concerning marriage (1 Corinthians 7:10); generosity (Acts 20:35); the support of Christian workers (1 Corinthians 9:14); the conduct of the Supper (1 Corinthians 11:23); the power of faith (1 Corinthians 13:2); the sufficiency of love as fulfilment of the law (Romans 13:8-10).

Where such appeal and quotation are impossible, through change of circumstance and the emergence of new problems, reference is made – for imitation – to (c) the *mind of Christ.* Two passages illumine this conception. Among questions posed at Corinth were some new to the Christian conscience: problems of mixed pagan-Christian marriage, and of the use for food of meat slaughtered in idol-temples. Paul prefaces his counsel with the reminder of the gift of the Spirit to believers, who rely not on human wisdom but on the wisdom which the Holy Spirit teaches, and adds "we have the mind of Christ" (1 Corinthians 2:12-16). Proceeding to advise, he carefully distinguishes his own counsel from remembered words of Jesus, and after expressing his judgement on a particular issue he repeats "And I think I have the Spirit of God." This is plainly a deliberate attempt to bring to bear upon day-to-day problems a moral wisdom and insight informed and guided by long pondering upon the story and the teaching of Jesus, and illumined by the Spirit as intellectual guide. Thus the remembered principles and insights of Jesus were translated into present, and unprecedented, ethical decisions.

W. D. Davies cites Resch for 1,096 parallels to the Synoptic Gospels in Paul, admitting that this grossly overstates the position but arguing nevertheless that the evidence is very impressive. Davies examines and accepts thirty-two clear quotations of Jesus by Paul: "It was the words of Jesus Himself that formed Paul's primary source . . . Paul is steeped in the mind and words of his Lord . . . Paul had the words of Jesus to which he turned for guidance, and he makes it clear that when there is an explicit word uttered by Christ on any question, that word is accepted by him as authoritative." It must be remembered that Paul was not among the Twelve who first heard Christ's teaching, and that no authorised translation of Christ's words into Greek yet existed.
Examining objections to the claimed prominence of imitation of Christ in Paul's thought, Davies declares "Again and again he holds up the historical Jesus for imitation . . . To him every Christian, like his Lord, was to have his Olivet and Calvary and Easter. All this does not refer to any pietistic or imaginative absorption of the individual in Christ . . . but to the facing of the harsh realities of the actual situations of life in His Spirit; it is in other words to have the mind of Christ and His obedience . . . For him, every Christian is pledged to an attempted ethical conformity to Christ; the imitation of Christ is part and parcel of Paul's ethic." Davies cites also C. H. Dodd: "The stamp of Christ will be upon the whole of the Christian's daily activity. The 'law of Christ' is binding upon him in all things. That law is apprehended inwardly by the activity of the indwelling Spirit of Christ, for it is the Spirit that gives us 'the mind of Christ'. But it would be a mistake to divorce this thought from a direct reference to the historic teaching of Jesus Christ. Paul in fact not only allows that teaching to mould and colour his own thought to a greater extent than is commonly realised, but he also definitely cites the words of Christ as morally authoritative."[27]

In the second passage, Philippians 2:1-11, "the mind of Christ" again directs behaviour: but here it is less a matter of moral insight and judgement than of virtue and graciousness of spirit. It imitates the renunciation of all selfishness and conceit, the embracing of unity, sympathy and love, which found its highest expression "in Christ Jesus", who emptied Himself to become the Servant of the Lord and the Saviour of men. This is the moral, rather than the intellectual, side of "the mind of Christ" – the adoption, as an act of will, of the attitude seen in Jesus.

Changing the language, but not the thought, Paul speaks (d) of our appropriating the *nature of Christ* – "putting on Christ . . . the new man created in the image of his Creator" – thinking now less of intellect or attitude than of Christlike motive and impulse, as the spring of Christian behaviour (Colossians 3:10, Ephesians 4:23f). And sometimes he speaks of our possessing (e) the *Spirit of Christ,* not in these instances as teacher and guide but as the indwelling source of all goodness, the power that controls from within, the Spirit of holiness, of purity, and of peaceableness, the origin and sustenance of all Christian graces, which flow naturally from His presence in the soul – love, joy, peace, longsuffering, gentleness, goodness, faithfulness, meekness, self-control – the lineaments of Jesus. "The fruits of the Spirit are the virtues of Christ" (Schleiermacher). The possession of this moral insight, this nature and this Spirit, in developing degree as Christian life matures, reproduces the likeness of Christ in the believer, even though the situations faced and the problems to be resolved differ widely from anything Jesus knew in the days of His flesh.

By such a process of salvation, aimed from the start at attaining the righteousness which the law failed to achieve, through the miracle of faith's recreating men in Christ, and moving always toward Christlikeness, man is redeemed from sinning. Positively, the continuing experience of salvation proves to be the source of a new moral life of unprecedented vigour, creativeness, and joy, which Paul expected would show itself, naturally and inevitably, in new qualities of character and behaviour. This is Paul's gospel of moral redemption.

9

Paul's Ethical Directives

THOUGH PAUL CONCEIVED THE work of Christ as the moral redemption of sinful men, and Christian morality as the natural and inevitable consequence of a true salvation-experience – the outflow, or "fruit" of the new life given in Christ – yet he knew that the development of Christian character would not proceed without effort, aspiration, and instruction. Much failure, and folly, arose from ignorance (Romans 6:3, 6, 16, 1 Corinthians 3:16, Galatians 5:21, Ephesians 4:20, 21, Colossians 1:28, 2:6, 7, 1 Thessalonians 4:1 etc). Paul would not, therefore, rely on the initial catechetical teaching received by converts as sufficient education in discipleship, but elaborated it in considerable depth and detail. His directives for Christian living emerge in scattered counsels and exhortations addressed always to concrete situations and informed by wide pastoral experience. The result is great richness of thought, metaphor, and themes, which can be expounded only by an artificial classification under main principles, of which the first, for Paul as for Jesus, was the pre-eminence accorded to love.

(1) THE NEW MORAL PRINCIPLE

Paul is usually designated the apostle of faith, but Marshall contends that "he was even more the apostle of love."[1] Defining what alone is effective, or has validity, in religion, Paul declares that neither heredity nor ritual (nor the lack of either) really matters: but faith, made an operative principle of moral life by love.

So Galatians 5:6: NEB – "faith active in love", margin "faith inspired by" (God's?) "love"; the context (note 13 and the great commandment in 14) strongly supports RSV "faith working through love."

Paul is unfailingly loyal to Christ's insight here: "He who loves his neighbour has fulfilled the law: the commandments, You shall not commit adultery, You shall not kill, You shall not steal, You shall not covet, or any other commandment, are summed up in this sentence, You shall love your neighbour as yourself. Love does no wrong to a neighbour: therefore love is the fulfilling of the law" (Romans 13:8-10) – this is almost a quotation from the interviews of Jesus with the enquiring lawyer and the rich young ruler. So in Galatians, Paul concludes discussion of the place of law in Christian life with "the law of Christ" – "Bear ye one another's burdens" – having just cited the same comment of Jesus: "For the whole law is fulfilled in one word, You shall love your neighbour as yourself" (6:2, 5:14).

The supremacy of love emerges equally clearly when Paul echoes the baptismal catechesis. In Colossians 3, the convert is to put on, in addition to and "above all" other graces, love – the sash (or, girdle) of perfection. Paul reinforces the primitive teaching on life in the new community by exhorting the Colossians to be "knit together in love" (2:2), and requiring the Ephesians to walk in love, all bitterness, wrath, anger, clamour being put away, and to become instead kind to one another, tender-hearted, forgiving one another. They had become *members* one of another: that is why they could no longer lie, steal, or nourish anger, or by any other unbrotherly attitude grieve the Holy Spirit who dwells within the Christian community. In Ephesians, the creation of one commonwealth, one household, one body, one holy temple, out of national, racial, social and religious diversity, is God's first step in fulfilment of the plan to unite all things under one head in Christ – the socialisation of men, in mutual Christian love, is the necessary corollary of that far-sweeping divine purpose (4:25 to 5:2, 2:17-22, 1:10 and see further (5) below).

The supremacy of love as the over-ruling principle of the new morality is seen again in Paul's great hymn to love (1 Corinthians 13). Here two fundamental contrasts are made. In the opening phrases Paul lists the manifestations of the religious spirit that have been highly valued through Christian history, five familiar and persistent conceptions of what is vital in religion: emotional experience, intellectual understanding, practical and energetic faith, generous philanthropy, courageous martyrdom. Each, Paul declares, is meaningless, profitless, mere "nothing", without the essential requirement – love. Similarly, 1 Corinthians 12-14 is concerned explicitly with the more spectacular manifestations of the Holy Spirit within the church. But all these could be counterfeited, and were in fact paralleled in heathenism: the supreme, the only infallible sign of the presence of the Spirit in the church – "the more excellent way" – is the evidence of love, the love created by and poured forth into the heart by the Holy Spirit (Romans 5:5; compare 15:30, Galatians 5:22, Philippians 2:2, Colossians 1:8). It is not surprising that Paul includes love among the enduring, eternal elements of religion, and then declares the specifically *moral* quality to be greater than either of the theological principles, faith or hope.

For all this, Paul nowhere defines this new moral principle. "Love does no wrong"; it shows liberality, zealous aid, cheerfulness in acts of mercy; it contributes to the needs of fellow-believers, and practises hospitality; it seeks to live in harmony, never repaying evil for evil. Love achieves identification with all sorts and conditions of men, enabling it both to weep and to rejoice with others, to be weak with the weak, feel shame with the fallen, and become all things to all men. It restores those overtaken in trespass, without self-righteousness; is kind, lowly, patient, forgiving, careful of the interests of others, promoting their honour and not its own. Love is careful for truth, and for whatever upbuilds other Christian lives, encouraging the fainthearted, avoiding criticism and judgement, seeking ever to do good, within the fellowship and beyond it.

Paul's most sustained description of Christian love shows it to be a *quality of activity,* kind, courteous, selfless, ambitious for others, never for itself, angry for others but never for itself; a *quality of thinking,* humble, sincere, never glad when others go wrong, never envious, suspicious, or cynical, but magnanimous, fair, and optimistic; and a *quality of suffering,* enduring adversity with patience, disappointment without bitterness, never petulant or vengeful; even when rejected, despised and crucified, "love never fails."

That portrait of love is the portrait of Jesus, and the only motive sufficient to sustain such goodwill in all circumstances is an experience of the love of Christ that passes knowledge. This reference back to Christ serves to emphasise two other details in Paul's description, out of many that could be recalled: (a) In Galatians 2:20 Paul's thought moves immediately, and revealingly, from "He loved me" to "He gave Himself for me"; and in Romans 5:5 Paul finds the unparalleled superiority of divine love to consist in this, that whereas others might peradventure sacrifice themselves for those they admire and count worthy, "God commends his love toward us in that while we were yet sinners, Christ died for us." This is the nearest Paul comes to a definition of what love *is:* goodwill carried to the point of unmeasured and uncalculating sacrifice for the admittedly unworthy.

W. Lillie discusses the view of Nygren that God's love for man is uncaused, spontaneous, not called out by anything outside itself, certainly not by anything lovely in man. It is wrong to suppose that God loves the godly for his godliness. "It is to something worthy, to the beauty in a person or object, that Plato's *eros* is drawn: 'that which is the object of love must indeed be fair, delicate, perfect, most happy'".[2] In Christian revelation, divine love, and the *agape* required of Christians, is precisely the love that extends to sinners, undeserved, inexplicable. That is the quality of love which alone is relevant in a sinful world.

(b) This is also the quality of love by which we ourselves are saved: "Concerning love of the brethren," Paul writes to the Thessalonians, "you have no need to have any one write to you, for you yourselves have been taught by God to love one another" (4:9). In Romans 5 the love commended to us by the death of Jesus is by the same token imparted to us, "poured into our hearts". When Paul urges upon the Philippians the loving spirit of mutual affection and service, he at once recalls the source of our own salvation in that same spirit shown in Christ (2:5f); when he urges the Ephesians to treat each other with tender-heartedness and forgiveness, he at once adds, "as God, for Christ's sake, has forgiven you" (4:32). Always, this evangelical motivation is part of Paul's exposition of love's meaning, anticipating John's unsurpassable summary, "We love, because he first loved us."

Thus, *to love is enough*. Within this supreme command, the multitudinous provisions of Judaist law and Torah are summarised and unified. All Christian insights, virtues, aims, disciplines, precepts, and valuations ultimately derive from this single principle. Love will not deceive its neighbour with falsehood, defraud him by dishonesty, defile him with impurity, nor corrupt him by bad example; it will not wound him by discourtesy, nor undermine him by temptation, over-reach him by injustice, nor exploit him for gain. Compared with the endless elaboration and complexity of most moral systems that rest upon codes of law and casuistry, this *formal simplification* of moral obligation into one over-riding precept, of active, universal, persistent and undiscourageable goodwill, offers immense clarity to the earnest mind and relief to the scrupulous conscience.

(2) NEW LIFE IN THE INDIVIDUAL

In what may loosely be called Paul's "individual ethics", emphasis falls mainly upon three themes: the Christian's mental life and qualities; the more negative discipline of sanctification, with related questions of freedom, and the indwelling Spirit; and the positive consecration of the Christian to Christ, with its constraining motives and effect.

(i) The importance which Paul attached to the Christian's *mind* is, at first sight, somewhat surprising, in view of his distrust of the wisdom of this world, and his warnings that knowledge merely "puffs up". Five times, in very varying contexts, he writes "I would not have you ignorant ..." He claims for the mature Christian a spiritual wisdom that the world could not comprehend, for "Christ is made unto us wisdom"; and desires that the Ephesians might be renewed in the spirit of their mind and given the spirit of wisdom and revelation in the knowledge of Christ, the eyes of their understanding being enlightened that they might know ...; that the Colossians, made complete in Him in whom are hid all the treasures of wisdom and knowledge, should remain established in the faith as they had been taught, being renewed in knowledge, and letting the word of Christ dwell in them richly; that the Corinthians should in understanding "be men"; that the Philippians' zeal may abound increasingly in all knowledge and discernment (1 Corinthians 1:30, Ephesians 4:23, 1:17, 18, Colossians 2:3, 7, 3:10, 16, 1 Corinthians 14:20, Philippians 1:9).

This unexpectedly intellectualist emphasis may arise from the polemic against incipient gnosticism's claims to advanced wisdom, but the inwardness of the Christian ethic demands it, too. Christian character is formed from within rather than imposed from without: the Christian's mental processes are therefore the key to his quality of living.

Qualities of mind especially commended by Paul include: *i. integrity* or sincerity, the candour and transparency which abhors craft and dishonesty, making its direct appeal to every man's conscience in the sight of God (2 Corinthians 2:17, 4:2, 15, 25). *ii. meekness* – for all his learning, and his argumentativeness, Paul had little patience with intellectual conceit: he counts himself debtor to the barbarian and the fool, urges that none think of himself more highly than he ought to think, but to count others better than himself and give place to others in matters of esteem (1 Corinthians 3:18, 8:2, Romans 1:14, 12:3, Philippians 2:3). *iii. the spiritual mind:* "Those who live according to the flesh set their minds on the things of the flesh, but those who live according to the Spirit ... on the things of the Spirit. To set the mind on the flesh is death, but to set the mind on the Spirit is life and peace" (Romans 8:5, 6). In such words, Paul is very close to the Sermon on the Mount: he is too good a psychologist to forget that the quality of the outward life depends in the long run upon the kind of thoughts – carnal, quarrelsome, envious, resentful or despondent – which are permitted and pursued in the inmost regions of the soul. *iv. The well-stored mind* – "Let the word of Christ dwell in you richly ... Whatever is true, honourable, just, pure, lovely, gracious, whatever is excellent or worthy of praise, think about these things ... All things are yours ... the world, life, death, present, future, all are yours ..." (Philippians 4:8, 1 Corinthians 3:21, 22). This is a faith sufficiently secure and unsuspicious to possess and appreciate all things good: a mind and heart at home in the Father's world. *v. The teachable mind* ever reaches forward, is ever ready to learn. "The Lord shall reveal even this unto you ... As babes ... I fed you with milk, not solid food; for you were not ready ... That you may comprehend with all saints the length, breadth, height and depth of the love that passes knowing ..." (Philippians 3:15, 1 Corinthians 3:2, Ephesians 3:18, 19). To the end, in Paul's thought as in Christ's, believers are but disciples.

But the primary quality of mind, essential to the Christian, is the *ability to discern God's will.* "Do not be fools, but try to understand what the will of the Lord is ... Being filled with the knowledge of God's will in all spiritual wisdom and understanding ... Being renewed in mind that you may discern the will of God, to know what is good and acceptable and perfect ... That you may approve what is excellent – have a sense of what is vital" (Ephesians 5:17, Colossians 1:9, Romans 12:2, Philippians 1:10). In matters ethically uncertain, each must stand or fall to his own Master. He must not merely conform to traditional or conventional opinions, nor simply submit to more aggressive minds, nor drift in confusion from one experiment to another, for whatever conduct does not proceed from Christian conviction is sin (Romans 14 *passim*). The weak, over-scrupulous conscience must be respected, but each must be fully persuaded in his own mind, and act as one possessing the mind of Christ, illumined by the teaching and example of Jesus and the guidance of the Spirit, not driven about by winds of fashion nor at the mercy of varying impulses and moods (1 Corinthians 2:16, Ephesians 4:14). In the deepest sense, the Christian character is for Paul autonomous and free, neither subservient to the world nor dependent on the world but the natural, visible outflow of a life hid with Christ in God, in which "every thought is brought into captivity to obey Christ" (Colossians 3:3, 2 Corinthians 10:5).

(ii) *Sanctification* is, in one sense, already accomplished as believers are set aside for God's exclusive possession and use, and accepted by Him (1 Corinthians 6:11). But sanctification is also a process which continues through Christian life, the will of God for all, prayed for by the apostle and enjoined upon the baptised (1 Thessalonians 4:3, 5:23, Ephesians 1:4, Romans 6:19, 22). The essential thought is of the religious purity required in persons, places and things reserved and dedicated to divine use.

This liturgical *purity before God* is holiness, in virtue of which Christians are "saints", sanctified by baptism and behaving in the world in holiness as befits a holy God (Ephesians 5:26, 1 Corinthians 6:11, 2 Corinthians 1:12, 7:1). *Purity before the law* is righteousness, which occupies so large a place in Paul's ideal. *Purity before the world* is blamelessness: "Do all things without grumbling or questioning, that you may be blameless and innocent, children of God without blemish in the midst of a crooked and perverse generation, among whom you shine as luminaries ... Holy, blameless and irreproachable" (Philippians 2:14f, Colossians 1:22). "Faultless", originally a sacrificial word (as of a lamb without spot or blemish) occurs in Ephesians of the church as Christ's bride, "presented before him in splendour, without spot, or wrinkle, or any such thing, holy ... without blemish".

In 1 Thessalonians 2:10 the three main terms occur together: "You are witnesses, and God also, how holy, righteous, and blameless was our behaviour." In the same letter (4:3, 7) mainly negative, even sexual, implications are noted: "This is the will of God, your sanctification: that you abstain from immorality ... God has not called us in uncleanness but in holiness." The context is similar in 1 Corinthians 6:11: mentioning the immoral, adulterers, homosexuals, drunkards, Paul declares "But you were sanctified." It is inaccurate to say Paul thought of sanctification only in these terms; he calls for cleansing "from every defilement of body *and spirit,* making holiness perfect" (2 Corinthians 7:1), as he prays that God will sanctify the Thessalonians in spirit and soul as well as body. Yet the immediate meaning of moral sanctification for many of Paul's readers lay in bodily self-discipline. As Inge well says, "St Paul dwells more on (sexual offences) than Christ ever did, but there is no reason to think that Christ would not have approved of all that he says ... St Paul is obliged to take account of the moral dangers to which his converts were exposed in such cities as Corinth."[3]

If Paul's teaching on "individual" sex morality is not to be grossly misrepresented, it is necessary to note carefully the motives to which he appeals for the self-discipline he urges. One is *the athletic motive,* self-discipline endured willingly for a chosen end. Phrases of the Pastoral epistles – "Exercise thyself unto godliness ... An athlete is not crowned unless he competes according to the rules" – are wholly in accord with Paul's use of the language of the gymnasium and the games in over fifty places:

"Do you not know that the runners in the stadium all run, but only one gets the prize? Run to win! ... I do not box as one beating the air; I pommel my body and subdue it. In the stadium every wrestler exercises self-control ... striving for mastery ... enduring the great contest." So the runner must not run uncertainly, but forgetting things that lie behind stretch forward to the things that are before him and press toward the finishing mark for the prize. "Every athlete exercises self-control in all things" (1 Corinthians 9:24-27, Philippians 3:13).

In such passages, censure falls upon everything that hinders strenuous and purposeful discipleship – indecision, love of money, instability of character, infirmity of purpose, uncertainty of aim, regrets for things left behind, weakness in dealing with the lust of the flesh – everything which might "disqualify" the competitor and forfeit the coveted prize. The word *asceticism,* which figures so prominently in Christian ethics in later generations, derives precisely from these athletic exhortations in the New Testament, but under the influence of Greek dualism it came to possess meanings which Paul would deny. The spiritual *athleticism* of Paul has in it nothing morbid, self-absorbed, dualistic or disabling: it consists in that self-discipline which is inseparable from all achievement, and aims at spiritual fitness, moral vigour, a personality tuned to high endeavour, and "the imperishable chaplet of divine approval."

Paul's second motive for self-discipline arises from *the advent perspective*. Spiritual sloth, the works of darkness, revelling, drunkenness, debauchery, licentiousness, even quarrelling and jealousy, are all, so to speak, short-term indulgences in immediate pleasures and moods: Paul deliberately sets them in the light of "what hour of the day it is," and the need for watchfulness as the Day of the Lord advances (Romans 13:11f). Once indeed, Paul tells the Ephesians, you were in darkness, indulging in things best hidden by darkness; now you are in the light of Christ's new day – Behave accordingly! (5:7-14). Once more we hear echoes of words of Jesus: eschatology reinforces ethics, and the Christian hope of the Lord's return imposes severe but intelligible moral restraint.

Paul's third motive for self-discipline is *the Christian's personal sacredness*. Essentially, this means the discipline of the lower natural life for the sake of the higher supernatural life to which the Christian has been called. But it is urged in two metaphors of peculiar power and daring. The individual Christian is a single member of the total body of Christ, an eye, ear, hand or foot (1 Corinthians 12:27, see 14-26). Once, in the heat of argument, Paul applies this language perhaps incautiously: "Do you not know that your bodies are members of Christ? Shall I therefore take the members of Christ and make them members of a prostitute? Never! Do you not know that he who joins himself to a prostitute becomes one body with her? For as it is written, The two shall become one. But he who is united to the Lord becomes one spirit with him. Shun immorality!" (1 Corinthians 6:12-18). Beneath the boldness of the metaphor lies a deep sense of the sacredness of the Christian person, body and spirit, made and redeemed by God, part of the body of Christ on earth, destined for eternal life.

The more attractive metaphor, in the same passage, represents not the Christian community (as in 3:16f) but the individual Christian as the shrine, the living temple, indwelt by the holy Spirit. "Do you not know that your body is a temple of the holy Spirit within you, which you have from God? you are not your own; you were bought with a price, so glorify God in your body" (6:18f). God's temple-site, like David's, had not been consecrated from that which cost Him nothing. And again the application is to sensual sin: "Every other sin which a man commits is outside the body, but the immoral man sins against his own body" – and the immoral Christian sins against God's shrine as well.

This is the heart of Paul's teaching upon sex and related themes of individual self-discipline. There is here no condemnation of pleasure, nothing of self-inflicted pain, or discipline, to atone for sin, none of the morbid fancies and self-mutilations popularly supposed to be implied in Pauline ethics. In the one reference, solitary and obscure, to such practices, Paul condemns them as of no value (Colossians 2:20-23). Instead, Paul urges that Christians keep themselves spiritually fit for Christ's service; that they shall ever be ready to meet Him at His coming; above all that each shall remember that he is sacred, divinely purchased and divinely indwelt, part of the body of Christ and a shrine of the holy Spirit.

Such self-discipline in no way conflicts with the freedom of the Christian man, one of the great issues for which Paul incessantly contended. He repudiated all attempts to impose Mosaic ritual regulations upon his converts, rejecting the whole legal system as a basis for salvation. "Stand fast in the liberty wherewith Christ has made you free" is the theme of Galatians; "The law of the Spirit of life ... has made me free" is his personal testimony; "Christ is the end of the law" is one of his slogans. The law of outward commands has passed away: Christians must not allow themselves to become entangled again with any yoke of bondage.

Yet, as Glover said, "If Paul escaped from the servitude of the law of Moses with a relief that never died away, he passed under the law of Christ" (1 Corinthians 9:21, Galatians 6:2).[4] Liberty is allegiance to a higher law, and there are laws that actually broaden and enlarge experience, as there are vows it were a shame a man should not be bound by. So, even in Galatians Paul recognises freedom's limits – the limit on thought imposed by loyalty to the gospel; the limit imposed by an accepted destiny and vocation; the limits implied by life in a moral universe where what is sown shall surely be reaped; most of all the limits imposed by the law of love – "You were called to freedom, brethren, only do not use your freedom as an opportunity for the flesh, but through love be servants of one another" (1:6f, 15, 6:7, 5:13, 6:2). Elsewhere, freedom of conduct is limited by consideration for the weaker brother's conscience; and always freedom is limited by responsibility to assist and advance other Christian lives – all things may be lawful, but not all things edify, or are profitable (1 Corinthians 8:9-13, 10:23).

Plainly, the Christian has exchanged the outward compulsion of imposed regulations for the inward constraints of a very high ideal. Yet this *is* a liberation, since the compulsions are now from within the self, and exercised by an ideal freely accepted. The law has become a delight; obligation has given place to inspiration by the Spirit of Christ. Christian self-discipline thus proves to be the "rule of the Spirit of life in Christ Jesus." The Christian turns from the works of the flesh to live in the Spirit, walk in the Spirit, be led of the Spirit; anyone who has not the Spirit of Christ is none of His (Galatians 5:16, 18, 25, Romans 8:9). Inge remarks that "this intimate relationship with the Spirit-Christ is unques-

tionably the core of Paul's religion."[5] From it he expected all the
graces and virtues of Christlike character to follow as naturally as
fruit from a vigorous tree. The figure was Christ's, and Paul
applies it variously, to the fruit of the gospel, the fruit of every
good work, the fruit of righteousness, the fruit of generosity, in
contrast both with the works of the flesh and the works of the law.
All the moral demands of the law are abundantly fulfilled by the
man living in the Spirit; and all Christlike qualities manifest themselves in him without conscious effort (Galatians 5:23). A similar
phrase, "the fruit of light, found in all that is good and right and
true" (Ephesians 5:9) may recall (as 2 Corinthians 4:6 certainly
does, and to the same effect) the story of creation, when divine
light breaking into a world of darkness brought forth from chaos
all order and beauty and fruitfulness.

It is evident that Paul's doctrine of sanctification, though basically concerned with the "negative" obligation of purity and holiness, is yet truly positive in its motives, its responsible freedom,
and its surrender to the Holy Spirit.

(iii) *Consecration*, Paul's third theme of "individual" ethics, may
fairly be described as what should be done with a sanctified personality – its practical dedication to the person and the cause of
Christ. Behind all Paul's exhortations in this connection pulse his
own tireless energy, his unsparing singleness of purpose, his consuming whole-heartedness in travelling, evangelising, writing,
organising, conflict, contention, imprisonment, and fearless
endurance. There is about Paul's commitment to Christ's work a
ruthlessness which breaks into something near impatience with
those of faint heart or faltering purpose (as John Mark), and
which gives depth of meaning to his glowing expressions of devotion.

Paul does not scruple to use the language (a) of *slavery* to
expound such consecration. As Christ is Lord, so the Christian is
slave, even bondslave, owing unquestioning obedience. Paul
explicitly compares spiritual with literal slavery (e.g. Colossians
3:22-24), speaks of slave-marks and seals of Christ's possession,
and works out in detail the conception of the Christian as purchased, belonging to his Lord: "Ye are not your own, ye are
bought with a price." To be alive at all "means fruitful labour" –
the slave exists only to work! (1 Corinthians 6:19, 20, Philippians
1:22) So represented, consecration is complete moral submission
to Christ's absolute claim and ownership.

There is another side to such slavery. Responsibility is limited to pleasing one Master: "If I were pleasing men, I would not be the slave of
Christ ... To his own master each stands or falls ... Who are you to
pass judgement on the slave of another? ... Be not slaves of men
..."(Galatians 1:10, Romans 14:4; contrast 1 Corinthians 9:19). And

the slave is valuable: Paul can speak confidently, on the doomed ship, of his own safety, not so much because God loves him, but because he is God's possession –"Whose I am and whom I serve" (Acts 27:23). According to John, Jesus had said "I call you not slaves, but friends"(15:15); yet Christians continued to use the word about themselves, perhaps with some justification from the parables concerning faithful and unfaithful servants, and the reminder that, do what they would, they must remain "unprofitable", costing more than they contributed.

In more religious terms, Paul speaks of consecration as (b) the offering of a *sacrificial victim,* not in ritual and material form but in the reasonable and spiritual worship of a living body and mind devoted to the good and acceptable and perfect will of God (Romans 12:1f). Gifts from the Philippians are harvest-offerings brought to God's temple, fragrant, pleasing to God; Paul's imminent martyrdom is a libation to be poured over the sacrificial offering of the church's faith; his mission among the gentiles had prepared a sacrificial offering to lay before God, his ministry a priestly service; in the Pastoral letters occur the brave words, "I am on the point of being sacrificed, I am now ready to be offered ..." (Philippians 4:18, 2:17, Romans 15:16, 2 Timothy 4:6).

For us this language has little power: we have never stood beside a reeking altar, nor partaken of Passover lambs. To appreciate Paul's feeling we must recall his native reverence for the ceremonial worship of the temple, which he never left behind. Fundamental to all his thought was the sacrificial pattern of man's approach to God: he saw Christ's death in these terms, as expiation in covenant blood. For him, sacrifice was no defaced metaphor, but a vivid, heart-moving figure linking Christian consecration with the measureless sacrifice of Christ for the sins of the world.

More emotional than strictly moral or religious is Paul's description of consecration as (c) the self-giving of *a man in love.* All the affective elements of Paul's deeply emotional nature were quickened and focused by Jesus. He speaks of the constraint of Christ's love, in a context of self-explanation which rebuts the charge that he was mad (2 Corinthians 5:11-15). Deissmann speaks of Paul's "mystical genitive" – the faith of Christ, the hope of Christ, the peace of Christ, the patience of Christ, the obedience of Christ, the suffering of Christ, the afflictions of Christ, and the rest.[6] The expression recurs with all the ardour and insistence associated with a beloved name, with a heart, a life, that has become irradiated by a single, exclusive emotional relationship. Paul "enjoys" Christ, with a trustful faith and self-abandonment for which the only analogue is human love.

This might give us pause, if Paul had not himself set the devotion felt for Christ in comparison with the love of wife or husband, and the desire to please Him in contrast to a rival desire to please another human soul (1

Corinthians 7). The unmarried are anxious about the affairs of the Lord; the married are distracted from that singleness of devotion. We might reply that loneliness, also, can bring distraction. But to remember Paul's strong emotional nature, his lack of family circle, his assertions of his right to marry, and his use of metaphors drawn from marriage and parenthood, is to realise what depth of meaning he would give to the phrase "love for Christ."

For Paul, life began with the apprehension of Christ, continued in the imitation of Christ, was directed to the service of Christ, sustained by union with Christ, rejoiced in the expectation of Christ, aimed at pleasing Christ; for him to live was Christ, and to be with Christ at last was all his hope. The opportunity of being found in Christ made worthless all that Jewry had offered him, and he lived only to know Christ better (Philippians 3:4-11). So he longs for the Corinthians, and for all Christians, that they shall not be enticed, or deceived, from a sincere and "virginal" devotion to Christ (2 Corinthians 11:2). Without doubt, Paul was a man in love.[7]

Such a conception of new life in the individual underlies all that Paul says about wider ethical questions. The bringing of every thought into captivity to Christ; sanctification from every defilement of flesh and spirit; consecration of all to the service of Christ – all are elements in that growth towards maturity by which a man approaches the goal of his redemption, conformity to the image of God's Son.

(3) THE NEW LIFE IN FAMILY AND HOME

Beyond individual character, the new life in Christ finds expression in the immediate circle of the family, the first school for community living. Paul had learned from Judaism the social and religious importance of well-ordered home-life, and the later Jewish ideal of monogamy seems everywhere assumed in his teaching. Apart from what he rehearses of the primitive catechesis, Paul's own thought on marriage, parenthood, and the place of woman seems strangely ambivalent, combining an idealist, even mystical, approach with the plainest practical and physical considerations.

(i) Concerning *marriage,* one side of his discussion gives very full recognition to the place of sexual desire in married love. In 1 Thessalonians 4:3-7, marriage is simply the antidote to immorality and uncleanness, and in 1 Corinthians 7 the same attitude is spelled out with great frankness. In verses 1 (which may quote words sent to Paul from Corinth), 7, 8, 26, 27, 32-35, 38-40, Paul is quite clear it is better to avoid marriage. His reasons are the impending distress, the imminent advent, the "worldly troubles of the married", and the division of loyalties which marriage entails.

Remarking that Paul had no interest in the continuance of the race, Moffatt adds an interesting parallel from Epictetus' reply to a young man who asked if a philosopher should regard marriage and a family as primary duties: "As things are, in the present state of the world, which is that of a battlefield, may it not be a philosopher's duty to be free from distraction in order to serve God utterly ... Ordinarily marriage is very liable to distraction, so that we do not find upon enquiry that marriage is a primary concern for the Cynic."[8]

Paul concedes of course that marriage is not wrong: "I say this for your benefit, not to lay any restraint upon you ... If you marry you do not sin ... Let them marry, it is no sin ... He who marries his betrothed (or, gives his daughter in marriage) does well: and he who refrains ... will do better." But the reason he gives for the "concession" is that not all have the gift of self-control. "It is better to marry than to be aflame with passion." "In many cases he thinks," says Inge[9] "the alternative is between marriage and the torments of repression; such persons are wise if they marry." This assumes, apparently, that they cannot rise to Paul's own position, "the complete sublimation of sexual energy in devotion to some high cause" (Marshall).

In verses 36-38 Paul uses the same argument concerning passionate couples who though engaged had intended for reasons of conscience to remain single (so RSV); others think the situation in view is that of a Christian father or guardian considering his duty towards a daughter or ward; others think the counsel is addressed to partners in so-called "spiritual marriage" (living together in virginity) referred to in Hermas and Irenaeus. Full marriage is Paul's solution to all problems so posed.

It is possible to plead that Paul is being realistic; that his counsel that marriage should not among Christians be merely on the level of lust common "among the heathen who do not know God" is sound enough; that, given the adventist foreshortening of perspective, the moral situation in Corinth, and his own intense consecration as "a eunuch for the kingdom of heaven", Paul's attitude is understandable. But the avoidance of lust is no very lofty basis upon which to build a Christian relationship and home, and it seems well below the valuation of human love, of home, of children, which most would feel to be part of Christian teaching.

On this side of his discussion, marriage remains for Paul a matter for personal judgement and decision, according to the gift which each has received from God. He is very careful not to lay down rules for others. He does not countenance the reaction against marriage altogether of some of the Qumran communities, the Essenes, some gnostic sects, and probably also some Christians. He gives no encouragement to the ultra-spiritual who would repudiate sex-relations within marriage, or renounce their mar-

riage vows for religious reasons. "In some of the Mystery-cults,"
says Moffatt,[10] "sexual relations were temporarily suspended during a period of religious ritual, and ... in Judaism on the day of
atonement ... or on the sabbath ... The wise ethic of Pharisaism
had forbidden prolonged abstention ... and for all his ascetic
instincts Paul was not blind to the danger of a husband or a wife
overstraining human nature by defrauding the other party
... even for the sake of spiritual ends." Those who regarded
marriage itself as immoral, so that husband and wife ought to
separate upon conversion, Paul answers with a direct negative:
"the wife should not separate from her husband ... the husband
should not divorce his wife."

An exception was necessary where subsequent conversion of one partner created a mixed pagan-Christian marriage. Here, said Rashdall,
"Paul defines a matter Christ had (naturally) not defined, the freedom to
depart from a heathen partner so desiring it, and apparently to
remarry."[11] But it is very doubtful if this freedom to remarry can be
assumed, in view of the clear prohibition of remarriage in verse 11. Paul
allows *separation*, for the sake of peace – the position would often
become intolerable – but not *divorce*. And the initiative must be that of
the heathen partner; the Christian should seek to sanctify the marriage,
and by considerate and faithful conduct to lead the other partner into
Christian salvation. This is to consecrate to Christian purpose a marriage
originally pagan, celebrated in an idol-temple – a far more optimistic
view of marriage than some have found in this chapter.
Realism guides Paul's decision on another question canvassed among
spiritual rigorists: Whether it was Christian for a widow to remarry. The
Pastoral epistles suggest that economic, social and sexual reasons combine to make this wise and humanitarian concession; in 1 Corinthians 7
Paul appears to think the same, even though he judged the widow would
be *happier* to remain single – a curiously hedonist argument for Paul to
use.

However, the other side of Paul's discussion of marriage is on
an altogether different plane. Here, not passion but Christian
agape is the essence of married love, and the Lordship of Christ
within the home creates a wholly new quality of relationship. A
high religious estimate of marriage is not entirely absent from 1
Corinthians 7: "To the married I give charge, not I but the Lord,
that the wife should not separate from her husband (but if she
does, let her remain single or else be reconciled to her husband) –
and that the husband should not divorce his wife ... A wife is
bound to her husband as long as he lives." The same estimate
underlies Paul's very sharp condemnation of incest, the most
appalling danger to marriage that can arise within the family; it is
echoed also in his total exclusion of adulterers from the kingdom
of God, and his warning that a Christian's projected marriage
should always be within the Christian loyalty – "only in the Lord"
(1 Corinthians 5:1, 6:9, 10, 7:39).

When we turn, however, from the moral problems of Corinth (and Thessalonia) to Paul's more positive exposition in Ephesians (5:21f) and Colossians (3:18f) of the catechetical teaching on marriage, the religious valuation and discipline of marriage becomes much more searching. He says nothing of the traditional dependency of women, due partly to their economic and physical vulnerability, especially during child-bearing: instead, he transforms the relationship of husband and wife in three distinct ways. First, though he begins with the catechetical theme of subordination he expressly avoids applying to the wife the word "obey" which he uses for children a few moments later. No absolute submission is in mind, only such as is "fitting in the Lord" and parallel exactly to the "subordination" of Christian to Christian (21), of the Christian and the church to Christ (22, 24), and (in 1 Corinthians 15:27f) of Christ Himself to God: it is subordination *of that kind,* the acceptance of clearly defined rank and function within an ordered group. Only such conscientious assent as may be fairly asked under Christ for the good order of the home, is implied in Paul's word.

Secondly, Paul imposes on the husband a precisely reciprocal obligation, in which a new notion of domestic equality emerges. "Husbands, love your wives" was sheer novelty when presented as a religious demand. Even in Judaism, though a husband could demand that his wife love him exclusively, she could make no such claim upon him, nor divorce him for any cause. Nor is the love which Paul demands left undefined: husbands are to love their wives as Christ loved the church and gave Himself for it – selflessly and sacrificially. Self-subjection in response to self-denying love is the very pattern of the gospel, and the necessary basis of any lasting union of strong personalities. It is on that premiss Paul counsels the wife's "subordination": if Christlike love be withheld, subordination cannot be required in Christ's name – the marriage has ceased to be Christian.

Thirdly, Paul's comment on the sexual tradition which gave to the husband both power and right over the wife's person, to which she was expected meekly to submit, is terse and specific – he simply *forbids* the harsh, overbearing demand (Colossians 3:19; compare 1 Peter 3:7). Christianity was steadily imposing a new standard of sexual behaviour within marriage as well as outside it. At the same time, Paul appeals as Jesus had done to the ancient principle, "they shall become one *flesh*" (Ephesians 5:31 (Greek)).

Recall on 1 Corinthians 6:16 above, where Paul takes very literally and seriously the union of persons resulting from sexual relations; and on Matthew 19:5 where the new union in marriage is seen to resemble the union of parent and child which Jesus says it *replaces.* It is possible that behind Paul's use of the phrase lies the context in Genesis 2:23f – "This (Eve) at last is bone of my bones, and flesh of my flesh."

In marriage, two persons become so identified that the man leaves the existing, natural, indissoluble relationship with his parents to cleave to his wife in a unity so complete that his love for her becomes itself an exalted form of self-love (Ephesians 5:28), as well as a reflection of the love Christ has for His cherished bride, the church. Thus Paul's realism is balanced in the end with mysticism: of the Ephesians exposition, Marshall comments "Married life and love could hardly be placed on a higher footing than that."[12]

(ii) Such a view of marriage plainly looks towards that equality of spiritual status and value, between man and woman, which found expression in the new Christian principle that in Christ "there is neither male nor female: for you are all one in Christ Jesus" (Galatians 3:28). The occurrence in Paul's correspondence of so many women's names, with warm approval of the part they played in Christian work, shows how fully that principle governed his own relationships – to Phebe, deaconness of the church at Cenchrea, to Priscilla, to Mary, Tryphaena, Tryphosa, Persis, Euodia, Syntyche, and the "other women" at Philippi, including surely Lydia.

1 Corinthians 11:5 and 13 leave no doubt that women took part in Christian worship, in prayer and in prophecy, just as the mention of Phebe shows that women held church office. Defending his counsel that women should participate in worship with head veiled, while men should not, Paul appeals to the creation story, "For man was not made from woman, but woman from man. Neither was man created for woman, but woman for man." Then, in one of his always stimulating asides, Paul *amends both points:* "And yet, in Christ's fellowship woman is as essential to man as man to woman. If woman was made out of man, it is through woman that man now comes to be; and God is the source of all" (1 Corinthians 11:11 NEB). For Paul so to correct the inferences usually drawn from the Genesis story is surprising: if woman derived from man at the beginning, man is derived from woman at every subsequent birth; man and woman are *equally* necessary, the one to the other; and both derive, and equally, from God. Even more surprising is to find in Paul a statement so near to a definition of the spiritual equality of the sexes – in Christ.

There is every reason why Paul should urge that in public worship women should be especially careful to give no offence to the suspicious outsider. No respectable Greek woman would appear in public unveiled, or with the short hair of the women who aped men, or with the unbound hair of the prostitute. Paul wishes that the Christian women of Corinth shall not outrage local *mores,* though he acknowledges that this wish was nothing more than the approved custom of the churches. If he appeals to ancient ideas to press his counsel home, that does not lessen the expediency of what he advises. Paul was, after all, a Jew, to whom feminine immodesty was especially disgusting.

1 Corinthians 14:34f – "Let the women keep silence in the churches, for it is not permitted to them to speak; but let them be in subjection, as the law also says. And if they desire to learn something, let them ask their husbands at home; for it is a disgraceful thing for a woman to speak in church" – apparently contradicts 11:5 and 13. It is possible, from comparison with "keep silent" in 28, 30f that no universal ban may be intended, but only a temporary requirement of order. Moffatt's suggestion, that though considered contributions to the service were permitted the putting of questions, and discussion, were to be discouraged, reads much into the passage. In a few manuscripts, versions and ancient citations, these verses appear at the end of the chapter; they certainly interrupt the sense, which moves from 33 to 36; the appeal by Paul to the *law* to direct gentile Christian worship is unexpected; and the instructions offered to "the churches" in a letter closely addressed throughout to Corinth, is also odd. Whether early scribes, seeing the inconsistency with chapter 11, and doubting the authenticity of these verses, moved them into a footnote, or whether they are in fact a marginal comment by someone else (having the same views as the writer of 1 Timothy 2:11-12), it is now impossible to say. We have to choose whether 14:34f, or 11:5, 13 (and 11) with Galatians 3:28, best represent Paul's usual thought and practice concerning the place of women in Christian worship and work.

(iii) Paul's teaching on the relation of parent and child again follows closely that of the primitive catechesis. The child's "subordination" is that of discipline rather than of accepted rank, for the child begins its moral education by obeying before understanding – though understanding, leading to assent, is always the goal. Hence, parental rules should be reasonable and persuasive: but until insight brings maturity, obedience must guide and guard the growing life. So the child is sheltered, and relieved from too early responsibility for moral decisions. Yet Paul offers no charter of unlimited parental authority. The obedience to others' judgement which is pleasant in the young child is pitiable, and perilous, in the adolescent: parents' first duty, therefore, is so to exercise authority as to cultivate a self-reliant responsibility which gradually assumes greater freedom of informed, individual choice. Paul's additions to the primitive rule of subordination appear to reflect this need.

For the obedience he requires is to be "in the Lord", which (whether limitation or motive) places the parent-child relationship on a Christian basis of mutual respect and affection, in which the parents' own obedience to Christ sets example and robs submission of all humiliation. Moreover the parents must educate –

"nurture and admonish" – and not simply command: Paul inherited the Jewish concept of home as school of piety and centre of domestic religion, and he coveted the same role for Christian homes throughout pagan society.

Secondly, the required obedience is balanced by counsel that fathers shall not "provoke" their children – whether by overstrictness, by too many rules, or by harshness, is not clear. The effect in one type of child, adventurous, daring, self-willed, would be "exasperation", rebelliousness, resentment, a continual clash of wills. In the other type of child, sensitive, timid, introspective, the effect of "provocation" will be "discouragement", a crushed and introverted spirit, and perpetual fear of rebuke.

The result in the one case will be an undisciplined, anti-social young adult; in the other, a weak character, vulnerable to every pressure and exploitation of society. Remembering that (so far as we know) Paul had no children, his insight and shrewdness here are remarkable, born perhaps of memories of a strict Jewish home amid the temples, barracks, athletic games and theatres of a pagan city, forbidden to his lively curiosity and imagination. Paul may well have known from experience both the rebellious exasperation with family rules, and the feeling of being vulnerable as he grew away from that sheltering discipline among students in Jerusalem.

Thirdly, the motives urged for such obedience are, that it is "right" (which may hint that even if parents are unreasonable, or not Christian, the obligation to be a Christian at home remains); that "it pleases the Lord" (perhaps an appeal to the child's own growing response to the gospel); and that such is the first commandment with promise, or "a primary commandment, and carries with it a promise". Obedience is not said to be for the parents' sake, or for the home's sake, or because the parents deserve to be obeyed, but on the highest grounds of morality, religion, and ultimate personal welfare.

Sooner or later, every child has to learn that this is a world where self-will confronts boundaries of freedom, beyond which no one can do entirely as he likes; a world where knowledge, experience, truth and right possess authority, against which it is foolish to rebel. If this wisdom is not learned within the affection of home, it will be learned less pleasantly at school, more harshly at work, painfully before the law, or at last in the tragedy of a corrupted life. Paul knew that to learn obedience to truth and right while still at home is easiest, happiest, and the will of God.

"Children ought not to lay up for their parents but parents for their children" (2 Corinthians 12:14) is another of Paul's significant asides, explaining why he is willing to be spent for the converts at Corinth. Its evaluation of the child, as in Christian eyes *an end in himself,* is plain. Marshall effectively contrasts

typical attitudes of the ancient world: "If God gives us children
... we shall need them to help us and support us in our old age"
(Xenophon); no father would cast off his son and thereby rob
himself of his son's assistance in old age, said Aristotle; Medea,
about to slay her children, bewails that "at one time I, unhappy
that I am, had many hopes that you would feed me in my old
age".[13] Paul's principle, of parent-for-child not child-for-parent,
remains the Christian ideal: even the rule of obedience must sub-
serve the child's welfare, not the parents' whim.

Paul believed that the decay of marriage, the lack of filial affection, and increasing disobedience to parents, were symptoms of
the breaking up of Roman society, and warnings of worse to come
(Romans 1:30). His domestic ideal would be hard to excel: the
husband loyal, gentle, accepting ultimate responsibility; the wife
loved, content with lesser responsibility within an equal partnership; children learning their moral lessons by obedience before
they have to decide for themselves; parents exercising authority
always with an eye to the child's freedom and maturity; all with
the caring consideration that stems from shared loyalty to the
Lord they love and serve.

(4) THE NEW LIFE AND DAILY WORK

In New Testament times, employed workers might include
hired labourers, whether fishermen or agricultural workers, con-
tracting their labour on the best available terms; household servants, both organising "stewards" or bailiffs, and more menial
porters and maids; slaves, belonging entirely to the master,
though sharing the protection and provision of the household;
and business "stewards" or managers, possessing varying degrees
of authority.

There could be within Christianity no contempt for manual
work. Judaism had honoured it, requiring *all* boys to learn a
trade; Jesus, Paul, and other apostles were accustomed to toil.
The divine command, "Subdue the earth", assumes that God will
bless human labour with the fruits of the earth, and Paul expresses traditional Jewish attitudes when he says "If any man will
not work, neither shall he eat", and quotes (as Jesus had done)
the proverb "The labourer is worthy of his hire."

It is misleading, nevertheless, to speak of a "secular vocation" in the
New Testament, for this conception arose as a "protest against the
medieval tendency to limit the idea of vocation to a monastic life"
(Lillie).[14] Within the New Testament, "vocation" is to Christian life
itself, or to specifically Christian service: the "calling wherein you were
called" (1 Corinthians 7) refers to status in society – slave or free,
married or unmarried.

Paul himself, while maintaining his right to "live of the gospel" in accord with Christ's own precept, yet preferred to remain independent (1 Thessalonians 2:9, 2 Thessalonians 3:7 etc). He twice uses the phrase "working with our hands", which recalls vividly the painful labour of sewing leather with wooden needles.

To the Thessalonian church, unduly excited about the advent, Paul sends stern warning to mind their affairs and work with their own hands, so that they might command the respect of outsiders and be dependent upon no one (1 Thessalonians 4:11, 12); "For we hear that some of you are living in idleness, mere busybodies, not doing any work. Now such persons we command and exhort in the Lord Jesus Christ to do their work in quietness and to earn their own living" (2 Thessalonians 3:10-12).

The dangers of indolence, infecting even those engaged in Christ's work, are illustrated in Didache xii: If he that cometh is a passer-by, succour him as far as you can; but he shall not abide with you more than two or three days unless there be necessity. But if he be minded to settle among you, and if he be a craftsman, let him work and eat. But, if he have no trade, according to your understanding provide that he shall not live idly among you, being a Christian. But if he will not do this, he is a trafficker on Christ: of such beware.

An honest Christian workman is an eloquent evangelist: a religious scrounger, living by faith in others' folly, is an offence to the gospel.

Elsewhere, Paul urges that the slaves shall work "not with eye-service", as needing to be watched continually to give their best; nor as "men pleasers", as currying favour with their masters at any cost of loyalty to God. Work is to be done "in singleness of purpose", and this because "Whatever your task ... you are serving the Lord Christ." The slack, dishonest worker will be "paid back for the wrong he has done. There is no partiality" – even for the slave against his master (Colossians 3:23f). Daily work is "the will of God" which the Christian can do "from the heart'; whatever good a man does, he shall receive the same from the Lord, whatever his place in society (Ephesians 6:5-8). "Doing the will of God", like the phrase "working with his hands the thing that is good" (Ephesians 4:28), may seem more relevant in situations where one's work may be chosen than in the compulsory labour of slaves. Doubtless, wherever possible a man should choose work of positive value: but Paul may be thinking of the slave's attitude to the task more than of the product.

The motives urged in these passages are illuminating: "So that you may command the respect of outsiders" reappears in the Pastoral epistles as "that the teaching may not be defamed ... to adorn the doctrine": a good Christian slave was a living testimony to the gospel. "That you may be dependent on nobody" seems to be echoed in Ephesians 4:28, where unnecessary dependence on the bounty of the Christian fellowship is called *stealing:* a Christian may not expect others to labour for what he eats. "That you may be able to give to those in need" recalls Paul's speech at Miletus, "I have shown you that by so toiling one must help the weak, remembering the words of the Lord Jesus, how he said, It is more blessed to give than to receive": the good workman serves Christ not only in his work but with his wages.

Modern Christians are surprised at Paul's acceptance of the master-slave relationship, even though it was a *household* arrangement, sanctioned by Jewish law, universal in the first century, and extremely dangerous to attack.

Slaves are said to have outnumbered citizens by five to one; one master bequeathed freedom to over four thousand of his own household. A proposal that slaves should adopt distinctive dress was defeated on the ground that it would demonstrate their numerical strength. After several slave uprisings, Rome was ever on guard against emancipation movements that could destroy social order. Paul's concern for outsiders' reactions to the attitude of Christian slaves shows him aware of the danger that if to other slanders aimed at the church it could be whispered that Christianity fomented slave-rebellion, then all toleration, and all opportunity for evangelism, would cease.

Not only does Paul avoid open attack upon the institution, he counsels slaves not be be concerned about their condition – though, if the opportunity to be free was given them, they should take it (the probable meaning of 1 Corinthians 7:21f). And Paul on one occasion returns a runaway slave-thief, now converted, to his master, though with many urgent pleas for clemency and a Christian welcome.

The advent hope foreshortened Paul's perspective on this subject also (1 Corinthians 7:21 with 29f), but it is probable that he was temperamentally more interested in the slave's advancement, in his being treated as a brother, than in his emancipation. The church was to find later that social and political freedom is no boon when combined with economic subservience or starvation. Nevertheless, though "Paul never concedes the rightness of slavery nor appears as its opponent" (Marshall)[15] yet he defined, and demanded, two attitudes which were ultimately to end it.

Three times, to gentile churches, Paul insists that in Christ there is neither slave nor free man, but all are one (Galatians 3:28, Colossians 3:11, 1 Corinthians 12:13). Immediately he stepped within the Christian fellowship, or the worship-service, the slave ceased to be a slave and became "the Lord's free man". So Paul says he is to regard himself, and to be regarded: not as the slave of man – he is bought with a higher price, valued at a higher rate, than any master on earth would give for him. At the Lord's Table he, no less than his master, is a brother for whom Christ died. Thus to send a man out into that ancient society with his

head high, with new dignity born of the sense of heavenly freedom, value and citizenship, must not be under-rated. It was an
answer to slavery far more practical and immediate than any
movement for emancipation. There are always *two* ways of overcoming a social handicap – to end it, or to disregard it. Each is
triumph.

The other attitude Paul defined and demanded was recognition
that masters themselves are Christ's slaves, also purchased at a
price; they shall answer to their Master in heaven for their treatment of their slaves. They must treat slaves justly and fairly,
knowing that their Master will show to them no partiality (Colossians 3:25, 4:1; Ephesians 6:9). But this demand for "fairness"
contradicted the very meaning of slavery. To treat the slave
"justly" was to end at once the characteristic feature of his slave-
condition, his lack of all rights; to assert an authority superior to
the master's will was to deny his absolute right as owner and lord.

We rightly regret that Christianity, when it came to political
power, took so long to apply its own principles to this inhuman
situation. But to teach the slave to walk with freedom in his soul;
to set him in a fellowship where he was equal with his brethren; to
demand for him justice and warn his master of judgement – these
were in principle revolutionary positions. As Rashdall says, Paul
did not oppose slavery as an institution, but the principles he laid
down contained its condemnation.[16] They also, in time, destroyed
it.

(5) THE NEW LIFE IN THE CHURCH

Conversion to Christ cost Jews their membership of the
synagogue, cost some gentiles the fellowship of pagan religious
groups, and cost many their family ties; all would therefore turn
eagerly to their new Christian friends for communal support and
sympathy. Yet lack of precedents, the want of any authoritative
definition of Christian ways, the widely diverse backgrounds from
which converts came, the charismatic spontaneity of some Christian worship, and the inherent individualism of the gospel, all
made achievement of a cohesive church life a serious problem.

Recognising the need, Paul enjoins attendance at corporate
worship-occasions (Colossians 3:16f), and condemns sharply all
self-assertive disunity and discourtesy, especially at the Love-
feast and the Lord's Supper (1 Corinthians 11:17-22). The gifts
and abilities of all are to contribute to the harmony of the
church's total service (Romans 12:6f, 1 Corinthians 12:7), though
each member's personal inspiration by the Holy Spirit is to be
strictly subject to the order required in public worship for the
good of all (1 Corinthians 12-14). The community's leaders are to

be given material support and spiritual esteem (1 Thessalonians 5:12f, 1 Corinthians 9:1-14, 14:37, 16:15-18, Galatians 6:6, Philippians 2:19-30 – the repetition is significant); but none should seek the honour of office for himself (Romans 12:10, Philippians 2:3). Far more is intended than an institutional ethic based upon expediency: the controlling principle is the new moral concept of love, extended into a bond of loyalty, "brotherliness" in Christ. The presentation of this ideal may owe something to Stoic teaching on the world-brotherhood of the like-minded, but Paul traces it to the common experience of Christ's love, and membership together in His own body, the church.

Brotherly concern imposed the duty of "edification" – encouraging, instructing, warning, exhorting and setting each other a good example, always with wisdom and humility. Brother cannot be indifferent to brother's progress in Christ. The same brotherly concern illumines the appalling lists of *sins against community* which occur in Paul's letters. The Thessalonians are firmly exhorted to warn the unruly, comfort the feeble-minded, support the weak, be patient toward all – which seems to imply some lack of compassion in that church. The Colossians must put off anger, malice, slander, foul talk, lying, and put on their opposites. The Philippians must do nothing through strife or vain glory, but in lowliness stand fast in one spirit. Paul fears lest at Corinth he might find quarrelling, jealousy, anger, selfishness, slander, gossip, conceit, disorder, and the sad spectacle of Christian appealing for vengeance against Christian before heathen courts. And he warns the Galatians, somewhat tartly, that if they persist in snapping at each other they might devour one another, and no church be left in Galatia! (1 Thessalonians 5:12f, Colossians 3:8f, Philippians 2:1f, 2 Corinthians 12:20, 1 Corinthians 6:6, Galatians 5:15).

Standing together in trouble and persecution; wanting, and striving, to think alike – differing only with regret; ignoring social and intellectual distinctions that could divide fellowship; taking care that so far as lies with you, peace is maintained with all men – many such insights into the technique of Christian fellowship may be gathered from Paul's counsel. His own protracted and untiring effort to stir the sympathy of his widespread gentile churches for their brethren in Judea is the best evidence of the importance Paul attached to healing any rift between Jew and gentile in Christ's one people. The real and manifest unity of all believers was for Paul both a theological necessity and a moral imperative – if any believer was to be assisted to attain maturity.

This theme of Christians in community, the "socialisation" of alienated men as they find their common unity in the unifying Christ, is fully expounded in Ephesians. It is God's eternal purpose in Christ to reduce again to unity and peace the whole fragmented and divided universe (1:10). The one church, formed out of many races, classes, and types of men, once themselves alienated, strangers, and far-off, is God's first step towards that universal reconciliation (chapter 2). In the process, each individual Christian is drawn out of his loneliness and isolation into fellowship: we are quickened *together,* raised up *together,* made to sit *together* in heavenly places, to learn *together* the length and breadth of the love of Christ, and to grow, *in the unity of the faith,* into the one perfect Man.

It follows that every sin against fellowship is a direct contradiction of God's whole purpose. Untruthfulness, want of integrity and candour, breeds mistrust and suspicion, and denies that we are members one of another. Anger, uncurbed and prolonged into resentment, gives Satan his opportunity to defeat God's intention. Unnecessary dependence upon common resources is a form of stealing which must destroy Christian generosity. Careless conversation – slander, criticism, the whispered question, the ill-natured comment – dissolves fellowship. The result is to "lower the spiritual temperature" of the Christian group; in Paul's more radical language, to grieve the Holy Spirit, who dwells within the Christian community but withdraws when fellowship is affronted. In a charismatic church this is more vividly demonstrated than in liturgical churches: every word or silence, every act or absence that injures fellowship is *seen* to be an offence to the Spirit within the community. Only tender-heartedness, kindness, generosity, the will to forgive, the imitating of God in lives of love, can ensure the continuing presence of the Spirit in the church on earth (Ephesians 4:25 – 5:2).

The Christian community-ethic confronts two especial problems: the tendency toward individualism in the evangelical formulation of the faith, and the relation of this obligation of unity to individual freedom. (a) The emphasis laid upon individual faith, personal experience, and private devotion to Christ, often reduces the church to a mere assembly of convenience, comprising self-sufficient individual Christians who choose to belong together because "they like it". This humanistic conception of the church as a sociological contrivance – or accident – loses the whole biblical truth of the one people of God, the body of Christ, the chosen nation, the divine family, the kingdom, the remnant, the messianic community, the household of faith, the bride of Christ, the Vine, the temple of the Spirit, the building of God. Where that corporate understanding of God's historic purpose is lacking, every individual Christian is infinitely the poorer. That is why Paul rebuked the excessive individualism that rent the church at Corinth, emphasising

the common tradition concerning the faith – "I received of the Lord that which I also delivered unto you ...";
the common gospel ordinances of baptism and the Lord's Supper;

the common demand for unselfishness and courtesy in all their relationships;

the common duty of upbuilding each other, giving no occasion to others to stumble;

the common discipline of order in worship and purity in morals, to which the whole church is subject and which Paul "ordains" in all the churches;

the common need of Christians for each other – the eye utterly dependent upon the hand, the foot upon the head; no part able to pretend it has no need of another part – each member alive only so long as it is united with others in one body;

the common "more excellent way" of Christian love, without which all that passes for individual excellence in religion is but sounding brass and profitless pretence.

In its own way, the Corinthian correspondence no less than the Ephesian letter, insists on membership of the community as a *necessary* element of a fully Christian life.

(b) The obligation to maintain fellowship creates problems for individual freedom when equally sincere consciences differ on what is permissible. Inevitably, "broad" and "narrow" attitudes emerge; a lax, tolerant, robust type of Christian, fearless of scruples, enjoying spiritual freedom, in conflict with a cautious, strict, intensely conscientious type, often miscalled "puritan", perpetually fearful of sinning, and often unhappy. In Paul's churches, three questions produced these divergent attitudes.

The *sabbath* was to Jewish Christians a sacred obligation and priceless privilege; to gentile Christians a novel idea resembling pagans' days of ill omen – at worst, a remnant of legalism. *Meat* sold in gentile cities was usually slaughtered on idol altars, very rarely prepared according to Jewish rules; some Christians felt this imposed strict abstinence from meat upon all enlightened consciences: but most family festive and funeral occasions, business conferences, civic functions, involved attendance at idol temples – the village halls and only available catering. The use of *wine* was forbidden by some Jewish sects, and some stricter Christians, because of the prevailing drunkenness: others felt no obligation to abstain.

The "clear sighted" were convinced that meat, drink, holy days, did not constitute religion, and idols were nothing; taking a "strong" line, claiming to be free, they tended to hold in contempt all scruples about trifles. Others, tender in conscience, fearing pitfalls everywhere, careful of others' misconstruction of their actions and distrusting argument about such things, took the "weaker" line of keeping a safe distance from all "doubtful" things.

Brotherliness demands that each respect the other's conscience. Every man, said Paul (Romans 14, 15), must answer to his own Lord, and must be fully persuaded of what is right: negligence, carelessness of principle, mere conformity, is certain to be sin. None shall sit in judgement; freedom, respect, responsibility must be allowed to all. *Each* has freedom – to do, or not to do: there must be no mutual accusation, and no contempt.

Yet there is no perfect equality here. Brotherliness requires the strong to bear the infirmity of the weak, and not the weak to bear the strong. If your brother, led to act against his conscience by following your example, is injured by eating what you eat, you no longer walk in love. "Do not, for the sake of mere food, hinder the work of God in another soul, nor let what you permit yourself cause the ruin of one for whom Christ died ... It is right not to eat meat, or drink wine, or do anything that makes your brother stumble."

In reply to the objection that individual liberty here is made subservient not only to the conscience of the community, but to the conscience of the weakest, Paul would probably ask – What is the alternative? should the strong Christian simply go his own way, contemptuous of the fears and scruples of the young, more timid convert? Is that brotherly love? Moreover, the weaker brother's conscience is not to be deferred to indefinitely: the duty of mutual edification remains. From his two chapters of instruction sent to Rome, and one to Corinth (1 Corinthians 8), Paul plainly expects the discussion of such problems to lead at least to understanding. Meanwhile, brotherly kindness unquestionably lays upon the strong the responsibility to deny themselves things they could defend, lest the weak be made to stumble.

It is a high demand – the ethic of Christian fellowship must be so. To encourage, Paul adduces first his own example: he was "strong" – "the kingdom of God does not consist in meat and drink – everything is clean –food will not commend you to God – we are no worse off if we do not eat and no better off if we do – all things are pure, and the idol is a mere nothing." Yet, "If food is a cause of my brother's falling, I will not eat meat ... while the world stands!" For a second encouraging example, Paul points further: "For even Christ pleased not himself ..."

Paul's exposition of the new life in the church gained steadily in importance as the division between the church and the world became sharper, and the Christian community became for more and more converts the substitute for family and social circle – as it had become for Paul himself. In his family, his work, and his church fellowship, the new man, possessing new moral life, was matured and trained for the wider witness of Christian living in society and the State.

(6) THE NEW LIFE IN SOCIETY AND THE STATE

For all his transfiguring experience, the "man in Christ" remained also a man in Corinth, in Philippi, in Rome, and the new moral life had to be lived within the secular world, organised politically as the *State,* constituting the daily theatre of discipleship as *society.*

(i) Paul summarises the Christian's relation to the State in Romans 13:1-7, sometimes assumed to contain all that Paul has to say. Attention to other facts and passages yields a more balanced view. Proud of his Roman citizenship, by temperament prudent and realist, this Jew from the provinces shared the gratitude of most provincials for Roman peace, order, justice and administration, which had made possible his missionary journeyings, frequently rescued him from the violence of mobs, and often restrained social evils (2 Thessalonians 2). It is not surprising that Paul's attitude to Roman rule should be positive and loyal, that he wished to forestall any suspicion that Christians were political agitators, and counselled believers to win if possible the favour of the watching world.

He urges therefore that Christians be subject to the governing authorities, offer no resistance, do what is good in order to win authority's approval, pay taxes, dues, respect and honour, and be in all things complaisant, law-abiding citizens. In part, this is to avoid punishment, and win public approval, but it is also for conscience sake. There is no authority except from God; those human authorities that exist have been instituted by God, and he who resists them resists what God has appointed His servant for society's good. They do not bear the sword in vain, but to punish wrong in God's name, and the Christian conscience supports their rule.

That Paul is writing to a church at the heart of the empire lends his words added weight. His view looks beyond social contract and expediency to a religious "mystique" of rule, essentially Samuel's doctrine of theocracy, perpetuated in the anointing of Judean kings by priests and prophets, and by utterances like that of Wisdom of Solomon (6:3):

Hear, therefore, O ye kings, and understand; learn, ye that be judges of the ends of the earth; give ear, ye that rule the people, and glory in the multitude of nations. For power is given you of the Lord, and sovereignty from the Highest, who shall try your works and search out your counsels.
So Jesus to Pilate: "You could have no power at all against me unless it were given you from above" (John 19:11). According to Josephus, the Essenes required sworn fidelity to authority "because no one obtains the government without God's assistance".[17] Orthodox Jews offered

sacrifice daily, and prayers in the synagogues, for the Roman Emperor
and people.

Behind this attitude lies the deep faith that God is Lord of
history, making and dispersing nations, raising up and dispensing
with world-powers, determining beforehand their times of flour-
ishing and the bounds of their occupation (Acts 17:26); the
confidence that human rule reflected the divine authority of *right*.

In a sinful and divided world, government is "the indispensable
precondition of a worth-while existence;" as Lillie says, "Bad
government may appear to the Christian a lesser evil than no
government at all."[18] That Paul forbade Christians to take their
breaches of fellowship before pagan courts (1 Corinthians 6:1, 7)
in no way weakens his assertion that human authority derives
from divine authority, and merits Christian support; he himself
appealed to Caesar.

This impression of entirely uncritical acceptance of all human
government is considerably modified, however, when attention
turns from Romans 13. Paul was an internationalist, in consequence of his universalist gospel, with his eyes fixed upon a day
when Christ would put down all rule, authority, and power, and
deliver up the throne of the world to God the Father (1 Corinthians 15:24). An inter-racial fellowship, and a supra-national
goal, must qualify all lesser patriotisms. Paul saw human government as after all a *temporary* expedient, restraining evil until the
Day of Christ. And a *fallible* one: Paul was well aware that human
authority could be disastrously wrong; none of the rulers of the
present age understood the wisdom of God – they had crucified
the Lord of glory! (1 Corinthians 2:8). By the time Paul wrote to
the Philippians, he himself had begun to suffer at the hands of
misguided authority, and to set his hope of justice on the power
above the State.

Moreover, Paul preached the kingdom of God, in terms that
led to charges of preaching another king, rival to Caesar, and
proclaiming things not lawful for Romans to receive (Acts 17:7,
16:21). Implicit in his message of the Lordship of Christ is that
priority of *divine* rule which was to bring many to martyrdom,
once Rome exerted her own total claim. To the most patriotic and
Romanised of all eastern Mediterranean cities, Philippi, Paul –
freeman of Rome and yet her prisoner – declared, "our citizenship is in heaven" (Philippians 3:20).

In the end, therefore, Paul counselled subjection to human
authority as appointed by God, yet nourished a vision, rehearsed
a story of governmental folly, and preached a higher rule, that
together leave no doubt where he would stand if caught in any
conflict between Caesar and Christ. Because effective opposition
to Roman power was impossible, and the very attempt suicidal,

no form of resistance was available, when Roman government over-stepped the just limits of human authority, but to refuse obedience and suffer the consequences. The death of Paul shows clearly the limits he placed upon subservience to the State when it *ceased* to be "the minister of God for good."

(ii) The pressures of society posed a more dangerous, because more subtle, threat to Christian living, much more serious than the minor ethical problems that harassed weaker consciences. Marshall describes[19] with sufficient evidence, the appalling viciousness of some circles, explaining the emphasis with which Paul places sexual perversions, drunkenness, carousing, among sins which totally exclude from the kingdom of God (1 Corinthians 6:9, 10).

The *defensive* principle of separation from the world was alone safe counsel for infant converts: "come out from among ... Be separate" (2 Corinthians 6:17) is the beginning of Christian holiness. The Ephesians are reminded that God saved them out of a lustful, disobedient, shameful life: such things must not again be so much as named among them! Paul tells the Galatians that the world which crucified his Lord is thereby crucified to him – as he is to the world. The same defensiveness probably explains why in 1 Corinthians 10 Paul urges that Christians abstain from attendance at idol temples. He admits (as to the Romans) that idols are nothing, that meats offered to idols are not forbidden food, that such detailed questioning of conscience should not be initiated by Christians. Yet to the Corinthians, in an exceptionally corrupt environment, and themselves emotionally immature, Paul seems to say, Keep away from such places, lest you find yourselves eating at the altar of devils and having fellowship with demons: keep your distance from temptation. The provisional, protective basis of this somewhat tortuous advice could hardly be plainer.

But self-protective isolation is not all that Paul teaches. The very epistle which declares that Christian citizenship is in heaven, illustrates the three positive, mature attitudes to which separation is only preliminary. Philippians 1 recalls that the Christian is *involved in the social context* of life, whether he will or no. Paul is hindered, imprisoned, endangered, by the secular world of which he is – though a servant of God – a member and a captive. His movements, plans, and safety, are all subject to society's decision; in due course, the supreme question of the status and freedom of the church within society will be decided *by Caesar*. However the Christian insists upon moral separation, he yet lives within society, is a part of society, depends upon society, witnesses to it, suffers with it, and must express his faith within it. That Paul evangelised his jailers is in keeping with his own counsel to the slave, to the Christian partner in a mixed home, to "stay there, with God" (1 Corinthians 7:24). The duty of positive involvement cannot be denied.

Philippians 2 shows the Christian *commissioned to society*, as a child of God in the midst of a crooked and perverse generation. On the one hand he is to "live shiningly" without grumbling or complaint, blamelessly, in innocence. Elsewhere this is elaborated as "walking circumspectly – looking around you – giving no offence;" walking in wisdom towards outsiders, careful to provide things honest in their eyes, paying one's debts (Ephesians 5:15, Colossians 4:5, Romans 12:17, 13:8). On the other hand the Christian is commissioned both to hold fast to, and hold out to a dying world, the word of life. Though Christians are not to love the world, they know that God loves it, and must tell it so. Not only an irreproachable example, but a bold, winsome, and convincing presentation of the truth, is the Christian's obligation to society; not to abandon the world in despair, but to redeem the generation in which he lives, all the more zealously because he thinks the days are evil (Ephesians 5:16).

Philippians 3 shows the Christian at the same time *detached from society,* living not like many shamefully, their minds set on earthly things, but as citizen of another realm, whence he looks for a Saviour. One can be involved with the world, without becoming immersed in it, or identified with it. We are at heart strangers in an alien society which we confidently expect Christ to change, subduing all to Himself. This is the eschatological perspective of Romans 13 also: "It is high time to awake from sleep: salvation is nearer now than when we first believed. The night is far gone, the Day is at hand. So let us cast off the works of darkness ... revelling, drunkenness, debauchery, licentiousness, quarrelling, jealousy, and conduct ourselves becomingly ..." The effect is a moral detachment that sees the present world always in the clear light of the world that is to come.

Within these general attitudes towards society, the Christian makes his particular contribution to social improvement through family, employment, and church. The total impression left by this teaching is of varied, even contradictory, counsel. But allowance must be made for changing pressures of circumstance, temptation, and danger; for lack of precedents and experience; and for the occasional, often urgent, nature of Paul's surviving correspondence. Even so, the general picture – of Christians saved out of the world, separated from it for their own spiritual safety, yet with growing maturity becoming involved in its life and problems, commissioned to it for the sake of the gospel, yet detached from it in inner independence and ultimate hope – has relevance still as Christians pass once more into a minority position within a largely "post-Christian" society.

It is not surprising that Paul's ethical directives are addressed directly to actual situations and problems of his time, as indeed were those of the law, the prophets, and of the Master. It follows that in language, occasion, and form, some of Paul's pronouncements are relative to historical circumstances that have long changed or quite passed away. Incarnation is the master-principle of Christianity – we have divine treasure in earthen vessels, eternal truth enfolded in temporary conditions. The long history of the development of Christian ethical thought is the record of the sifting-out of what is timeless, essential, and revelatory, from what was of its age and circumstance. Thus to some degree, and inevitably, Paul's ethical teaching was defined over against the contention against Jewish legalism, the church's political helplessness, the expectation of the imminent advent of Christ, a traditional antipathy towards art, a recoil from "Corinthian" sexual laxity, and possibly a lingering "Jewish" feeling towards women –all of which were to fade or change with time. And Paul himself confesses to misgivings about some things he has written (2 Corinthians 11:1, 17, 23; cf 7:8, and the outburst in Galatians 5:12).

But there can be no doubt of Paul's enduement with the Spirit, nor of his sacrificial devotion to the ideal of Jesus and his loyalty to Christ's words. Nor any question of his penetration into Christ's inner meaning and profoundest demands. In ethics (as in theology) we owe to Paul the universalising of that which God did in Palestine in three short years; and the translation of the message of the divine family, the kingdom of God, and the imitation of Christ, into terms that gentiles could understand. We owe to Paul also the confidence that the ethic of Jesus *can* be so transplanted, the assurance that it is relevant for every age and people. Most of all, we find the clue to the changing continuity of Christian ethics in Paul's conception of the "mind of Christ". The Christian goes forward into new situations, to face novel problems, striving to be loyal to the Christ of history, but walking in the company of the ascended Lord, prompted always in mind and moral judgement by the indwelling Spirit of Jesus.

Thus Paul makes plain just how the rule of law has finally given place to the rule of the Spirit of life in Christ Jesus (Romans 8:2).

10

Petrine Counsels

TO ASSUME THAT AFTER Paul "no new ethical note is struck" in the New Testament is to dismiss nearly one-fifth in length and about one-third in time of the available material. Certainly, by Paul's death the great principles of Christian ethics have become clear, but it is wrong to conclude that Peter, James, and John have nothing original to say, or to let Paul's interpretation of the gospel overshadow all others. Moreover, in ethical matters the latest pages of the New Testament are in some respects those nearest to our own situation.

The warmth and winsome spirit of 1 Peter, its background of suffering and its generally accepted basis in baptismal instruction, all lend peculiar interest to its counsel. The usual difficulty arises of disentangling ethical from theological themes. As E. G. Selwyn shows: "From the side of theology we find faith issuing in holiness, and holiness expressing itself in brotherly love; the 'fear' or reverence proper to belief in God is reflected in the respect and courtesy which must govern men's relations to one another: man's attitude of obedience and humility before Him bespeaks a similar temper in social and domestic life. From the side of ethics, we note how regularly St Peter bases his moral injunctions upon general principles, often of a definitely theological kind: his 'because' (twelve times, 1:16, 18 etc.) is a characteristic of his thought, tracing the motives of action or of endurance to the divine will ... to the example of Christ ... or to the eschatological End of human destiny."[1] That admirable summary highlights the characteristic Petrine approach, which lays all emphasis upon subordination – respect for authority – and the imitation of Christ.

(1) SUBORDINATION

The catechetical theme of submission to just authority becomes in 1 Peter the pre-eminent concept, applied with exceptional thoroughness both as a religious attitude and as a social code

Subordination towards God is emphasised in 1:17, where those who call upon the Father should conduct themselves with *fear* before Him throughout the time of their exile; in 2:17, where "fear God" stands among the briefest definitions of Christian attitudes; and in 3:15, where we are bidden to reverence Christ in our hearts as Lord, to whom all angels, powers and authorities are subject (22). The same emphasis underlies the constant use of the category of obedience to describe a right reaction to the gospel – the obedience of children (1:14); obedience to Christ (1:2); obedience to the truth (1:22). The epistle's severest warnings of judgement are for those who, like Noah's generation, did not obey (3:20); those on whom the rock will fall for disobedience (2:8); those on whom the final judgement will fall, also for disobedience (4:17). Selwyn[2] notes that obedience is a characteristic of Jewish ethical thought, and especially of Deuteronomy, with which book other features of the epistle are in accord.

To appreciate the importance of subordination and obedience in New Testament ethics, it is necessary to recall again the fundamental biblical conception of sin as self-will, disobedience of divine command; and the relation to this of the main themes of law, kingdom, faith as obedience, the Lordship of Christ: see chapter 7 (3) (v).

The frame of piety that enshrines such obedient subjection is humility under the mighty hand of God, who opposes the proud and gives His grace to the humble (5:5, 6). It would be wrong to infer that Peter knows nothing of joy, of peace, and of a warmer emotion of love towards Christ: but it remains true that (in the words of C. Bigg) "the predominant feeling towards God is one of intense awe".[3]

Subordination elaborated as a social code is simply the application to daily life of this theological virtue of reverence. The whole exhortation beginning at 2:11 follows this theme, each paragraph either beginning "Be subject ... be submissive ...", or focussing upon consideration of others' claims or upon meek acceptance of persecution, the section closing with "Humble yourselves ..."

(i) 2:13-17 applies the exhortation to *civic relationships.* "Be subject, for the Lord's sake, to every human institution, whether to the emperor, as supreme, or to governors as sent by him to punish those who do wrong and to praise those who do right." This will answer foolish criticism: Christian freedom must not be – and must be seen not to be – a pretext for law-breaking and evil-doing. Paul's advice, to honour all authorities, is here repeated with added weight from the approach of persecution.

Peter can ask, as Paul might have done, "Who is there to harm you, if you are zealous for what is right?" But Peter can add, "But even if you do suffer for righteousness' sake, you will be blessed ... Have no fear

... Arm yourselves for suffering in the flesh, rejoice that you share
Christ's sufferings. If you are reproached for the name of Christ, you are
blessed ... If one suffers as a Christian let him not be ashamed, but
under that name let him glorify God ... Know that the same experience
of suffering is required of your brethren throughout the world."

Submission is thus carried to the point of unresisting acceptance of undeserved sufferings. But "Let none of you suffer as a
murderer, or a thief, or a wrongdoer, or a mischief-maker."
Neither the injustice of the State, nor Christian freedom, provide
excuse for breaking the State's laws. One gains the impression (as
in Matthew 17:24f) that some Christians were interpreting their
freedom in this way, which may help to explain, as Lillie suggests,
the New Testament's emphasis on submission to civil authority.[4]
For Peter as for Paul, the Roman emperor and his officials are the
fountain-heads of law and order, "performing a certain indispensable function in human society ... the heathen officials were
divinely commissioned" (Selwyn).[5] Yet here again, the fact that
Christians suffered, and accepted suffering, is the best proof that
conformity had limits. Peter would still say, "We ought to obey
God rather than men" (Acts 5:29).

(ii) 2:18-25 applies subordination to *slaves,* even in relation to
over-bearing masters, and calls for the patience of Christ when,
while doing good, the slave suffers unjustly. The slave may rise to
this if "mindful of God", and sure of "God's approval"; especially if he recalls that by precisely such unjust sufferings he had
been redeemed. So submissive a spirit, enduring wrongs instead
of asserting rights, could be justified by nothing less than an
appeal to the spirit of Jesus Himself. In effect, it is a call to accept
the inevitable, when it truly cannot be changed, with a Christlike
spirit: it says nothing of the Christian's duty when the opportunity
to change the total situation might arise. It is *an adjustment-
attitude* within an existing institution, not an assessment of that
institution as a whole.

In so short and immediate a letter we would not expect to find
the far-reaching principles which were eventually to destroy slavery; but we do miss any appeal or warning addressed to masters.
C. E. B. Cranfield thinks masters may have been few in the
churches Peter addressed; or their position presented no urgent
problem. It may be that Peter concentrated on the humbler side
of each relationship –on the duties of the citizen rather than of the
State, the slave rather than the master, the wife rather than the
husband – and the nature of the counsel, and the difficulty of
accepting it, may explain why. But even so, its one-sidedness
sharply reminds us that we have no complete and balanced exposition of Peter's thought.

(iii) 3:1-7 applies subordination to *wives,* urging the power of

reverent and chaste conduct, "the imperishable jewel of a gentle and quiet spirit", to win for Christ an unbelieving husband. Such behaviour is in God's sight "precious". The example of holy women of the past, espcially of Sarah's submissiveness before Abraham, is urged to encourage obedience. Allowing for the catechetical precedent, the threefold emphasis upon submissiveness seems excessive. Perhaps the new freedom practised within the Christian fellowship was giving cause for criticism or for domestic disharmony. Both Selwyn and Cranfield think the phrase "their own husbands" (3:1, 5) limits the counsel within marriage, implying nothing of general "inferiority" of women to men in other spheres, but only relative function within an ordered home.

This, too, is an adjustment-ethic affecting an existing institution, not an evaluation of marriage in the abstract. It was of no use, as Cranfield points out, for Christian wives to suggest to their pagan husbands that in Christ there can be no male or female, but all are one. "Peter cannot, by his letter, suddenly alter the legal position of wives in Asia Minor. What he can do is to help these women to see their situation in a new light."[6] By doing freely what would promote harmony and admiration, they would help to break down the prejudice of pagans against the gospel.

Peter balances this counsel to wives with a brief but very significant reminder to husbands. As in Paul, the obligations of marriage are reciprocal – a revolutionary proposal for many pagan homes. Husband and wife are spiritually equal, in their prayer life and before God. More significant still, sexual relationships are to be so disciplined by consideration, by joint responsibility, by reverence for the gift of creating life which the partners share together, that prayer fellowship shall not be destroyed or hindered. Brief as it is, this provides a remarkable compendium of Christian marriage-counselling. Since it is addressed to the husband, it implies that the submissiveness expected of the wife is set within a fine relationship of consideration and care. Comparing the word "honour" in 2: 17 and 2:13, Cranfield argues that some subjection is here required of the husband also: the subordination of selfish desire to the physical and spiritual needs of the wife. "Where it is recognised that husband and wife are spiritually equals, there is an end of domestic tyranny. It means that women are taken seriously as persons, and can no more be thought of, or treated, as mere drudges, mere child-bearing machines, or mere playthings."[7]

(iv) 3:8-9, 4:8-11, 5:5-6 pursue (with digressions mainly upon Christian suffering) the application of subordination to *life within the church*. In 3:8f it is suggested that unity of spirit, sympathy, love of the brethren, will be especially tested when any wrong occurs: then there must be no returning evil for evil, but a meek acceptance of wrong, for this is approved and blessed by God. Following discussion of the duties of pastors, Peter urges "younger" members to submit themselves to the elders, with humility towards each other and towards God. But this is to apply to pastors as to people; leadership within the church does not permit the dominating, imperious spirit, nor any self-seeking. The heritage, the flock, is God's: all are to subject themselves to the common good, remembering always that God resists the proud.

Among the humbler servants of the church, as among the leaders, all self-assertiveness, all self-promotion, is out of place. "As each has received a gift, employ it for one another, as good stewards of God's varied grace." Whoever speaks should do so as one who utters oracles of God; whoever renders service, as one who renders it by the strength which God supplies – that in everything God may be glorified through Jesus Christ. Whatever a man does, or offers, is assessed by its usefulness to others, and its contribution to God's glory.

So the same principle governs church life as governs the Christian home, the Christian at work, and the Christian as citizen: a gentle and humble-minded submissiveness. Whatever theological motives may lie behind this formulation, Peter appeals mainly to the divine honour that exalts the humble, and even more to the emulation of Christ.

(2) THE IMITATION OF CHRIST

The example of Jesus is appealed to, first, in the counsel to slaves to accept patiently unjust suffering – "for to this you have been called, because Christ also suffered for you, leaving you an example, that you should follow in his steps" (2:21f; note Christ's "faith", 23). There follows a reminder of the innocence of Jesus, His patient silence before His tormentors, born of the quiet trust that committed His cause to God.

Christ's example is appealed to again to support the injunction that all Christians shall arm themselves to meet abuse and suffering: "it is better to suffer for doing right, if that be God's will, than for doing wrong. For Christ also died for sins, once for all, the righteous for the unrighteous ... Since therefore Christ suffered in the flesh, arm yourselves with the same thought" (or, mental attitude, "mind"): "Rejoice in so far as you share Christ's sufferings" (3:15 – 4:1, 13).

But the imitation of Christ is assumed in the *form* of Peter's argument even more eloquently than it is expounded. Again and again, ten or eleven times, an exhortation is followed immediately by appeal to something Christ did, did not do, suffered, or revealed in His own spirit. These references back to Christ are not more brief, nor more infrequent, than we might expect in so short a letter; what is more significant is that the example of Jesus is brought clearly into relation with both the main themes of the epistle, the principle of subordination, and readiness to suffer. The humble situation of the slave, the fears of the threatened young convert, the most private life of the Christian home, are all transfigured by the light of His perfection.

"If one were asked," says Selwyn, "what trait of all others in the character of our Lord is dear to St Peter, the answer is plain: it is His meekness. And he writes about it as one who himself had witnessed it."[8] Christ, Peter cannot forget, is He who when He was reviled, reviled not again; when He suffered, He threatened not. Perhaps Peter could not help recalling his own very different reaction to threatened suffering.

Selwyn thinks this provides the clue to much that Peter would say about Christ's passion. His doctrine of the atonement grows, *in part,* out of Christ's meekness and patience under suffering. In meek acceptance of unjust death for our sakes, Christ gives the central and all-transforming ethical example by which our lives are to be illumined. And as in Paul, the saving example is not merely something which Jesus has set before our eyes, but something He has done and suffered on our behalf.

Inevitably, our Lord's words are recalled: the call to save life by losing it, and to take up His cross; and also His experience: Christ, through death, ascended to heaven, to the right hand of God, where angels, authorities, and powers became subject to Him (3:22). Even so we, by binding the towel of humility about us, can discover how God gives grace to the humble (5:5); and by the principle of dying to live, we can through meekness in service and suffering find exaltation and joy. It is here, almost exclusively, that the example of Jesus – as meek and lowly in heart – bore upon Peter's conscience. Perhaps something in his earlier temperament, his mistakes, or his discipline by Christ, best explains why.

(3) WELL-DOING, HOLINESS

Two lesser strands in Peter's ethical teaching should not be ignored. Six times he refers to the Christian's *well-doing,* meaning thereby the active kindness, and social usefulness, of hearts open to others' needs. The phrase occurs in 1 Peter more often than in all the rest of the New Testament; elsewhere it is found almost exclusively on the lips of Jesus Himself. The meaning includes loving one another earnestly from the heart; putting away all malice, guile, insincerity, envy, slander; exercising the charity that covers sins rather than exposing them; and the open-heartedness of ungrudging generosity. Usually, Peter couples with well-doing the duty of witnessing for the faith: those who do well will earn praise of the authorities appointed to uphold good in society. We are to maintain good conduct so that in case any slander us as evil-doers, they may see our good deeds and glorify God: "It is God's will that by doing right you should put to silence the ignorance of foolish men." Right doing will not shield from all suffering, but by doing well we commit our souls to God's safe keeping. The reason we give for the faith that is within us will thus gain confirmation from a good conscience within ourselves and a good reputation among those who watch us. Nevertheless, evangelistic witness is more the consequence of well-doing than its motive: the deepest reason for doing well is again Christlikeness. It was Peter who summed up those three glorious years in the unforgettable phrase, "He went about doing good ... for God was with him" (Act 10:38).

The other lesser strand in Peter's teaching concerns *holiness,* one ethical element in the Christian's priestly service of God. "As he who called you is holy, so be holy yourselves in all your conduct, since it is written, 'You shall be holy, for I am holy'" (1:15-16) enters Christian exhortation straight from the Levitical Holiness Code, through the primitive catechesis. In 1 Peter it is closely associated with the building of Christians into a spiritual house (or shrine), a holy priesthood, to offer spiritual sacrifices acceptable to God through Jesus Christ (2:5); and with the other side of Peter's exposition of the death of Christ, as a spotless sacrifice that ransoms from futility through sprinkled blood. Such overtones of worship, privilege, sacrifice, (recalling Romans 12:1f) set Christian consecration in unusual but attractive light, especially for those who feel that the heart of all Christian morality is self-offering to God, rather than social adjustment to one's fellows.

Describing such holiness, Peter speaks of the "girded" mind, the soul purified by obedience to truth, the exile's detachment from the world about him, the need to keep clear of the fleshly passions that war against the soul. Former gentile companions are surprised that converts no longer join them in wild profligacy: but they will give account to Him who is ready to judge the living and the dead (4:3-5, recalling Peter in Acts 2:40). Sensuality, and all forms of lawlessness, are left behind by those called out of darkness into Christ's marvellous light, constituted a royal priesthood, a holy nation, a people for God's own possession. The experience of high privilege, and the sense of conferred sacredness, preserve the Christian from all that is unholy.

Peter's brief letter may not break new, adventurous ground in ethics, but it sets the challenge to Christlike living in a hostile world in very clear light. By isolating one particular quality in Christ, meekness and patience under injustice and suffering,

Peter has touched for most of us the very nerve of Christian morality, where selfishness and personal pride – our concern for our "rights" – instantly recoil.

11

Johannine Rigour

" " IN THE LETTERS OF John the great ethical note is the insistence on the inseparability of the love of God and the love of man, a point already noticed both in the gospels and in Paul." So Marshall,[1] and Inge[2] is scarcely more respectful: speaking of the Johannine literature as a whole, "The ethical standpoint is mystical and Pauline. The command of love is very strongly emphasised, but there are perhaps signs that it is 'the brotherhood', that is to say the society of believers, rather than mankind, ... who are now regarded as the objects of affection and sympathy. The moral dualism is very strongly marked: the evangelist seems to see the world in black and white ... he is not thinking of problems of conduct, but depicting the incarnation as a cosmic drama in which the principles of good and evil stand face to face ..."

Both comments are true, of course, but scarcely sufficient. "Johannine Christianity" is one of the richest and most enduring streams of the historic faith; it could hardly have become so without some more satisfying ethical content than is here summarised. Within its own idiom, the fourth Gospel is as concerned with ethical insights as are the Synoptics; the brief First Epistle, too, in its condensed, forthright way contributes much to ethical understanding.

(1) THE FOURTH GOSPEL

Whatever we decide about the historicity of John's Gospel, its contribution to the portrait of Christ became part of the heritage of the church, and the Johannine themes of devotion to Jesus and imitation of Jesus became part of Christian ethics. We saw (in Chapter 6) that devotion represented as a *love* for Jesus whose reality is in loyalty, not emotion, and whose expression is obedience; the imitation of Christ is analysed rigorously into love, obedience, suffering, and humble service, in each of which Christ had explicitly provided example. The Gospel's central purpose, however, is to bring men to believe that Jesus is the Christ, and so to have life in His name (20:30). Ethically, this places emphasis, not on specific forms of well-doing but on the possession of divine life: John joins Paul and Peter in declaring that to possess life is prior to living, that character determines conduct. What matters is that men shall come to Christ, be born anew, receive life, and in consequence live as He lived.

Since possessing divine life depends upon faith, the acceptance of truth, "coming to the light" so that conduct might be judged and pardoned, rejection of divine life, through unbelief and avoidance of the light, is the supreme sin, the sufficient and only condemnation: "He who does not believe is condemned already because he has not believed ... This is the judgement ... that the light has come ... and men loved darkness" (John 3:18, 19). Specific forms of ill-doing are less important than this sin of unbelief, which by cutting men off from life proves to be the root of all wrong conduct. For John, man's choice of faith or unbelief is inextricably both intellectual and moral: judgement falls on unbelief as a moral attitude, resistance offered wilfully to God's initiative in Christ. Nor does John allow for intermediate positions; all is sharply defined – truth or lies, light or darkness, death or life, faith or unbelief, God or the devil. One accepts, or one rejects, life in Christ: and by that both character and destiny are determined.

The severity of this presentation must be measured by John's insistence that God's initiative in Christ is one of love. The love of God for the world is fundamental; the love of the Father for the Son, of the Son for the Father, of the Father and the Son for the disciples, and of the disciples for the Father and the Son, constitutes one reciprocal relationship upon which life and salvation entirely depend. For definition of love, John's mind turns ever to obedience and to sacrifice: "If you keep my commandments, you will abide in my love, just as I have kept my Father's commandments and abide in his love ... Greater love has no man than this, that a man lay down his life for his friends" (John 15:10, 13).

But Inge is right: the disciples' love is seen almost exclusively as an inward-looking brotherly-love binding together the like-minded, rather than an outward-looking compassion for all sorts and conditions of men. The outside world is hostile: awareness of future peril through rejection by society gives to love its Johannine dimension of loyalty to the brethren. To that mutual loyalty in shared persecution Christ calls the disciples in the upper room, that the vine may remain one, that the world may know these men unbreakably united in Him. The record may owe something to John's later experience of the world's hostility, and of the divisiveness of gnosticism, but there is no need to doubt that Jesus did so emphasise the need for Christians to stand together in persecution and in testimony. Nevertheless, John understood very well that divine love is far wider in scope than the Christian fellowship – "God so loved *the world* . . ." But the practice of love begins within the fellowship, among those who share the creative experience of being loved. If it fail there, love towards all mankind becomes, as John's epistle says, mere words (1 John 3:18).

(2) THE FIRST EPISTLE

First John is the earliest systematic reply to the major challenge presented to Christian ethics – a reply all the more powerful because the writer is intellectually sympathetic to Hellenism, yet convinced of gnosticism's threat. Teachers of certain secession-groups (2:18, 19, 26, 4:1f), claiming "advanced" spiritual experience, professed to lead their adherents beyond "elementary" concern with merely moral questions into a new amoral freedom: John meets the doctrinal and the ethical heresies with equal forthrightness and vigour.

(i) Gnosticism was dualistic. Everything material was naturally, essentially, and therefore incurably, evil; everything spiritual was good. Two ethical reactions were possible. One sought to discipline, even to abuse, the evil body in order to save the soul (cf Colossians 2:20f, 1 Timothy 4:3); the other, to treat all deeds done with the body as ethically irrelevant. Since the body cannot be made more, or less, evil than it is, moral discipline or immoral delight are alike indifferent to the life of spirit – which is, and must by nature remain, undefiled. The spiritual, or enlightened, therefore have no sin; they are *above good and evil*. According to Irenaeus, Basilides (circa 130 AD) "bids men despise, and take no account of, things offered to idols, but to use them without fearfulness; and to treat as a matter of indifference the indulgence in other practices and in lust of all kinds".[3]

That this seductive amoralism affected the church is clear not only from 1 John but from Titus 1:10, 16, 2 Timothy 3:1-7, 2 Peter 2:12-22, Jude 4, 7-19, Revelation 2:14f, 20. Irenaeus says of certain "spiritual gnostics" that "they affirm that good moral conduct is necessary for us (that is, for ordinary Christians), but they themselves will unquestionably be saved not from moral conduct but because they are by nature spiritual . . . The spiritual are incapable of receiving corruption, whatever moral conduct they practise . . . Hence the most perfect among them perform all forbidden things without any scruple, and some of them, obeying the lusts of the flesh even to satiety, say that carnal things are repaid by carnal and spiritual things by spiritual."[4] Clement speaks of the Basilidians as "having power to sin because of their perfection, being altogether assured by nature of future salvation;" and of the Prodicians that they live as they choose, and they choose lasciviously, "as belonging to a kind of superior race ... The law, they say, is not written for kings."[5]

Towards this moral indifferentism, John is merciless. In fifteen different ways he emphasises the peril of tolerating sin in Christian life. Not specific sins, but the seriousness of all sin, is one of his themes. *Sin* consists in lawlessness, the denial of moral obligation, repudiation of the rule of right; *sins* include all acts which express that attitude, every form of unrighteousness.

Sin is defiance of God's rule, rebellion against the constitution of the universe; Christ appeared to take away sins; He Himself was sinless; to be accounted righteous (="justification") cannot be divorced from actual righteousness; all sin is of the devil, and Christ keeps guard over His own that the evil one touch him not; a divine life abides in the Christian, and he cannot tolerate sin; he whose hope is built on Christ purifies himself, and prays for others who sin (3:3-10, 5:16-18). John could scarcely make more clear the position of the child of God, unable to claim sinlessness (1:8) yet fixed in relentless antagonism to sin. Answering the contention that morality is beneath the notice of the spiritual man, John insists, roundly and variously, that "he who commits sin is of the devil." "God is light ... If we say we have fellowship with him and walk in darkness, we lie ..." (3:8, 1:5, 6).

(ii) Gnosticism was intensely intellectualist, offering salvation through knowledge, so engendering pride and individualism. As a movement, gnosticism (in Dodd's phrase) possessed little sense of social obligation; as Robert Law said, "It was loveless to the core." Ignatius records that the gnostics "give no heed to love, caring not for the widow, the orphan, or the afflicted, nor for those who are released from bonds, neither for the hungry, nor the thirsty".[6]

John's reply is again brusque: "He that loveth not knoweth not ..." (4:8) Twelve times he stresses the duty of mutual loyalty and detailed, practical love, shown in compassion towards a brother's need. To illustrate this adequately would be to rewrite 1 John. Love is John's purpose, the message we heard from Christ, the commandment He gave; love shows that we are in the light, that we have life; love is the meaning of the cross, and the nature of God. Christian love is the reflex of divine love in human hearts – they who have been so loved cannot help loving. Man's love towards man is God's love overflowing the heart on which it is "bestowed", flooding unconfined into a love-starved world. Not to love is not to know God, or Christ, or the gospel (4:7-21, and *passim*).

John does not illustrate love's activities as Jesus did, and Paul; he is concerned with the basic attitude, countering gnostic lovelessness. But what John does say, in his terse way, about love *seeing* a brother's need, and then *sharing* this world's goods, or, if we do not, then keeping silent about love (3:17, 18), is as telling as anything in Paul. Like the fourth Gospel, 1 John appears to limit the scope of Christian love to "the brethren", narrowing the "neighbour" of the great commandment to the fellow-Christian (4:21). John does not at all suggest that others are excluded from love, nor that brotherly-love fulfils the law of Christ completely. He speaks to the immediate situation of Christian division, sharpened by controversy. But he also emphasises (as does the fourth Gospel) that God's love in Christ is universal – "not for ours only ..." (2:2, cf 4:14 – 'the world') He fully recognises, and reminds his readers, that Christian love, though learned and first practised within the Christian fellowship, must extend beyond it, as God's love does.

This is the more important in that John insists so clearly that love is divine, is "of God" in nature and in initiative. The situation is "not that we loved God, but that he loved us ... If God so loved us, we ought also to love the brethren ... We love, because he first loved us." That is John's ultimate word about love.

He could hardly say more, unless it be that he who hates his brother is lost in darkness; he who does not love his brother is not of God, but of the breed of Cain, and abiding in death. Love is known in the death of Christ, and its obligation flows from the same event (3:15, 16). Christian theology (4:7-12) and Christian experience (4:13-16) alike demonstrate that God is love and the origin of all love. Thus, for John, as for Jesus and Paul, gospel and ethic *coincide* – in love.

By these two tests, of antagonism to sin on the one hand and love like God's on the other, John examines ruthlessly all claims to spiritual experience, and to the knowledge of God. Emotional ecstasies, eloquent professions, are worthless without appropriate behaviour: only *doing* righteousness, *doing* love, prove that we know God. So John sifts claims to new birth by applying uncompromisingly ethical tests: "Whosoever believeth that Jesus is the Christ is born of God" (5:1 Greek), but

Every one who does right is born of him (2:29)
No one born of God commits sin (3:9)
He who loves is born of God (4:7)
Whatever is born of God overcomes the world (5:4)
Any one born of God does not sin (5:18)

because God Himself is righteous, and God Himself is love. That is the Johannine rigour of assessment.

Three other themes recur strongly in John's ethical thought: (a) surprisingly – against the background of love – no less than fourteen references to "commandments" must be added to what John says about "lawlessness", and about the word of Christ controlling Christian thought (3:4 etc, 2:4, 5 etc). Keeping His com-

mandments is the evidence that we know God; disobedience dis-
proves all spiritual claims; to keep God's word is to show our love
matured, to believe in Christ, to abide in Him, to be assured that
prayer is answered. This principle of moral *obligation* is no new
commandment, but part of Christianity "from the beginning";
though there is also a new commandment – to love one another.
Nor are Christ's commandments burdensome, for love delights to
please (2:7 etc, 5:3, 3:22).

John's summary is a fairly complete exposition of Christian
moral law. While he keeps Christian obedience firmly within the
context of Christian privilege – the experience of God's love –
John is yet not afraid of the idea of obligation. He is no sentimen-
talist, assuming that high ideals work by their own fascination; he
would never say, "Love God, then do as you please": John says
instead, "Love God, and you will do what He pleases" – delighting to do it, but not free not to do it, and still doing it when
obligation rather than delight impels you. God's commandments
are still commandments, and God's.

(b) John is equally uncompromising in hostility towards "the
world". In general, his attitude is "world-renouncing". The
separatist sect-consciousness which emerged in scripture with the
doctrine of the remnant and the post-exilic "saints", and
deepened with Qumran and the Baptist, is here intensified: we
miss almost entirely the social ethic of Paul and Peter. The world
in its moral blindness did not know Christ, and does not know the
Christian (3:1). It hates the children of God, being more hospit-
able towards the spirit of anti-Christ – and the heretical leaders
(4:3-5). Lust and pride being the controlling factors of the world's
life, and to "pass away" being its destiny, both loyalty to Christ
and simple common sense require that the Christian shall not love
the world, but having been delivered from it shall "stay delivered". The world is not "of the Father" but lies in the power of
the evil one (5:19); to be "of the world" is to betray love of the
Father (2:15).

The phrase "the world" has here acquired a moral sense. It represents
the crystallisation, so to speak, of sensual lust, external show, and boastful pride, and is "on the way out" (2:16f). It denotes not all men, but
human society as organised under the power of evil and opposed to
God. Dodd[7] points out that at this time the greater danger to the church
lay not in the world's persecution but in its sensuality, avarice, materialism, cruelty, and pride; while Barclay has shown[8], with a wealth of
illustration from seven or eight classical authors, an appalling picture of
the vicious immorality, extravagance, love of pleasure and of cruelty,
domestic infidelity, homosexuality, contempt for child-life, confessed
moral helplessness, which formed the less congenial environment of the
growing church. Neil Alexander[9] notes also the harm which "the world"
had already done in enticing away some of the church's leaders; while

from the epistle itself we may discern the power of gnosticism to compromise with, and to attract, popular opinion. All this lies behind, and
partly explains, John's intense hostility towards "the world".

Yet John counsels no escape from the world into outright ascetic rejection of it; he falls into no dualism – John could not think
of the flesh in which Christ was incarnate, or of the world which
God loved, as intrinsically evil. Nor does he doubt that Christ is
Saviour of *the world,* and His death a propitiation for the sins of
the whole world. Here once more John concentrates on the
immediate issue: the world has produced the gnostic heresy, and
eagerly welcomes and supports its exponents; Christians therefore must not follow it, must contend against it, must overcome it
by faith (5:5).

In spite of all this (whatever may be true of the "second" and
"third" epistles), it is quite wrong to speak of bitterness, or any
decline from earlier standards of tolerance. Brooke[10] speaks of
the pressing sense of danger; the definitions of faith are razor-
sharp; the analysis of Christian obligation is unrelenting; the
method of argument an either-or confrontation with truth, that
allows no midway positions. The whole is clearly aimed at known,
local, and urgent problems and attitudes, yet John *never once* says
that any identifiable person or group takes up the attitudes or
professes the doctrines that he condemns. The references to error
are always oblique: "If any man say ... Who is a liar but he who
... Take care lest any man deceive you ... If we say ..." No
one is forced into impossible situations from which it would be
humiliating to retreat. With skill and courtesy exceedingly rare in
religious controversy, all is said clearly, uncompromisingly, yet
never merely to justify the writer or to vindicate friends, and
never so presented as to alienate further those who differ. All is
written only with a view to agreement. John is very much in
earnest; he writes to define, to clarify, to persuade, even to warn,
but much more to reconcile – "that you might have fellowship
with us" (1:3). So he will not deepen division by sharpening
personal antipathies: in all contention for the truth and against
the world, the supreme law is still love.

(c) John's third emphasis is that found everywhere in the New
Testament: the imitation of Christ. The whole epistle is a comment upon John 13:15 – "I have given you an example, that you
should do as I have done to you." John says that we saw the
divine life of the Christian manifested in Christ. We understand
walking in the light by watching Him who is ever "in the light".
We walk as He walked; we test what is right by "the righteous
one"; we purify ourselves as He is pure. So too Jesus is the
standard and the exemplar of love: by this we know love, that He
laid down His life for us. The example of Jesus illumines our

experience: the world does not recognise us because it did not recognise Him; but we remain in God's love as He did. "As he is, so are we in this world." So close is the parallel drawn between the Christian's experience and Christ's, that John can even say, unexpectedly, that Christ also is "born of God" (5:18), and so able to keep from the evil one all who are one with Him in the divine family. Beyond this identification with Jesus and imitation of Jesus John can see no higher destiny or glory for the Christian: "It does not yet appear what we shall be, but we know that when he shall appear, we shall be like him, for we shall see him as he is" (3:2).

John, then, in Gospel and in epistle, makes no small contribution to Christian ethics. His vigorous opposition to the moral indifferentism of gnosticism as it began to infiltrate the churches applies equally to the modern relativism which denies the objectivity and obligation of ethical insights. John's evaluation of love as the basic ethical attitude is wholly modern, though John strengthens it with an appeal to the historic example of Jesus, and by his insistence upon Christian obedience. His demand that religious experience be tested always by its ethical and social consequences, has timeless relevance. The Christian is called, and by all he knows of Christ and of God he is compelled, to aim resolutely at righteousness and to cultivate Christian love. He must at all times obey the divine commandments, keep himself free of the enticements of the world, and in all things imitate the likeness of Christ. Only by so doing will his profession be vindicated, and his soul abide in Christ.[11]

12

"Sub-Apostolic" Discipline

ALTHOUGH INVESTIGATION OF THE precise dates and authorship of New Testament books lies outside the scope of biblical ethics, it is impossible to ignore entirely the passage of time and the change of conditions as the New Testament period draws to a close. The writer of *Hebrews,* for example, heard the gospel not "at first" directly from the Lord but indirectly from those who had heard Him; while the readers had themselves been believers for some time, and their first leaders had already passed away (2:3, 6:12, 10:32, 13:7). The exhortation and instruction in 1 Timothy 4:1-5 presupposes that the "later times" mentioned there have at least begun. The advice of 1 Timothy 5:14 that younger widows should marry reflects a different situation from that presupposed in 1 Corinthians 7 (8, 25ff, and 39f); and the tone of *Revelation* in its references to the State is very different from *Romans* 13. With the *Pastoral* epistles, *Hebrews* and *Revelation* may conveniently be grouped *James, Second Peter,* and *Jude;* while the Gospels of *Matthew* and *Luke* evidently belong to the same milieu.

It is the change of conditions and its effect upon the church's thought, as reflected in this literature, that alone concern ethics. The term "sub-apostolic" deliberately avoids the assumption of "post-apostolic" date, while yet characterising the Christian life described in these sections of the New Testament as below the level of freshness and vigour that prevailed earlier. If "apostolic" is a convenient epithet for the quality of Christian life characteristic of the first decades, when the power of the Spirit was plainly evident in joyous exuberance, overflowing zeal, fluidity, freedom and variety of experiment, headlong expansion, immediacy of inspiration – the exciting, throbbing, unpredictable and invincible church-life depicted by Luke in *Acts* – then "sub-apostolic" is an equally convenient epithet for that phase of the church's development when excitement gave place to calmer though equally strong conviction, expansion gave place to consolidation, fluidity to organisation, variety to tested and approved patterns of belief and behaviour, and the characteristic note of Christian exhortation came to be "discipline" rather than fervour.

Such a phase, whatever dates be assigned to it, was an inevitable and necessary preparation for the long centuries of development that followed. This constitutes beyond question the immense value of these parts of the New Testament. In all this literature, the first generation is rapidly passing away; Palestine falls further into the background, and Christianity moves out into the Graeco-Roman world to face pagan criticisms and rival moralities. In numerous respects, the later pages of the New Testament speak to a situation *much nearer to our own;* while some of the perennial issues, the areas of repeated misunderstanding, the points constantly needing clarification, begin to appear.

For example, some firmer church organisation was necessary, and some compromise too, if Christianity was to survive after the hope of an immediate advent receded: it could not remain a way of perfection for an élite with a brief future. As Scott says, because the Pastoral letters (in particular) make Christianity "a working religion for ordinary men, the author . . . may justly be ranked among the great Christian teachers."[1] We ought therefore to value highly the plain practical wisdom offered in these difficult years, when the first fire died down and Christianity had to brace itself for the long haul through history. To preserve the legacy of the first years in two precious Gospels and related counsel; to establish the church as an institution while still demanding (as the Pastoral epistles do) that the personal quality of men and women be held more important than their office; to adjust the lofty insights and ideals of the early apostolic age to the more pedestrian, more bitterly persecuted, church in the pagan world, without losing their essential truth and challenge, was no mean accomplishment.

Moreover, the changes in emphasis necessitated by the changing circumstances illustrate clearly the growth of insight, the flexibility of application, required by any living ethic. Some adaptation of the teaching of Jesus was evident already, of course, in the primitive catechesis; Paul had to defend the Christian position on new fronts; John faced an unprecedented ethical challenge. E. F. Scott pointed out that as Christianity moved away from Judaism, the assumption of an underlying ethico-religious sentiment could no longer be made; morality had to evoke a new set of motives of a more prudential kind, promising reward and warning of judgement.[2] This principle of development, thus inherent in Christian ethics from the beginning, grows steadily more plain as the New Testament closes.

(1) 2 PETER: JUDE

The change which Scott mentions may be exemplified by the ethical material common to 2 Peter and Jude. The situation addressed resembles that of 1 John, the emergence of gnostic-type groups for whom morality does not count. But where 1 John argues from the original commandment, the example of Jesus, the nature of spiritual experience, Jude and 2 Peter are content to abuse, and to prophesy doom upon the opponents. The language of these letters itself becomes violent and "sub-apostolic" in tone. No doubt the condemnation was deserved: but it probably had more effect in stiffening waverers than in persuading or frightening heretics. It would scarcely succeed in reconciling them, as John would have striven to do.

Nevertheless, 2 Peter contains one passage of a very different kind, the analysis of Christian moral growth in 1:5-8. Beginning with *faith,* as the morally creative vision of Christ and of a better life made possible in Him, 2 Peter urges that if faith is to become fruitful it must develop *resolution,* the "virtue" (by derivation, manliness) which moves from vision to valour, from admiring goodness to achieving it. Yet vision and resolution will not build character without *knowledge* – of oneself, of the world, and of the will of God. So many fall through ignorance, naivety, and want of thought. At this point of growth a double conflict is certain to arise: that within oneself against all that is unworthy of Christ demands *self-control;* that outside oneself against a tempting, threatening world demands patient *endurance.* But the experience of conflict itself brings new insights; it teaches a new dependence upon God and all the means of grace, what 2 Peter here means by *godliness,* the outward pattern of regular religious exercise which sustains the soul. Conflict will also teach new sympathy for other Christians, similarly tested, and a new appreciation of other Christians' help: in such sympathy and appreciation *brotherly-love* is born. Thus, step by step, through natural moral growth, the young Christian reaches that wider and more complete attitude of moral understanding and goodwill towards all men which is the climax of Christian character – Christlike *love.*

If only for this psychological analysis of "normal" Christian development, 2 Peter deserves place in the unfolding of Christian ethics.

(2) JAMES

Another change marked in the "sub-apostolic" literature is an increasing adjustment to pagan ethical thought, as Christian apologists sought to persuade gentiles of the superiority of Christian ethics. Pagan virtues like courage, honour, patriotism, were acknowledged to have a splendour of their own and came in time to stiffen Christian heroism. E. F. Scott remarks that eventually a composite ethic emerged, in which Christian and pagan elements were hard to distinguish, until Augustine, for example, could be turned towards Christian teaching by reading Cicero.[3] Some pagans accepted the Christian ethic while repudiating the faith. But as Greek religion declined, and Greek moralists appealed increasingly to ancient custom, or to common public opinion, in attempting to support ethical standards, the need that moral discipline rest on something more than fallible human judgement made others seek religious sanctions for morality. Thus for many, by the end of the first century, ethics combined some Christian, some Greek ideals, and some Christian beliefs accepted only for morality's sake. Hence arose the distinction between "merely moral" Christianity, a basically ethical viewpoint assuming some religious justification, and "spiritual" Christianity, a basically religious viewpoint acknowledging some ethical "consequences" – *a distinction which for Christianity is fundamentally invalid but of which the church has never since rid herself.*

In this way, later Christian writings, into the second century, tended to become "moralist". It is not entirely due to "the exhaustion of the first ardour", for "the church which braced the storm of persecution in the second century was no less devoted than the church which had seen visions in the first" (Scott).[4] But the wider world needed moral guidance, and the church sought to supply it. This change of emphasis is often illustrated from the letter of James, despite widely different opinions as to its date. Some think that James echoes continually the Stoic moralists, as later Christian apologists were to do; others emphasise the debt of James to the Jewish Wisdom literature with its strongly practical aim; others again note that James' forcefulness is paralleled in the New Testament only in the discourses of Jesus Himself, with their stress on conduct – which would support an early date. That James is preoccupied with ethics is clear: in his 108 verses fifty-four contain imperatives; he thinks of Christianity as "primarily a new ethic."

Massey Shepherd[5] isolates eight meditations upon sayings of Jesus, concerning endurance of trials, hearing and doing, respect of persons, faith and works, evil speaking, factiousness, the dangers of wealth, and the need of patience. The fifth includes a vigorous diatribe on the use of the tongue; the seventh, a castigation of the wealthy in the style of an Old Testament prophet. Shepherd points to fourteen echoes of the mountain sermon, and five from elsewhere in Matthew, with other Matthean parallels and allusions. The concentration upon questions of behaviour, even of good manners, and the description of Christianity as a new "law", obedience to which is the only cogent proof of faith, are likewise close to

Matthew's portrait of Jesus as the new Rabbi – whether we think the likeness of message arises from common sources or from common environment and needs.

James' purpose is to persuade earnest Jewish readers, who reverence the ethical instruction of the old Wisdom school, to listen again to *the moral wisdom* of Jesus. For sincere men of a moralist cast of mind and synagogue training, it was an approach that could well lead eventually to deeper understanding. The "moralism" of James must not, however, be overstated. Scott suggested that James differs from Jesus in making love a binding obligation instead of a personal inspiration arising from a deep relationship with God[6]; yet it was the Master who defined love as the "great" and the "new" *commandment,* and who warned of divine judgement on failure to obey. Nor is James' position very different from Paul's. Paul perceived the deadness of the law's letter, and substituted the inward constraint of life in the Spirit that the law might be fulfilled freely, from within; James speaks of reverence for divine wisdom, given from above, which transforms "the law" into the perfect law of *liberty,* a law which such inner wisdom constrains one to obey. The difference is formal, not substantial. Similarly, when James discusses an issue much debated in Judaism, the relation of Abraham's justification by faith to his righteousness through keeping the law ("by anticipation"), he is not answering Paul, but saying much the same things. James holds that conduct alone shows faith to be valid: Paul declares that nothing avails except faith which works, by love.

When James declares that faith alone is not sufficient, he is thinking of the kind of faith which devils may possess, and which merely makes them frightened, not the Pauline faith-union in which the believer dies and rises again with the dying and rising Christ. When James demands works to prove that faith is alive, he is not asking for the fulfilment of the legal code – which Paul decries as "works" – but for mercy and kindness to the widow and fatherless, sacrifice like Abraham's, loyalty to God's purpose like Rahab's. Paul would fully concur with James in the definition of true religion (James 1:27).

It is not true then that James retreats from the position established by Jesus and Paul into a neo-Judaism; nor that gospel teaching is wanting in his epistle. James expects his readers to recognise who "the Lord" is; what faith, new birth, prayer, confession of sin, involve. He assumes knowledge of the law of Christ, the law of love. Probably, too, the accusation against the powerful rich among his Jewish readers, that they have condemned "the righteous One" (cf Acts 3:14, 7:52, 1 John 2:1) contains at least an allusion to the death of Jesus;[7] while 2:7 refers to the customary invocation of Christ's name at baptism. Throughout, Jesus is Messiah, Lord, "in glory", coming again, and Judge; and the mind and words of Jesus are the controlling influence in all that James writes. He knows that the law, however "royal" and "free", cannot be fulfilled except by those born again by the implanted seed, the word of truth (1:18f). He can speak, obscurely, of "the spirit which God has made to dwell in us", and more clearly of the need of divine grace (4:5, 6). The necessity of more than earthly wisdom is especially stressed (3:13f and *passim*), and the readiness of God to give wisdom from above, without rebuke. What faith is to Paul, hope to Peter, and love to John, wisdom is to James – or wisdom and grace together.

James' examples of the kind of works that prove faith true are very close to the parables and sayings of Jesus. James condemns the heartlessness that can say to the hungry and unsheltered "Go, be filled, and warmed" without raising a hand to help them (2:15f); he warns all who practise oppression by the power of wealth; he criticises the excessive deference paid to the rich in religious assemblies. This is the outlook of the parables of the sheep and goats, of Lazarus, of the rich farmer. Crisply and unforgettably James asserts the essential truth: "Pure religion, undefiled before God our Father, is this – to visit the fatherless and widows in their affliction, and to keep oneself unstained from the world" (1:26, 27). "A twofold sensitiveness, to the need and suffering of others, and to personal purity amid the contaminating risks of the age – such is the moral ideal of James for anyone who claims to be devout."[8] Charity and chastity, pursued in the sight of God the Father, is for James the only true religion. It may not amount to a new ethical discovery; its temperature and power may be below that of apostolic experience at its best; yet James' summary is not yet outgrown, while his forceful presentation of a moral faith in down-to-earth terms has timeless value in the continuing church.

(3) HEBREWS

Hebrews is almost the converse of James: for here high theology is asserted with great force and eloquence, the implied ethic being assumed rather than expounded. The example of Christ is appealed to once again. His temptation and His tears are held before the timid and the wavering, who should learn from His steadfastness, and from His rising through humiliation to sit at God's right hand, how they should face the enticements of evil and the menace of the world. The intercession of Christ, the divine sympathy which it implies, and the grace which it guarantees, provide inner resource for courageous living to those who draw near with full assurance of faith, emulating the endurance of the heroes who in every age have lived by faith. While this faith has dimensions that reach beyond ethics, it is also plainly a moral quality, the spring of moral attitudes of considerable ethical significance.

Abel's approval as a righteous man, Enoch's pleasing God, Noah's steadfastness in an evil age, Abraham's vision and venturing, Moses' moral choice for God and Israel against the pleasures and rewards of Egypt, all are ascribed to the faith by which the righteous live. Justice, courage, strength and victory, the heroism of great leadership, the resistance that saves society in dark days, all spring from faith rooted in things unseen. With a larger canvas then any other New Testament writer, and with full awareness of the moral value of religious faith to social welfare, the author depicts dramatically the ethical outcome of life lived in the sight of God (ch 11)

In chapter 12, the peaceful fruit of righteousness is a goal to be pursued even through pain and discipline. Peace is to be striven for, and holiness, without which none shall see the Lord – for the immoral and irreligious like Esau forfeit their spiritual birthright, the vision of God. In the brief sentences of chapter 13, familiar but vital counsels of the primitive catechesis are recalled. The brotherly love that creates the Christian fellowship must be safeguarded; hospitality must be shown, especially to travelling strangers, and not withheld when identification with fellow-Christians in prison, fleeing from persecution, or suffering social ostracism, brings danger. Contentment, freed from avarice, springing from confidence in God's faithfulness, will keep the heart strong. Certain ascetic tendencies, the rejection of marriage, the toleration of immorality, and regulations about particular foods, may well have arisen from that "gnostic" Judaism which the Qumran and Essene communities attest: against such things the readers are clearly warned.

It is surprising how many themes of Christian social responsibility may be gathered from 13:1-5, 16, 17: brotherly love, hospitality, kindness to strangers and the persecuted, prison-care, defence of the ill-used, marriage, sexual discipline, wealth and the sharing of goods, and loyalty to the community. Respect and support for Christian leaders is especially enjoined, as promoting that unity and courage which will enable Christians to suffer for Christ when thrust out by a hostile society, inwardly sustained by the moral conviction that God will in the end vindicate the right in a divine kingdom which shall never be moved.

Though his strength is given to other themes, the writer to the Hebrews is well aware that the life of faith has to be lived in a faithless world, and only faithfulness will save.

(4) THE PASTORALS

The "later times" described in 1 Timothy 4:1ff (cf 2 Timothy 3:1 "the last days") set the scene for all three Pastoral epistles. The authority conferred upon Timothy and Titus, the detailed regulations about church offices, the existence of an order of enrolled widows (1 Timothy 5:9), the distinct change of spiritual "climate", all reveal an "ecclesiastical" background more developed than we meet in 1 Corinthians, Ephesians or even Philippians. "Behind the writer", says A. J. B. Higgins, "lies the church as an established institution with its organised ministry, its clear-cut set of doctrines, and its system of worship."[9] Consonant with this growth of organisation is a marked diminution in explicit mention of the Holy Spirit: apart from a quotation from inspired prophets (1 Timothy 4:1), the only two clear references in thirteen chapters are 2 Timothy 1:14, which alludes to truth entrusted by the Spirit who indwells us, and Titus 3:5 – "the washing of regeneration and renewal in the Holy Spirit, which he poured out upon us richly ...". This contrasts sharply with the prominence of the Spirit as the driving force in Christian living (in Romans) and in the life of the church (as in 1 Corinthians, Acts). Similarly, heresy is not here met with reasoned and creative argument, exploring new truth under the challenge of denial, but with denunciation: discussion itself is condemned as "stupid, senseless" (1 Timothy 1:4-6, 4:7, 2 Timothy 2:14, 23 Titus 3:9).

Certainly the teaching of Paul's earlier epistles is here reaffirmed:

1 Timothy 5:23 (against over-scrupulousness concerning wine) recalls Romans 14 and 15; 1 Timothy 2:1f (positive support given to State officials) recalls Romans 13; Titus 3:14 (importance of honest work, and the reason, "so as to help cases of urgent need") recalls Ephesians 5:28, Thessalonians *passim*; Titus 2:9f, 1 Timothy 6:1 (slaves to be submissive, faithful, honest – more so when their masters are Christians) recall 1 Corinthians 7:20f, Colossians 3:22f etc.; and 2 Timothy 2:8 recalls the problematic 1 Corinthians 14:33f.

But time has modified some earlier attitudes, and shifted some emphases. The permissive approval of marriage expressed in 1 Corinthians 7 gives place to positive counselling of marriage and family life (1 Timothy 5:13f, Titus 2:3-5) – though the underlying reason is much the same. Experience of the evils consequent upon indiscriminate almsgiving prompts the advice that any believer who has widowed relatives should regard them as a personal obligation; a widow should be able to look first to children and grandchildren for support, for provision by children for their parents is acceptable and approved in the sight of God (1 Timothy 5:3, 4; contrast 2 Corinthians 12:14). Increasing numbers of

women deserted, widowed, or (since conversion) repudiated by
their families, had intensified the problem first faced in Jerusalem
(Acts 6:1f); now, "if any one does not provide for his relatives,
and especially for his own family, he has disowned the faith, and is
worse than an unbeliever" (1 Timothy 5:8, 16) – a surprising
judgement.

A morbid taste for controversy, breeding dissension; profitless
discussion of genealogies; "the godless chatter and contradictions
of what is falsely called knowledge"; ascetic tendencies, with
some rejection of marriage; "myths" associated with a circumcision party; doubts about the resurrection of the body, and some
emphasis upon legal regulations, especially concerning abstinence
from certain foods, all recall the type of heresy which Paul confronted at Colossae. Moral obligation seems here not to be denied
outright, as in 1 John, but the peril is seen (1 Timothy 1:19f). All
manner of immoral and antisocial behaviour is charged against
such teachers, and the folly and weakness of those who listen to
them is severely castigated.[10] A gnostic slogan – "to the pure all
things are pure" – is cited in Titus 1:15f, and the claim to "know
God" while denying Him in behaviour recalls the language of 1
John. Sensual sins are less emphasised than in 1 Corinthians (and
2 Peter), though the danger is not overlooked (1 Timothy 1:8f, 2
Timothy 2:22, Titus 2:12, 3:3).

But the attitude to gnosticism has hardened, compared with the
reasonable arguments of Colossians. "The Lord will requite
... Whom I have delivered to Satan that they may learn not to
blaspheme ... They must be silenced" (2 Timothy 4:14, 1
Timothy 1:20, Titus 1:11). The association of heresy with moral
laxity may partly explain this stiffening of attitude, but it is
scarcely surprising that some have found here the germ of what
later became fierce intolerance towards unorthodoxy of belief and
irregularity of behaviour.[11]

Another symptom of moral change appears in the warnings
against love of wealth, a sign of the altered position of Christians
in the world. Demas' desertion is explained by his love of this
present world; bishops are warned not to be greedy for gain,
lovers of money; and so are deacons (2 Timothy 4:10, 1 Timothy
3:3, 8). All are counselled against imagining that godliness is a
means of gain. Desire to be rich is a temptation and a snare, the
origin of other ruinous desires – love of money is the root of all
kinds of evil. Those already rich must therefore be warned against
pride, and the uncertainty of riches (a clear echo of Jesus); true
wealth lies in liberal and generous deeds, and the sure hope of
eternal life (1 Timothy 6:5-10, 17-19). In part, these warnings are
linked to heresy: false teachers "teach for base gain what they
have no right to teach", being lovers of money (Titus 1:11, 2
Timothy 3:2, 6); but they are related also (as in 1 Peter) to the

growing importance of official position in the churches, bringing dangerous opportunities for social ambition and personal gain.

Two over-riding impressions remain concerning the moral atmosphere of these epistles:

(i) The lowered spiritual temperature

Scott finds something "arid, commonplace, superficial" in the writing;[12] certainly we miss the earlier spiritual glow. The Christian is a good parent, a sound citizen, dutiful, genial, benevolent, practising all the virtues; the principles of Jesus are primary, but the Christian is careful also of personal dignity, moderation, concern for material as well as spiritual needs. He is admirable, but scarcely saintly (Titus 2:7, 12, 14, 3:8, 1 Timothy 6:3, 2:1).

This impression is confirmed by the pedestrian qualities required in church officials. Doubtless every point mentioned deserves notice: sad experience underlies the warnings about money, gossip, arrogance, intemperance, quick temper, for the circumstances of church office present just such temptations. Nevertheless, the instructions have a defensive air; they show a lack of confidence in individuals, and seek to hedge about a vulnerable position. Gone is the abounding joy in Christian character so vigorous and victorious that mean temptations present no perils. Men of whom only these correct recommendations for office can be predicated would never "turn the world upside down." Gone too, apparently, are the men and women supernaturally "gifted" for their tasks by the Holy Spirit.

The same is true of the Pastorals' whole ethical ideal. Much is said of keeping a clear conscience; of love issuing from a pure heart, a good conscience, a sincere faith; of life quiet and peaceable, godly and respectful in every way, well thought of by outsiders, avoiding all controversy, submissive, obedient, showing perfect courtesy to all men, doing good deeds because these are excellent and profitable (1 Timothy 1:5, 18, 2:2, 3:7, 9, 5:10f, 2 Timothy 1:3, Titus 3:1f, 8). It is fitting, even valuable, counsel for Christians – but hardly revolutionary. Such character would give no offence, even to the devil; it would accomplish little, destroy nothing. What has become of the explosive, transfiguring, radiant dynamic of apostolic experience? A phrase like "holding the form of religion but denying the power of it" serves to reveal what it condemns: would it have been necessary in the height of apostolic inspiration? The excellent summaries of Titus 2 and 3 have the same muted tone:

The grace of God has appeared for the salvation of all men, training us to renounce irreligion and worldly passions, and to live sober, upright, and godly lives in this world, awaiting our blessed hope, the appearing of our great God and Saviour, Jesus Christ, who gave himself for us to redeem us from all iniquity and to purify for himself a people of his own who are zealous of good deeds ... We ourselves were once foolish, disobedient, slaves to various passions ... but when the goodness and loving kindness of God our Saviour appeared, he saved us not because of deeds done by us in righteousness, but in virtue of his own mercy, by the washing of regeneration and renewal in the Holy Spirit, which he poured out upon us richly through Jesus Christ our Saviour, so that we might be justified by his grace and become heirs in hope of eternal life ...

– impeccably correct statements of Christian doctrine and ethics, accurate, cool, formal, but nothing more. This is the language, not of the slave, the devotee keyed for sacrifice, the man in love, but of the well-briefed lawyer defining his case (contrast ch 9 (2) (iii)). The fire, the passion, the excitement of the glorious gospel of Christ, have faded: the Pastorals breathe Christianity at moderate temperature, as most succeeding generations were to do.

(ii) The relation of sound doctrine to right behaviour

is consequently changed: in this, too, the Pastorals are prophetic of later developments. The relation is everywhere very close: a list of violent, antisocial, even murderous, crimes in 1 Timothy 1:8f ends unexpectedly with "and whatever else is contrary to sound doctrine"; in verse 19, rejection of conscience is sufficient explanation of shipwreck of faith; sober Christian citizenship is evidence of men saved and coming to the knowledge of the truth; perversions of ethics are due to departure from the faith and acceptance of the doctrines of demons. The very phrase, "sound doctrine" ("healthy, health-giving teaching") expresses the pragmatic assumption that right-doing is the test of right-thinking. The "sound words" comprise teaching *that accords with godliness* (1 Timothy 6:3); Titus is to insist on the gospel truths "so that those who have believed in God may be careful to apply themselves to good deeds ..." (3:5).

"Careful to apply themselves ..." The right ethical conclusions are to be drawn from right theological doctrines. In Romans and Colossians, true faith in the dying and rising Saviour so united men to Him as to transform them by the power inherent in the gospel. The indwelling Spirit of Christ produced the fruit of Christian character by the force of its own vitality; faith *was* obedience; the new man created in Christ Jesus was made in the image of its Creator, and redemption was itself a morally transforming experience. Now, the experience is the foundation upon which the new character remains to be built if a man is "careful" to be consistent. The Christian faith is a rock of right living, but not its living root; a blue print, an intellectual justification, for morality, but no longer a moral dynamic transfiguring helpless sinners.

This combination of right theological opinions with right principles of conduct is in the Pastorals "godliness": says Scott, "This is still the popular conception of the Christian life. To be a Christian you require to hold certain beliefs ... you must take care to act in accordance with the principles laid down in the Gospels. These two obligations of faith and conduct must go together, but little attempt is made to relate them to one another."[13] Still more recently, the attempt has often been made to divorce them entirely, preserving the principles while repudiating the beliefs. At first, Christianity would have said they *are* inseparable; the Pastorals say merely that they *ought not* to be separated.

The Pastoral epistles, of course, make no attempt to reduce morality to the pagan level of doing right because it is right – admirable for the man no longer in need of such counsel, useless for the unregenerate sinner to whom Christianity addresses itself. For motivation, the Pastorals offer divine approval, the promise of redemption, the strength of Christian fellowship and discipline, "the washing of regeneration and renewing of the Holy Spirit", the sure facts of Christ's incarnation and death to save sinners, the hope of His coming again. Even so, the doctrine and the ethic are becoming separated; the gospel is *almost* the theology which will make morality expedient. Whenever this position is reached, the ethic is liable to be first appreciated for its own sake, then found to be impracticable, and then discarded. The Pastoral epistles clearly avoid that: "The foundation of God stands sure" upon the gospel history, and Christian morality is related to it, and to the Lord of Whose coming, death, and coming again, the gospel tells. The relation is now one of obligation and consistency, rather than of inspiration and creative constraint; yet because the church taught and nourished a morality so based, she remained a school of virtue in the midst of a steadily deteriorating society.

(5) MATTHEW'S GOSPEL

As the break between church and synagogue became complete, Christian Jews needed reassurance that their adherence to Jesus as Christ was well-founded, and at the same time an apologetic which might convince hesitating Jews of the validity of Christ's claims. Matthew arranges his exceptionally rich tradition of the sayings of Jesus into five great discourses – the sermon on the mount (5 – 7), the mission charge (10), the parables of the kingdom (13), the discourse on the church (16-18), and that on the end of the age ((23) 24-25) – perhaps in significant parallel with the five books of the law, certainly with the intent to present Jesus as the greatest of all rabbis, the final interpreter of the will of God. The ethical weight of Matthew's argument falls upon:
(i) *the work of Jesus* as Messiah, the righteous One (27:4, 19, 24f), in establishing righteousness on earth, the rule of God, the

ultimate aim of the whole law. "Thus it becometh us to fulfil all righteousness", is Christ's first public word, and the programme announced in 3:14f.[14] He called men to seek first the kingdom of God and His righteousness, even at the cost of suffering for righteousness' sake; He declared that except a man's righteousness *exceed* that of the scribes and Pharisees, he would in no wise enter the kingdom. The righteous law of God cannot be abolished, only fulfilled (5:17-19). In a key passage, Jesus is described as God's Servant to bring righteousness to victory in the earth (12:20 – Matthew alone adds "to victory"). Then will the righteous shine, and those serving the righteous will be rewarded (13:43, 10:41). (ii) Matthew presents Jesus also as *the authoritative interpreter of the law* –

of the law of murder, adultery, oaths, retaliation (5:21f, 27f, 33f, 38f); of love of neighbour (5:43, again 19:19f, yet again 22:37f); of the rules of piety – almsgiving, prayer, fasting (6:1f); of leprosy (8:1f); of the sabbath (12:3-7, 9-14); of filial duty (15:1-9); of defilement (15:10-20); of temple tribute (17:24f); of marriage (19:3-12); of perfection and eternal life (19:16f); of worship (21:12-17); of levirate marriage (22:23f); and of the greatest commandment (22:34).

Plainly, this question of the authority of Jesus to interpret God's will was central for Matthew (21:23, where chief priests and elders publicly demand "By what authority ..."; cf 12:8, 17:5). The final clash with Jewry was concerned with the relative authority possessed by Jesus and by the scribes and Pharisees (23); in the end, the ascending Lord sends forth His disciples expressly to teach men all that *He* has commanded.

Thus the law stands for Christians, down to the last yod and accent (5:18; cf "all" in 3:15, 23:3, 28:20). Till heaven and earth pass, all that the law says must be fulfilled, and greatness belongs only to those who do and teach the new righteousness undiminished (5:19). Rabbis held that the messianic age would see the Torah fulfilled – and so does Matthew. But all turns upon who is to interpret God's law, and in 5:17f Jesus does precisely this – "It hath been said ... but I say unto you ..." The sermon ends with warnings against the workers of *lawlessness;* neither baptismal profession ("Lord, Lord,"), charismatic gifts ("done many wonderful works"), nor knowledge of the truth ("heareth these sayings of mine"), will avail for those who fail to do the will of the Father (7:21-27). Whereas Paul could argue that Christ was the end of the law as a way of salvation, Matthew argues equally strongly that Christ –and the Christian disciple – fulfil the law as a way of life.

But Matthew insists that the contention between Jesus and the Jewish leaders was not merely concerning the law's validity, on which both agreed; nor concerning failure to keep the law ("hypocrisy" 21:28f, chapter 23 passim); but concerning who interprets the law aright (15:6, 9, 14; 16:6, 11f; 22:34 etc). Jesus' authoritative interpretation proceeds (a) by *radicalising the law,* breaking through formal legal statements to the disobedient heart, with its anger, lust, lovelessness (5:21-48); (b) by *appealing to original principles* and the divine intention, behind the rules and concessions demanded by the hardness of evil hearts (19:1-12, cf 12:3-7, 5:45); (c) by *epitomising the law* in the great commandment of love (7:12, 9:13 = 12:7, and more explicitly in 22:34-40). For Matthew, righteousness is allegiance to the law as Jesus interprets it; in following Jesus, the perfect demand of the law as Jesus interprets it, is fulfilled: it is *not* abandoned.

(iii) Matthew makes this *summary of the law as love* quite fundamental to ethical thought (5:43f, 7:12, 9:13, 19:19, 21, 22:34f, cf 24:12). In 22:34f the "testing" of Jesus does not lie in seeing if He will give the wrong commandment precedence, or will dare to summarise the law in one or two commandments: opinions varied on both points.

Rabbis asked, "What is the smallest portion of scripture on which all the regulations of the Torah hang?" One suggested reply was, "In all thy ways remember Him"; rabbis also said, "The rules concerning the sabbath are like mountains which hang upon a hair, for there is little scripture to support them". Note twice here Jesus' word "hang" = exegetically deduce (cf Matthew 22:40). The question and answer in 22:34f do raise the question of precedence, but this was no matter of contention. It is said many times that each commandment is equally important: "the scriptures make the easiest among the easy commandments equal to the hardest among the hard."

The real issue in the "testing" lay in Jesus' making the love commandment not only "greatest" but the *norm,* in the performance of which all are performed. Love is the "essence" of the law; law and prophets "hang" upon love for God and neighbour. The formal equality of all commandments is abandoned, and the love-commandment is made the canon for the interpretation of the whole Torah and the principle by which the relative validity of different parts of the law may be determined. In 12:9-14, the love-principle controls the law of the sabbath; in 5:43-47 love is the sum of all the foregoing injunctions and constitutes the "better righteousness" required of disciples; in 15:16-20, sins against love alone defile a man, controlling interpretation of the levitical laws of uncleanness. As Gerhard Barth suggests,[15] the prominence of the command to love doubtless derives from Jesus and the whole Christian tradition, but Matthew's "editing" of the tradition in this respect is unique, and fundamental for the relation of Christian and Jew.

The rabbis also were concerned with interpreting, and "hedging" the law; but they knew no interpretation deduced from a central principle like Matthew's love-commandment. Matthew not only saw the law so

summarised, but saw Jesus as the ideal both of law-keeping and of love.
It followed that the imitation of Jesus became a second mode of law-
interpretation.

(iv) Matthew is concerned about *the church,* no less than about
relations with unbelieving Jews:

There is more about the church in Matthew's Gospel than in any other –
in 16, Christ's church is built by Christ, who assigns the keys and assures
the church of permanence against the "gates of Hades"; in 18, Matthew
elaborates the discipline of the church's erring members, and the presence of the Lord with the two or three met in His name to act, or to
pray; in 26 the worship of the church centres in the Lord's Supper; in 10
and 28, the programme of the church is described in detail.

Matthew's concern arises from the mixed nature of the church, no
longer as pure in membership and loyalty as at the beginning.
Only Matthew has the parable of wheat and tares, and that of the
dragnet; among the guests at Messiah's banquet some have
proved to be without wedding garments; among the Messiah's
bridesmaids are some wise but some foolish; among those who
hear Christ's word are some wise, some foolish builders; there are
faithful servants, and others wicked, drunken, slothful; some have
ten talents for Christian service, others five, others again are useless, lazy, full of excuses; there are sheep and goats within the
flock; many are called but few prove to be chosen; one son says
readily "I go, sir" and does not: the other declines – and goes!

Many call Jesus "Lord" and do not the things He says. Many fall away,
betray their fellows, "hate one another"; because wickedness is multip-
lied *most* men's love grows cold. In part, this declension is caused by the
fading of the advent hope: the wicked servant says, "My lord delayeth
his coming;" the bridesmaids are blamed, not for sleeping (for they all
slept) but for not providing against delay; the master of the house
returns to take account of his servants "after a long time" – to all of
which Matthew replies, "The Lord of those servants comes at a time
when you look not for him, when you have ceased to expect him, at an
hour you do not know." Moral safety lies only in constant vigilance:
"What I say to you, I say to all – Watch."

Matthew's prescription for a morally decadent church is, first,
to recall the great words of Jesus about the sifting-out that must
take place, the separation of true from false, of wheat from tares,
of good fish from bad, of faithful from unfaithful servants, wise
bridesmaids from foolish, those remaining at the banquet from
those cast out.

One passage of the mountain sermon emphasises the *choice* that must be
made, on man's part, and then maintained: one must choose God or
mammon, the broad way or the narrow, wisdom or folly in building,
good fruit from good trees, or bad fruit from corrupt trees, to be acknowledged servants, or repudiated ones, in the last day.

The purgation of the church by the sifting of souls is one of Matthew's themes: but it is not man's task, it is God's (13:28-30, 49).

Matthew recalls, secondly, more fully than either of the other Gospel-writers, words of Jesus about the coming judgement. In all, judgement is mentioned sixteen times – on the holders of the vineyard, the bridesmaids, the faithless servants, God's flock, and others. Christ shall sit on the throne of His glory, and He shall decide who shall inherit the kingdom prepared by the Father. That will be the judgement – to miss the coming manifestation of the kingdom of Christ in glory. The verdict is strictly according to deeds – not faith, or profession, but according to whether we have fed the hungry, visited the sick and the prisoner, clothed the naked, obeyed the supreme and essential law of love towards our neighbour (16:27, 25:34f).

Thus Matthew shares with James the right to be called the moralist of the New Testament. For his version of the traditions about Jesus reveals an ethical insight, concentration, and earnestness beyond almost any other New Testament writer's. The "sub-apostolic" situation, both within the church and in the church's approach to the world, demanded – as Matthew clearly taught – the most meticulous observance of the ethical standards of Jesus, Himself *par excellence* the spokesman of divine law and exemplar of divine love.

(6) LUKE'S GOSPEL

Luke's purpose, to explain and commend the gospel to the cultured and responsible aristocracy of the Graeco-Roman world, determines the content and shapes the form of all that he writes.

"It is clear" writes Professor Barclay, "that by Luke's time Christianity had reached the highest level of Roman society. For this new kind of clientele Christianity clearly needed a new kind of literary approach. Something must be written which would not jar on the literary taste of educated and cultured Romans and Greeks."[16] Theophilus (Luke 1:3) was of this class, and awareness of the susceptibilities of the readers prompts the sheer beauty, the dramatic power, the historical care, the persuasive style, and the ethical emphasis, of both Gospel and Acts.

(i) One ethical element in Luke's apologia is (as in Acts) his gallery of characters influenced by the gospel. Zaccheus the corrupt official, the woman of the city streets, Martha and her sister, the centurion of the cross, Levi, another civil servant, the demoniac at Gadara restored to sanity, decency and a quiet mind, are all vividly described. Peter is clearly and sympathetically drawn, while Joseph "the good and righteous councillor", the penitent thief saved at the eleventh hour, Mary of Nazareth, each makes a telling point in commending the ethics of Christianity to the readers Luke has in mind.

Qualities especially admired, or envied, by such an audience were courage and good sense, the manliness and strength of mind of the Stoic ideal cultivated among Romans; and joyousness –"the gladness of the Greeks." Luke alone preserves Christ's counsel to sit down first and count the cost before engaging upon discipleship, lest you be unable to see it through. Impulsive offers of discipleship were discouraged: to put the hand to the plough and look back shows one to be "unfit" for the kingdom. In Luke, the cross is to be taken up *daily* as a continuing discipline of Christian life, and a hardened, experienced Roman commander admires deeply the courageous, self-controlled manner of Jesus' death (14:28, 9:57-62, 23, 23:47).

Similarly, from Mary's opening song and the praise that heralded Christ's birth, to the children singing in the temple and the swift and joyful hearts that proclaim the resurrection, there are more happy scenes of youth and health, of music, feasting, dancing, in Luke's Gospel than in either of the others. These – Luke is saying – are the kind of people the gospel breeds: manly, heroic, happy people, for the gospel is "good tidings of great joy to all people." The basis of that attitude to life was ultimately religious, but it has no small significance for Christian ethics that Luke should keep alive that human and joyous ideal into the sub-apostolic age.

(ii) The other ethical element prominent in Luke's apologia is his deep sympathy with what Christianity could do for under-privileged, despised individuals and groups, the outsiders, the outcast, the needy, sinful, sick, alien or lost. Many such crowd Luke's pages, with an insistence that cannot be purposeless.

The sick appear in all the Gospels, but Luke sees them with a doctor's eye and describes with a doctor's accuracy. When John sent to Jesus to ask "Are you he that should come?" Luke comments that "Jesus in that hour cured many of diseases and plagues and evil spirits ..." For Luke, it was answer enough that the blind received their sight, the lame walked, lepers were cleansed, the deaf heard, the dead were raised, and to the poor the gospel was preached. He took care to keep the example and ideal of compassionate ministry to the afflicted ever before the church.

Women, too, are everywhere in Luke's Gospel, finding in Christ a new dignity and value – Joanna, Susanna, Elizabeth, Mary and Martha, Anna, the woman who touched Christ's robe, the woman who lost her bridal decoration, the widow of Nain, another widow who persuaded a reluctant judge, the women at the cradle, at the cross, at the tomb, and the magnificent scene in the house of Simon when Jesus blazed against snobbery in defence of the woman of the city. Luke tells us more of the mother of the Lord than all other Bible writers together. And Luke saved that dramatic story of the "freeing" of the woman bowed with infirmity for eighteen years – "bent over, and could not fully straighten herself": Luke sees, and he suggests the spectators saw, what Christ was able to do for womanhood at large here set forth in a single example.

The poor have a similar place in Christian compassion, as Luke describes it. Mary's song has almost revolutionary flavour –
He hath put down the mighty from their seats
And exalted them of low degree;
He hath filled the hungry with good things
And the rich he hath sent empty away:
– and so has Luke's form of the Beatitudes: "Blessed are you poor, for yours is the kingdom ... Blessed are you that hunger now, for you shall be satisfied ... Woe to you rich, for you have received your consolation." Luke alone tells the parable of Lazarus neglected at the rich man's gate, and the judgement that awaited such callousness. Luke alone tells of the wealthy fool, bankrupt in God's sight; and of Zaccheus, whose conversion meant the restoring of ill-gotten wealth. The parable of the debtors is in Luke only, and with it repeated warnings against covetousness, anxiety, and avarice. Throughout, Luke shows unparalleled interest in the unequal distribution of wealth, a strong compassion for the needy, and a conviction that Christianity must ever preserve not only a generous heart but a sensitive conscience about the sins of property.

A gentile himself, Luke shows scarcely less interest in the *alien,* the immigrant exile, the displaced person. He carries the genealogy of Jesus back to Adam, making Jesus Brother to all mankind. He delights to tell of the Samaritan leper who alone returned to give thanks, and the Samaritan who shamed the priest and levite by his understanding of love for one's neighbour; of the widow of distant Zarephath who cared for the Israelite prophet; of Naaman the Syrian cured by Elisha. Christ is the light to lighten the gentiles, who come not only from north and south (as in Matthew) but from east and west also, for "all flesh shall see His salvation". So long as the church possesses Luke's gospel she can never forget the world-vision of universal redemption that makes her ethic inter-national, inter-racial, and *human* in the widest sense.

Luke's compassion does not fail the undeserving, the *sinners.* His is the matchless chapter 15 on evangelism of the lost, and only Luke mentions the joy in heaven over sinners being saved. Jesus has come to proclaim liberty to the captives; He is Himself numbered with transgressors. The quisling taxgatherer, the convicted thief, the prostitute who now loves as ardently as once she sinned, the contrast between the self-righteous Pharisee and the humble taxgatherer pleading for mercy, the prayer of the dying Christ "Father, forgive them ..." are all for Luke at the heart of the gospel which offers redemption even for the worst among mankind.

Of all New Testament writers, Luke is clearest in his presentation of Christ as the Friend of all who else are friendless, the

Hope of all who without Him must despair – with all the far-reaching implications which that portrait has for men in every age who profess to follow Him.

Placed side by side, these closely related emphases reveal Luke's especial understanding of Christ and of the Christian ideal. As he sees Christianity, it demands a wide charity, a broad sympathy with all sorts and conditions of men, a syllabus of Christian social activity. In this, he looks forward directly from the sub-apostolic period into the second century. Luke's interpretation of Christ's concern for society's least and lowest and most resistant to improvement, approaches a Christian humanism, which must have commended itself to those leaders of Roman society responsible for good government in an age when social discontents and dangers were already becoming acute.

For ethical resource, Luke looked to the power everywhere manifest in Christ, the "power from on high" which the disciples must await in Jerusalem before beginning their mission, the power of the Holy Spirit. Luke does not relate Christian character to the presence of the Spirit in the soul as directly as Paul does, but the Spirit pervades the Gospel, from Christ's conception to the ascension promise. There is no doubt that Luke regarded the quality of life he met in the individuals he describes, and the social and redemptive energies released within the church, as the consequences of the invasion – first in Christ, and then through Christ into the lives of all who follow Him – of the loving, healing, redeeming power of God. As the Pastorals' prescription for sub-apostolic "decline" was greater moral discipline, so Luke's is to recall the beginnings, and especially the original faith and experience, that only by the Spirit of Christ could Christlike life and service of men be attained.

(7) REVELATION

In Revelation, the situation of the church has changed so radically that the book has often been represented as not simply sub-apostolic but sub-Christian. Its "ferocity towards persecutors", the fierce taunt-song over the anticipated fall of Rome (18), its prayers for vengeance and "sensuous" conceptions of the hereafter, its "scant ethical instruction", and the language used towards heretics, are all said to breathe a spirit of vengeance, a gladness that in due course it will be the enemies' turn to suffer, which is directly contrary to the attitude of Jesus. It is said that the book contains no teaching upon brotherly kindness, patience under persecution, help towards the distressed, or love of enemies; "nowhere a suggestion that Christ may take pity on the heathen and turn them to repentance." All in all, the last book of the New Testament reveals "a bitterness and intolerance which paganism itself rarely showed." "If it nad been the only book in the New Testament we should never have guessed that Jesus had once lived a human life on earth, and that He had brought a gospel of love, goodness, brotherhood."[17]

On the other hand, the seven churches of Asia are called to purify their membership in readiness for great endurance. Throughout, it is insisted that Christ's servants must be worthy of Him – the prayers of true saints rise like incense before God, their white garments are their righteous acts. When the city of God replaces that of Rome, in it will be found nothing that defiles, or is abominable, or that makes a lie: all will be purity and light. The fierce taunt-song condemns Rome for her vicious impurity, her iniquities, wantonness, luxury, extravagance, her trade in human souls, and only in the last line adds that "in her was found the blood of prophets and of saints". Real concern for personal purity is evident also in the condemnation of certain teaching at Pergamos and Thyatira (2:14, 20); in the final judgement upon "the abominable, murderers, whoremongers, sorcerers, idolaters, liars" (21:8), and in the banishment of the same evil-doers from the city of God (22:15). At the last, healing and universal peace are the ultimate goal. Plainly, the book of Revelation is *not* entirely without concern for ethical questions, and a better world.

14:4 – those who "follow the Lamb whither he goeth" and attain to foremost honour in heaven, are those who "have not defiled themselves with women, for they are chaste" (so RSV, NEB, Greek "*virgins*") – expresses a more extreme view on sexual purity than appears elsewhere in the New Testament. Kiddle, C. A. Scott argue that the words must be taken literally, the former holding that it is a recognition of the ancient feeling that the highest spiritual state was open only to celibates; the latter, that it represents a high estimate of Christian asceticism, probably a reaction against prevailing corruption and a counterpoise to "the doctrine of Balaam." M. Ashcraft lists among possible interpretations: praise of complete celibacy ("difficult to harmonize with other New Testament passages" favouring marriage); freedom from idolatry (= adultery in biblical language); chastity in general (not defiled by "adultery, fornication" – assuming that *marriage* does not defile); a later interpolation by a monk defending celibacy (R. H. Charles); or – which Ashcraft prefers – ritual purification in readiness for battle (G. B. Caird). This last suggestion scarcely avoids the implication that all sexual intercourse is defiling. The literal meaning seems inescapable: this verse, perhaps with Matthew 19:12, illustrates the earliest step towards that asceticism which was to mark the second century's reaction to, and infiltration by, Greek dualism.[18]

Something of the author's intolerance of heresy springs from his intolerance of evil: the letters to the churches presuppose that the heresy in view is some form of gnostic amoralism, tending not merely to mislead opinion but to corrupt character. Similarly, in resisting the State, the author recognises that the "immediate enemy is Rome, but behind Rome is the world ... the domain of Satan, inherently opposed to the will of God".[19]

Many Jews believed the heathen world to be under the control of the gods of idolatry, ruled by demons for the prince of this world; some gnostics held the whole material world essentially evil – including the State. In either light, Rome's declared hostility to Christianity and her exaltation of Caesar-worship must have appeared as deliberate enmity towards all that Christ stood for ("anti-Christ") directed by "the mother of harlots" (17:1, 5), the agent of Satan, the capital of the kingdom of evil as the new Jerusalem would be the capital of the kingdom of God.

This view contradicts Paul's, and Peter's, for whom the Roman State was ordained of God, the minister of God for good, deserving of all Christian support. But the new doctrine concerning Christian citizenship and the individual's relation to the State was not the result of deeper insight, but a pragmatic adjustment to a change of circumstances. In the words of Oscar Cullmann, "According as the State remains within its limits or transgresses them, the Christian will describe it as the servant of God or as the instrument of the Devil."[20] Moreover, the implied view of salvation, as being *gathered out* of every kindred and people and nation (5:9, 7:9 Greek), recalls that of Peter at Pentecost, who bade men save themselves from a wicked and perverse generation. The world is identified in the mind of John with evil, and evil must be destroyed. The domain of Satan must fall if God's will is to be done: compromise was impossible.

This view of relentless war between church and State explains the high value attributed to martyrdom. The writer's immediate purpose is neither to expound the gospel nor to enforce Christian ethics, but to call to heroic resistance. The faithfulness of Christ, and His triumphant death, are therefore emphasised. Martyrs are said to overcome because they love not their lives unto the end; they shelter beneath heaven's High Altar until God shall vindicate their steadfast loyalty. Those who seal their testimony with their blood have washed their robes and made them white in the blood of the Lamb; they are above accusation; on them the second death has no power; they intercede for their brethren; they live and reign with Christ without waiting (6:9f, 7:14, 12:10f, 20:4-6). The exaltation of martyrdom later led to abuses: to spiritual pride, even to assumption of powers of absolution and intercession by *intending* martyrs. Martyrdom may sometimes express pride, stubbornness, dogmatism, more than devout conviction and loyalty. But it is unfair to read later exaggerations into Revelation. The church needed the heroic spirit; self-sacrifice, like that of Jesus, was the ultimate testimony, and the ultimate protest. Given the prevailing circumstances, it proved too the ultimate test of love and allegiance towards Christ. To give one's life for Christ's sake, when necessary, remains a disciple's moral obligation.

The final goal is a world redeemed, cleansed, made beautiful, from which vice and violence, oppression and cruelty, drunkenness and lies, avarice, darkness, and pain shall be banished. The gates stand ever open for freedom; there shall be no night there; the river of the water of life flows freely for all peoples, and the leaves of the trees which line its banks are given for the healing of the nations. Here the redeemed walk, and sorrow and sighing have fled: for the city of God is centre of a world so unified that kings of all nations bring their pride and their power in tribute. And it has no temple: for the Lord God Almighty and the Lamb are the temple of it.

That prophetic vision is *not* unworthy to close the long story of biblical ethics. Nor does the writer day-dream about imagined potentialities of humanist social reform: the ideal city descends out of heaven, from God. To the end, the Bible relates morality to religion, and sees man's only hope to lie in the beneficent purposes of God. The God who at the first set man in a garden, alone, leads him at last to fullness of life in the social community of a city: but the city, like the garden, is only secure and satisfying when man walks there with his God.

Thus in the closing pages of the New Testament there begins that long development which was to produce the kind of Christianity which the following centuries were to know, in which the institution ever tended to repress individual inspiration, and a disciplined loyalty to Christian "principles" replaced the passionate personal loyalty to the living Christ which nourished itself upon stirring memories. Many of the characteristics of second and third-century Christian ethics already begin to appear. Christian morality is seen as the addition of right conduct to a right faith, a matter of consistency, rather than a natural, irresistible consequence of a transforming experience. Decreasing place is given to imitation of Christ as the figure of the Master recedes – though it is not forgotten entirely. The beginnings appear both of antinomianism and of asceticism, and also of a greater emphasis upon Church life and its duties. Some adjustment occurs in the Christian approach to the pagan mind – a greater concern for ethical than for theological solutions to contemporary needs: this is a movement of thought that was to preoccupy the second and third centuries. A more complicated attitude is required towards the State, and towards society, as the original, theocratic principle is modified by bitter experience of human injustice, and of persecution. And a new heroism emerges, for which taking up the cross comes to mean again a literal acceptance of martyrdom. All these features strengthen and intermingle in the Christianity of the immediately succeeding centuries.

13

Looking Backwards – and Forwards

THE DISTINCTIVE CHARACTER OF biblical ethics is best illustrated by comparison with alternative approaches to the perpetual question, What is the nature of the good, the right? Extra-biblical ethics rests upon various foundations, different formulations being broadly classifiable as those which do, and those which do not, recognise some basis of moral obligation "external" to man himself. Among the former are ethical systems which appeal to ancient laws, the custom of the tribe, to proverbs and to case-law, resting ultimately upon the accumulated wisdom of experience discovering what the world and life are actually like. Also those which appeal to some eternal "real" world of ideas behind the fluctuating, unreal world of the senses, which beckons man to attain eternal ideals of truth, beauty, and goodness in his own striving after reality (Plato); or the cool, rational appraisal of the logical, balanced form of things – the discomfort and danger of all extremes – which prompts the cultivation of the happy mean in all attitudes and conduct (Aristotle). The appeal to an innate sense of moral obligation, inherent in human nature (Kant, Butler), or to some over-riding "evolutionary principle" of progress through increasing fitness to survive in a competitive universe, making moral development one inescapable factor in the biological process, is of the same kind. All such moral theories tend to assume that ethics deals with some *objective* feature of the universe, to which man adjusts his life by wisdom and obedience.

Psychological analysis of morality has concentrated either upon the innate self-respect, pride, and self-determination that makes for manliness (Stoicism); or upon the universal desire for happiness, supposed to imply that all reasonable men desire the greatest happiness of the greatest number (Utilitarianism); upon the craving for self-realisation and self-fulfilment (Perfectionism); or upon the intuitive awareness of moral distinctions (Shaftesbury, Hume, the Moral Taste and Intuitionist schools). A teleological view of the universe will see man as above all a purposive agent, and ethics as the systematisation of his controlling purposes according to their "value", judged usually by their permanence, breadth, and purity. These formulations of ethics tend to assume as a basis a *subjective* attitude, perception, or feeling, a tendency of the mind, a moral taste or capacity varying with individuals as the capacity for mathematics, or aesthetics, varies. In this case, moral living is not an adjustment to an objective moral "order", but a personal preference for what gives satisfaction to one's nature.

Insights so widely and so persistently affirmed cannot be wholly wrong: in fact most of these ways of expressing man's ethical experience can find illustration somewhere in the long biblical record. The sense of objective obligation, the voice *within* the soul, the conception of a moral goal to be striven after, of varying temporary or permanent "valuations" to be made, even the search for happiness (as "blessing"), are all biblical, and so is the vision of a perfect world, "a pattern shown thee in the mount", to which behaviour in this world should approximate. The notion of an onward-moving purpose behind all things, in conformity to which man finds his true significance, is likewise basic to scriptural morality. To admit all this is but to say, with Paul, that even beyond the sphere of historic revelation, God has not left Himself without a witness; that the fundamental law of human life is writ-ten within the human soul itself (Romans 2:14, 15).

(1) THE RELIGIOUS ROOT OF BIBLICAL MORALITY

When we attempt, however, to summarise the main ideas of biblical ethics, it is to *the religious root of morality,* and the moral nature of religion, that we must give first place. In the story of Adam, in the Noahic covenant, in the Mosaic law and the prophets, the terms upon which man lives are framed by God as the conditions of human welfare. Old Testament ethics is founded in the constitution of man's life as God's creature, while the sanc-tions, motives and resources of morality are all conceived as terms of a covenant offered by God for man's acceptance. In the New Testament, the religious experience of salvation, fellowship with God, prayer, the indwelling of the Spirit, all the operations and means of divine grace, are presupposed in Christian ethics, in the teaching of Jesus, in the primitive catechesis, in Paul, Peter, John, and in the later books alike. Admittedly, within the Bible, as outside it, religion is sometimes amoral, occasionally immoral, so that in Amos, Isaiah, Malachi, the strongest criticism of "relig-ion" comes from prophets of moral reform. But this only confirms the main thrust of the biblical message: the touchstone of religion is morality, the proof of faith is obedience, while the spring and vindication of morality is always ultimately religious; and hope for the immoral lies not in self-reform but in divine salvation.

One consequence is that biblical ethics assumes *the objectivity of moral distinctions* and the obligation of moral law. Objectivity is plainly implied in the religious basis and sanction; obligation is asserted, continuously and variously, in the fundamental notion of law, in the Torah, in the conception of God as King which is basic to both Testaments, and in the messianic metaphor of divine-human relations. It reappears in the unvarying requirement of "righteousness", which presupposes both a standard of right and an obligation to observe it. It is fully expounded in the New Testament ideal of the kingdom – of life under the divine reign, passes into gentile terminology in the confession of Jesus as Lord, and is worked out in detail in the catechetical teaching on subordination. Behind all lies the conviction that God makes the final demand upon human life, that His will is the ultimately unanswerable "categorical imperative" under which man lives.

The objectivity of moral judgements, though much debated, is not without philosophical support: (i) the *universality* of the faculty of moral judgement, signifying that it concerns more than individual taste, preference or experience; (ii) the large measure of *agreement* in particular moral decisions – *for* justice, courage, loyalty, social cohesion, *against* cruelty, deceit, murder, sexual promiscuity; (iii) the fact of moral *obligation,* involving self-accusation, remorse, the condemnation of others for not accepting obligations; (iv) the *social necessity* of moral standards – without which neither praise, blame, moral education, punishment, moral restraint, social reform (as of slavery or child labour) can be justified, since without objective standards all opinions are equally valid, all attitudes equally defensible, and social control is mere bullying by the majority.

In the last resort, whatever is true of moral judgements is true also of scientific ("factual", intellectual) judgements; the same arguments that tell against moral objectivity (variety and changes of opinion, elitism, intuitive basis) tell equally against intellectual objectivity – we can no more prove that the principles of reason apply to the real, objective world, than that the principles of morality do so. Only the naive suppose that our fallible sense experience gives certain and direct knowledge of the "world-in-itself'. All knowledge and wisdom are ultimately intuitive, the construction of insights confirmed and justified by experience: moral and intellectual judgements, in respect of their objectivity, stand or fall together. The biblical view, of course, avoids argument, and intuits directly from the sense of moral obligation to the origin of the moral law in God as Author of creation and of man.

But God is more than King and Creator: He is Father, Redeemer, Saviour. The crowning revelation is that God is not only law but love, man's ultimate succour, always willing man's highest good. Trust and worship, prayer and promise of reward, are also part of biblical morality, therefore, as well as obedience and surrender. Man's immediate goal is a life "unseparated" by

sin from the abiding sense of divine love; his ultimate goal is
self-fulfilment in conformity with the will of God, perfect self-
realisation in eternal life; morality and welfare at the last coincide. In conformity with God's nature as eternal love, the central
and essential divine law is discovered in the end to be the law of
love: in true love all the law that matters is sufficiently fulfilled.
But the same law of love is discovered also to be the law of man's
own being, since man is set by creation, by nature, and by redemption, in inescapable social relationships. And since to fulfil the
law of one's own being is perfect liberty, man's highest freedom is
found in experience to consist in living in accordance with the law
of God, the law of love.

Thus though the language of biblical ethics is that of law, kingship, lordship, obedience, the service of God proves to be the
highest liberty man can know. God is Spirit as well as law, and
love: man's obedience, like his worship, is the response of spirit to
Spirit, the obedience of *faith,* of true wisdom, of love, a surrender
that springs from within, where union with Christ, gratitude for
salvation, the indwelling Spirit, operate upon the inmost motivation of the soul. Man's most complete obedience is the constraint
of an *inward* law: objective moral obligation is transmuted into
subjective, intuitive discernment, an inward illumination that
prompts and sustains an inward devotion to the "external" will of
God.

(2) THE SOCIAL AND EARTHLY CONTEXT

Nevertheless, though the basis of the biblical ethic is thus
intensely personal, it is never merely individual. The single soul is
always seen within the family, within "the people of God", the
remnant, the kingdom, within a community embracing at least
oneself and one's neighbour, a disciple-band, a church, a teeming
world, a network of interacting civic and social relationships.
Social pressures and social obligations everywhere operate upon
the private conscience, and from the first pages of the Bible to the
end, duty is extended beyond the individual's own concerns to
involve all that is implied in being his "brother's keeper". The
reduction of all morality at last to the law of love leaves no possible doubt of the corporate, social dimension of biblical ethics.

Similarly, though rooted in a spiritual reality, and realm,
beyond the present, the biblical ethic is never entirely other-
worldly. The doctrine of creation carries with it the perception
that all visible, material things reflect an invisible, spiritual world,
and the clear implication that all material things are, or may
become, sanctified as vehicles of creative power and purpose. The
Old Testament never ceases to assert, in its ethics as in its theol-

ogy, that the earth is the Lord's. For Christians, this truth is tremendously reinforced by the incarnation. To say that the Word became flesh is to bring all flesh, all that sustains the life, the health, the destiny, of the material world, into direct relation with the Christian conscience. Christianity can never consistently be world-renouncing while it continues to proclaim that God loved the world, that Christ came into the world to be the Saviour of the world. Since the practical ministry of Jesus to man's physical and material needs lies at the heart of Christian origins, both responsibility and compassion for the conditions of human existence must ever remain integral to Christian morality. In this sense at least, Christian ethics is characteristically *incarnational.*

(3) THE FOCUS UPON CHRIST

But it is incarnational also in the further sense that the biblical ideal is finally embodied in the person of Jesus Himself. The imitation of Christ is the ethical implicate of the incarnation not only because the nature and character of the divine Son are thus revealed in human terms, but because His is by definition a perfect humanity, sharing fully the limitations, temptations, adversity and obligations of mankind, yet achieving within these temporal conditions a *human* perfection. The persistence, and the varied exploration, of the idea of *Christus Exemplar* in New Testament ethics, whether in the simplest form of "following Christ" (Synoptics), in His qualities of character (John), in His attitude towards all evil (1 John), in His acceptance of suffering (Peter), in His deep sympathy with men (Hebrews) or in the recapitulation of Christ's dying and rising and the possession of His "mind" and nature (Paul), shows beyond question that in ethics as in soteriology "Christ is the end of the law to everyone who believes." In Him, all Christian idealism is wedded indissolubly to all Christian incentive.

This is Christianity's unique contribution to ethics: the identification of the moral ideal with a historical person; the translation of ethical theory into concrete terms in a real human life; the expression of moral obligation in the language of personal loyalty; and the linking of the highest moral aspiration with the most powerful motives of personal admiration, devotion, gratitude, and love. In thus uniting the only hope of eternal salvation with the highest expression of the moral ideal in one historic person, lies the unique power of the Christian gospel.

Here also lies its potential of continuous development. The fatal weakness of every legal system is historical relativity: a continuously elaborating Torah is essential if the ethical enactments of one age are to have any relevance for the next. The same is true of ethics based upon any philosophic system, which advances in psychology or in science may render out-of-date. The progress of the world's thought and experience affects Christian ethics too, for Christian formulations cannot escape the intellectual climate in which they are framed. Though the fact of moral obligation is timeless, its form is as changeable as the experience of men. Yet – audacious as the claim is – Christian testimony through twenty centuries has confirmed that the embodiment of the ideal in the life, the words, and the example of Jesus has provided moral inspiration, guidance, and power for every generation, race and culture from His day until now.

(4) THE CAPACITY FOR CONTINUAL DEVELOPMENT

But not without change. Biblical ethics closes with many queries unanswered, many unprecedented situations coming into view, some old problems and many new ones still to be resolved. The necessity for development is illustrated already within the New Testament, as insights are clarified, circumstances change, priorities are rethought, and the initial duty of making Christian adjustments in existing conditions gives place to attempts to change those conditions. Such changes and adjustments multip-lied greatly as the Christian community moved on into the second and succeeding centuries, out from Palestine's essentially religio-ethical culture into one in which religion and ethics were rarely connected and sometimes antagonistic and from an envi-ronment in which political theocracy was at least understood, into one in which absolute human dictatorship was imposed by force.

How much greater still must be the changes in priorities in depth of insight, in enlarging responsibilities, in sensitivity of con-science, in constantly re-clarified vision, as the church herself became first imperial, then corrupt, then was reformed and broken; and as dictatorship slowly gave place to democracy Meanwhile, the cultural and philosophic climate became inimical to faith – humanism replaced theism as the starting-point of seri-ous thought. And scientific "enlightenment" not only challenged the assumptions of the biblical world-view, but raised totally new ethical problems, affecting industrial morality, contraception, nuclear warfare, genetic engineering and the like, to which the Bible has no ready answer. At the same time, Christian scholar-ship itself began to despair of ever rediscovering the Jesus of history just when Christian moralists pointed more and more insistently back to Him. All that, however, is the story of the changing continuity of Christian ethics through twenty centuries.

How to change, so continuing to be relevant, *while remaining the same,* so continuing to be Christian, has been the challenge perpetually confronting Christian ethics.

Man's conscience moves more slowly than his mind, but in the end Christian ethics must keep pace with maturing faith; merely residual attitudes, conventional pieties, less rational inhibitions, must be left behind. That the canon of Christian ethics was never closed, any more than the canon of Christian theology, is the consequence of another great doctrine of the gospel – as influential in ethics as that of the incarnation – the doctrine of the presence of the living Spirit of Christ in the ongoing church. Already within the Old Testament, but much more clearly and consistently in the New, the heart and secret of man's moral development is seen to lie in the presence within human experience of the Divine Spirit, revealing in law and prophets the divine will, inspiring in reformers and apostles the divine protest against evil, creating and indwelling the divine community as the earnest and the agency of the ideal, and constantly renewing in godly men the hunger and the capacity for good.

Without the timeless presence of the Spirit, the imitation of Christ would descend to a mere antiquarian Hero-worship, disguising a moral retrogression from modern life and duty into profitless nostalgia for a lost age. And the supreme insight of the Bible concerning the Spirit is precisely that which sees Him less as the bestower of "gifts" and the generator of power than as the source of Christian morality and the form of the contemporary Christ in the experience of believers.

Here lies the quintessence and the crown of biblical ethics, in the final identification of the Spirit of Christian holiness with the living Spirit of Christ, with us always to the end of the age. Amid all the changes of the centuries, the imaginative re-interpretation of the figure of Jesus in each new age, and the capacity of the Spirit-led Christian conscience to re-limn His image in the colours of each new generation, has been the secret of Christianity's perennial appeal, moral authority, and redemptive power. In the end, no more penetrating, satisfying, or final word can be written about Christian ethics than Paul's splendid affirmation:

> We all, mirroring with face unveiled the glory of the Lord
> are being transformed into the same image,
> from one degree of glory to another,
> just as the Lord the Spirit works upon us.

BIBLIOGRAPHY

(and key to references)

Alexander A. B. D. *Christianity and Ethics,* Duckworth, London 1914

Alexander N. *The Epistles of John,* SCM Press, London 1962

Allegro J. M. *The Dead Sea Scrolls,* Penguin Books, Harmondsworth and Baltimore, 1956

Allen W. C. *Gospel of Matthew,* (International Critical Commentary) T. and T. Clark, Edinburgh 1907

Ashcraft M. *Revelation,* (Broadman Commentary) Broadman Press, Nashville 1972, Marshall, Morgan and Scott, London 1973

Barclay W. *"Hellenistic Thought in New Testament Times"* in *Expository Times,* vol LXXI 1959-60, T. and T. Clark, Edinburgh

   Ethics in a Permissive Society, Collins-Fontana, London 1971

   The Gospels and Acts, SCM Press, London 1976

Barrett C. K. *The Holy Spirit and the Gospel Tradition,* SPCK, London; Macmillan, New York 1947

Barry F. R. *Christian Ethics and Secular Society,* Hodder and Stoughton, London 1966

Bigg C. *St Peter and St Jude,* (International Critical Commentary), T. and T. Clark, Edinburgh 1902

Bornkamm G, Barth G, and Held H. J. *Tradition and Interpretation in St Matthew's Gospel,* (ET P. Scott) SCM Press, London 1963

Brooke A. E. *The Johannine Epistles,* (International Critical Commentary), T. and T. Clark, Edinburgh 1912

Bruce F. F. *The Spreading Flame,* Paternoster Press, Exeter 1958

Brunner E. *Justice and the Social Order,* Harper Bros., New York 1945

   The Divine Imperative, (ET Olive Wyon), Macmillan, New York; Lutterworth Press, London 1937

   The Mediator, Lutterworth Press, London 1934

Burnaby J. *Amor Dei,* Hodder and Stoughton, London 1938

Caird G. B. *The Apostolic Age,* Duckworth, London 1955

   Revelation, A. and C. Black, London 1966

Carrington P. *Primitive Christian Catechism,* Cambridge University Press, Cambridge 1940

Charlesworth J. H. (Editor) *John and Qumran,* Chapman, London 1972

Clark G. H *"Situation Ethics",* in Henry C (Editor) *Dictionary of Christian Ethics,* Baker, Grand Rapids 1973

Cranfield C E B *First Peter,* SCM Press, London 1950

Cullmann O *Baptism in the New Testament,* SCM Press, London 1950

   The State in the New Testament, SCM Press, London 1957

Davies W. D. *St Paul and Rabbinic Judaism,* SPCK, London 1948

Deissmann A. *Paul,* Hodder and Stoughton, London 1926

Dodd C. H. *The Johannine Epistles* (Moffatt Commentary), Hodder and Stoughton, London 1946

Ellis E. *St Luke* (New Century Bible), Oliphants-Nelson, London 1966

Ferguson J. *Politics of Love,* James Clarke, Cambridge nd

Fletcher J. *Situation Ethics,* SCM Press, London 1966

Glover T. R. *The Jesus of History,* SCM Press, London 1917
  Paul of Tarsus, SCM Press, London 1925

Harnack A. *History of Dogma,* Williams and Norgate, London 1894

Henry C. F. (Editor) *Dictionary of Christian Ethics,* Baker, Grand Rapids 1973

Henson H. H. *Christian Morality – Natural, Developing, Final,* Oxford University Press, London 1936

Hill D. *Gospel of Matthew* (New Century Bible), Oliphants, London 1972

Houlden J. H. *Ethics and the New Testament,* Mowbrays, London 1973

Hunter A. M. *St Paul and His Predecessors,* SCM Press, London 1940

Inge W. R. *Christian Ethics and Modern Problems,* Hodder and Stoughton, London 1930

Jacob E. *Theology of the Old Testament,* Hodder and Stoughton, London 1958

Kiddle M. *Revelation* (Moffatt Commentary), Hodder and Stoughton, London 1940

Kirk K. *The Vision of God,* Longmans Green, London 1931
  Conscience and Its Problems, Longmans Green, London 1927

Klausner J. *Jesus of Nazareth,* Collier-Macmillan, New York 1943

Ladd G. E. *"Eschatology and Ethics"* in C Henry (ed.) *Dictionary of Christian Ethics,* Baker, Grand Rapids 1973

Leany A. R. C (Editor) *Guide to the Scrolls,* SCM Press, London 1958

Lecky W. E. H. *History of European Morals,* Longmans Green, London 1905 edition

Lillie W. *Studies in New Testament Ethics,* Oliver and Boyd, Edinburgh 1961

Luthardt C. E. *History of Christian Ethics,* 1888-93 (only volume one translated)

Marshall L. H. *Challenge of New Testament Ethics,* Macmillan, London 1946

Maurice F. D. *The Gospel of the Kingdom of Heaven,* Macmillan, London 1893

Mitton C. L. *Epistle of James,* Marshall, Morgan and Scott, London and Eerdmans, Grand Rapids 1966

Moffatt J. *First Corinthians* (Moffatt Commentary), Hodder and Stoughton, London 1938
  General Epistles (Moffatt Commentary) Hodder and Stoughton, London 1928
  "War" in *Dictionary of the Apostolic Church* (edited James Hastings) T. and T. Clark, Edinburgh vol ii 1918

Moule C. F. D. *"The New Testament and Moral Decisions"* in *Expository Times,* vol 1xxiv 1962-63, T. and T. Clark, Edinburgh

Murray J. *Principles of Conduct,* Tyndale Press, London 1957

McNeile A. H. *Gospel According to St Matthew,* Macmillan, London and New York 1955

Macquarrie J. (Editor) *Dictionary of Christian Ethics,* SCM Press, London 1967

Neil W. *Epistles to Thessalonians* (Moffatt Commentary), Hodder and Stoughton, London 1950

Nygren A *Agape and Eros,* SPCK-Macmillan, London 1941

Oesterley W. O. E. and Robinson T. H. *Hebrew Religion, Its Origin and Development,* SPCK, London 1961 edition

Peabody F. *Jesus Christ and the Social Question,* Macmillan, London and New York 1900

Ramsey P. *Basic Christian Ethics,* SCM Press, London 1950

Rashdall H. *Conscience and Christ,* Duckworth, London 1916

Robinson H. W. *Inspiration and Revelation in the Old Testament,* Oxford University Press, London 1946

   Christian Doctrine of Man, T. and T. Clark, Edinburgh (3rd edition) 1926

Robinson T. H. *Prophecy and the Prophets,* Duckworth, London 1923

Ropes J. H. *Epistle of James* (International Nritical Commentary), T. and T. Clark, Edinburgh 1916

Rowley H. H. *Job* (New Century Bible) Oliphants, London 1970

Russell D. S. *Between the Testaments,* SCM Press, London 1960

Sanday W. and Headlam A. C. *Epistle to the Romans* (International Critical Commentary) T. and T. Clark, Edinburgh (fifth edition) 1902

Sanders J. T. *Ethics in the New Testament,* SCM Press, London 1975

Scott C. A. *Revelation,* Hodder and Stoughton, London 1905

Scott E. F. *Revelation,* SCM Press London (fourth edition) 1941

   Pastoral Epistles (Moffatt Commentary), Hodder and Stoughton, London 1936

   Ethical Teaching of Jesus, Macmillan, New York 1924 etc

   Varieties of New Testament Religion, Scribner's Sons, New York 1947

Selwyn E. G. *First Peter,* Macmillan, London 1949

Shepherd M. H. *"The Epistle of James and the Gospel of Matthew"* in *Authorship and Integrity of the New Testament,* (Theological Collections No 4) SPCK, London 1965

Songer H. S. *James* (Broadman Commentary), Broadman Press, Nashville 1972, Marshall Morgan and Scott, London 1973

Stewart J. S. *A Man in Christ,* Hodder and Stoughton, London 1935

Taylor V. *Gospel According to St Mark,* Macmillan, London 1952

Teaching Symposium (no editor named) *Teaching Christian Ethics,* SCM Press, London 1974

Vermes G. *The Dead Sea Scrolls in English,* Penguin Books, Harmondsworth and Baltimore 1968

White R. E. O. *Into the Same Image,* Marshall Morgan and Scott, London and Broadman Press, Nashville 1957

   Biblical Doctrine of Initiation, Hodder and Stoughton, London and Eerdmans, Grand Rapids 1960

   Apostle Extraordinary, Eerdmans, Grand Rapids 1962, Pickering and Inglis, London 1968

   Open Letter to Evangelicals (1 John), Eerdmans, Grand Rapids 1964, Paternoster Press, Exeter 1965

Yoder J. H. *The Politics of Jesus,* Eerdmans, Grand Rapids 1972

SOURCE – REFERENCES
AND
ACKNOWLEDGEMENTS

(for full titles see Bibliography: *Op cit* = work *just* cited)

FOREWORD
The Question is ...
(pages 7-12)

1. J. Fletcher *Situation* ... 31-33
2. J. Fletcher *op cit* 26
3. H. W. Robinson *Christian Experience of the Holy Spirit,* Nisbet, London 1928 26
4. J. H. Houlden *Ethics* ... 1-2
5. E. F. Scott *Varieties* ...; cf J. D. G. Dunn *Unity and Diversity in the New Testament,* SCM Press, London 1977, and J. T. Sanders *Ethics*
6. E. F. Scott *Varieties* ...vi
7. F. R. Barry *Secular* ... 16

CHAPTER 1
(pages 13-30)

1. T. H. Robinson *Prophecy* ... 4f
2. C. E. Luthardt *History* ... part II
3. H. W. Robinson *Inspiration* ... 55; cf E. Jacob *Theology* ... 103ff
4. W. O. E. Oesterley – T. H. Robinson *Hebrew Religion* ... 223
5. T. H. Robinson *Prophecy* ... 5f
6. G. Murray *Five Stages of Greek Religion* Oxford University Press, Oxford 1925 67ff
7. Oesterley-Robinson *op cit* 223
8. H. W. Robinson *Inspiration* ... 79
9. Oesterley-Robinson *op cit* 135; cf T. H. Robinson *Prophecy* ... 16; De Vaux *Ancient Israel* Darton, Longmans and Todd, London, and McGraw-Hill New York 1961 475; J. Murray *Principles* ... *passim*
10. H. H. Rowley cited in Hastings *Dictionary of the Bible* ed. F. C. Grant, H. H. Rowley, T. and T. Clark, Edinburgh and Charles Scribner's Sons, New York, 1963 970a
11. H. W. Robinson *Inspiration* ...83f citing T. H. Robinson
12. T. H. Robinson *Prophecy* ... 141
13. Full discussion in P. R. Ackroyd *Exile and Restoration* SCM Press, London 1968 87ff

CHAPTER 2
(pages 31-52)

1. A. B. D. Alexander *Christianity* ... 48f
2. W. O. E. Oesterley *The Psalms* SPCK London 1955 78f

3. Discussion in S. Mowinckel *Psalms in Israel's Worship* (ET D. R. Ap-Thomas) Blackwell Oxford 1962 vol II 12f
4. See J. Robertson *Poetry and Religion of the Psalms* Blackwood Edinburgh 1898 249ff
5. W. O. E. Oesterley *The Psalms* (above) 56f
6. S. Mowinckel *Psalms in Israel's Worship* (above) vol II 207f
7. A. B. D. Alexander *Christianity* ... 49
8. See H. W. Robinson *Inspiration* ... 244f; C. H. Toy *Proverbs* 10
9. D. S. Russell *Between* ... 81
10. A. H. McNeile on Ecclesiastes, Hastings *Dictionary of the Bible* ed. F. C. Grant, H. H. Rowley, T. and T. Clark, Edinburgh and Charles Scribner's Sons, New York 1963
11. W. O. E. Oesterley – T. H. Robinson *Introduction to the Books of the Old Testament* SPCK London 1934 171
12. H. H. Rowley *Job* 252-262 citing Duhm
13. T. H. Robinson *Prophecy* ... 206f (present author's italics)
14. Oesterley-Robinson *Introduction to OT* (above) 170
15. H. W. Robinson *Inspiration* ... 259
16. D. S. Russell *Between* ... 144
17. H. H. Rowley *Job* 174
18 D. S. Russell *Between* ... 24f, and 148 citing other passages from 1 Enoch, Testament of Benjamin, 2 Esdras
19. D. S. Russell *Between* ... 153f citing "practically all the apocalyptic books".
20. R. H. Charles *Apocrypha and Pseudepigrapha of the Old Testament* Oxford University Press, Oxford 1913 218
21. Evidence in R. E. O. White *Biblical* ... 44-46, especially Sirach 45:5, 8:9, 39:1-11, 1 Maccabees 2:42, Apocalypse of Baruch 57:2; also Sirach 44:20f, Testament of Levi 13: 3, 7-8, Pirke Aboth 2:8, 2 Baruch 32:1, 51:3, 48:22, 24
22. D. S. Russell *Between* ... 83
23. H Rashdall *Conscience* ...92f
24. D. S. Russell *Between* ...64
25. R. P. Hanson in A. R. C. Leaney (ed) *Guide* 55
26. Josephus *War* II viii 2, Eusebius of Caesarea *Praeparatio Evangelica* VIII ix 2, in J. H. Charlesworth (ed) *John* ... 159
27. D. S. Russell *Between* ... 55
28. G. Vermes *Dead Sea* ... 13
29. R. E. Brown, in Expository Times vol 1xxviii (1966-67) 19-23
30. J. H. Charlesworth *John* ... 88, 108
31. G. Vermes *Dead Sea* ... 26f, 36f, with references, reproduced on pages 72, 79 etc
32. 1QS4: 2-4 (see J. H. Charlesworth *John* ... 78f) corresponding to Community Rule in G. Vermes *Dead Sea* ... 76f
33. 1QS 7:1f with 2:24f, 5:3f, 24f and the Damascus Rule 6:20f, cited by Marie-Emile Boismard in J. H. Charlesworth *John* ... 159
34. G. Vermes *Dead Sea* ... 29
35. G. Vermes *Dead Sea* ... 39, 52
36 R. P. Hanson in A. R. C. Leaney *Guide* ... 60f
37. J. M. Allegro *The Dead Sea* ... 102f
38. G. Vermes *Dead Sea* ... 30
39. J. M. Allegro *The Dead Sea* ... 101
40. Full evidence and discussion in J. H. Charlesworth *John* ... 109f
41. G. Vermes *Dead Sea* ... 75ff
42. J. H. Charlesworth *John* ...13
43. J. H. Charlesworth *op cit* 111 note 11, 78

44. G. Vermes *Dead Sea* ... 77
45. G. Vermes *op cit* 75f. Charlesworth *(John* ... 110) gives copious other references
46. J. H. Charlesworth *op cit* 82; see 85f and 111
47. 1QS 4:18; J. H. Charlesworth *op cit* 85n and 42
48. J. L. Price in J. H. Charlesworth *op cit* 16

CHAPTER 3
(pages 53-63)

1. E. F. Scott *Ethical Teaching* ... 30f, 32
2. E. F. Scott *op cit* 17
3. J. Klausner *Jesus* ... 384
4. D. S. Russell *Between* ... 89
5. W. R. Inge *Ethics* ... 40; E. F. Scott *Ethical Teaching* ... 17, 128
6. E. F. Scott *op cit* 13
7. L. H. Marshall *Challenge* ... 5 citing Klausner *Jesus* ...
8. L. H. Marshall *op cit* 158f
9. T. R. Glover *Jesus* ... 49
10. E. F. Scott *Ethical Teaching* ... 34

CHAPTER 4
(pages 64-77)

1. E. F. Scott *Ethical Teaching* ... 27
2. W. R. Inge *Ethics* ... 45
3. L. H. Marshall *Challenge* ... 110
4. E. F. Scott *Ethical Teaching* ... 64
5. L. H. Marshall *Challenge* ... 207
6. W. R. Inge *Ethics* ... 69
7. T. R. Glover *Jesus* ... 168f
8. E. F. Scott *Ethical Teaching* 57

CHAPTER 5
(pages 78-108)

1. L. H. Marshall *Challenge* ... 29f
2. E. F. Scott *Ethical Teaching* ... 48
3. L. H. Marshall *op cit* 114
4. A. H. McNeile, W. C. Allen, D. Hill, each in commentaries on Matthew, *in loc*
5. A. B. D. Alexander *Christianity* ... 224
6. L. H. Marshall *Challenge* ... 161, B. Russell *History* ... 812
7. P. Ramsey *Basic* ... 266, 272
8. D. Hill *Gospel* ... 111; G. Vermes *Dead Sea* ... 76, 142
9. L. H. Marshall *Challenge* ... 153
10. 4 BC. Josephus *Antiquities* XVII x 4; E. F. Scott *Ethical Teaching* ... 77f. For thorough discussion, see Yoder: *Politics* ...
11. W. R. Inge *Ethics* ... 57
12. W. R. Inge *op cit* 55; L. H. Marshall *Challenge* ... *147* – apparently ascribing to Moses himself the later legalism which Jesus opposed
13. H. Rashdall *Conscience* ... 104
14. W. R. Inge *Ethics* ... 63, citing F. Peabody *Jesus Christ* ... 104
15. See L. H. Marshall *Challenge* ... 160
16. See R. E. O. White *Image* ... 176 and *passim*
17. T. R. Glover *Jesus* ... 167

18. See W. R. Inge *Ethics* ... 70
19. T. R. Glover *Jesus* ... 172

CHAPTER 6
(pages 109-123)

1. A. Harnack *History* ... vol i 67; W. R. Inge *Ethics* ... 42
2. G. Bornkamm, G. Barth, H. J. Held *Tradition* ... on Matthew 18:18 (see index)
3. Bornkamm-Barth-Held *op cit* on Matthew 11: 28-30
4. E. Ellis *St Luke* 12
5. See chapter 4 (3) (i)
6. C. K. Barrett *Holy Spirit* ... 160 Barrett rejects the evidence of the gospel tradition and argues that Jesus Himself did not promise or foresee the gift of the Spirit to the church; but that the expectation is present in the material now gathered into the Gospels, is manifest.
7. Bp Butler's *Sermons* – sermon XI
8. H. Rashdall *Conscience* ... chapter 2; G. E. Ladd *"Eschatology ..."*; J Jeremias (*The Parables of Jesus* SCM Press, London 1954 120-139) assesses the effects of 'catastrophe' and 'crisis' on the teaching of the parables, seeing it especially as underlining Christ's call to repentance (p. 126).
9. E. F. Scott *Ethical Teaching* ... 43 (paraphrased)
10. W. R. Inge *Ethics* ... 21f
11. H. H. Henson *Morality* ... chapter 7
12. E. F. Scott *Ethical Teaching* ... 128
13. R. E. O. White *Image* ... ch 11, and 158
14. W. E. H. Lecky *History* ... vol ii 8f

CHAPTER 7
(pages 124-133)

1. V. Taylor *Gospel* ... 78f, 86f
2. The assumptions here are plainly important. The evidence, and the tables of comparison, are fully set out in 'E. G. Selwyn *1 Peter* 18f and Essay II, following P. Carrington *Primitive* ... Almost simultaneously W. D. Davies *(Paul* ... 122f) was arguing similarly; A. M. Hunter *(St Paul ...)* had also pointed in the same direction, and twenty years later (revised edition 1961) spoke still more strongly. Varying degrees of support are expressed in G. B. Caird *Apostolic* ... 109f, 113, C. H. Dodd *1 John* 63, J. N. D. Kelly *Early Christian Creeds* (Longmans, London 1950) 17-19, 50f, V. Taylor *Gospel* ... 97, 103f, 133. J. Moffatt *1 Corinthians* 12, and W. Neil *Thessalonians* 184f both assume a catechetical tradition in the apostolic churches. The arguments are summarised in R. E. O. White *Biblical* ... chapter 10 and additional note 7. Nevertheless, not all scholars have accepted this reconstuction of primitive catechetical material; if it be rejected, extensive coincidences of content, language and order between very different New Testament books remain unexplained: but the moral instruction itself remains part of the New Testament, as evidence of the ethical concern of the primitive church.
3. Pattern tabulated, with references, in White *Biblical* ... 164f
4. Pattern tabulated, with references, in White *op cit* 168 and n 1
5. Pattern tabulated, with references, in White *op cit* 174 and n 1
6. Pattern tabulated, with references, in White *op cit* 175 and n 1

7. Pattern tabulated, with references, in White *op cit* 176 and n 2
8. Passages echoing this pattern are 1 Peter 2: 13-3: 8, 5: 5f, Romans 13: 1-7, Colossians 3: 12, 18-4: 1, Ephesians 5: 21-6: 9, 1 Timothy 2: 1-15, 6: 1f, Titus 2: 4-10, 3: 1, James 4: 6, 7, 10 Hebrews 12: 9, 13: 17. On subordination, see J. T. Sanders *Ethics* ... for a critical view.
9. Pattern explained in White *op cit* 177 and n 1
10. G. B. Caird *Apostolic* ... 113

CHAPTER 8
(pages 134-156)

1. 2 Thessalonians 2: 15, 3: 6, Romans 6: 17, Acts 20: 35, 1 Corinthians 7: 10-12, 11: 23, 15: 3f, Galatians 1: 11f
2. W. R. Inge *Ethics* ... 75f; T. R. Glover *Paul* ... 79; L. H. Marshall *Challenge* ... 267. W. D. Davies *Paul* ... 121-136 discusses fully the sources of Paul's ethical thought, emphasising the catechetical concern of the churches.
3. H. W. Robinson *Man* ... 104f
4. W. R. Inge *Ethics* ... 79; L. H. Marshall *Challenge* ... 268. Note the use of "flesh" in Romans 13: 14, 7: 25, 8: 4, 9-13, Galatians 5: 16f and 6: 8
5. J. S. Stewart *A Man* ... 104
6. L. H. Marshall *Challenge* ... 269
7. W. Lillie *Studies* ... 45f, 54
8. H. W. Robinson *Man* ... 107
9. W. Lillie *Studies* ... 12f, quoting E. Brunner *Justice* ... 84
10. T. R. Glover *Paul* 82
11. T. R. Glover *op cit* 83 citing 1 Timothy 4: 2, Titus 1: 15, Ephesians 4: 18, and 2: 12
12. T. R. Glover *op cit* 87f
13. H. W. Robinson *Man* ... 123f
14. L. H. Marshall *Challenge* ... 269
15. H. W. Robinson *Man* ... 125f
16. J. S. Stewart *A Man* ... 177f
17. H. W. Robinson *Man* ... 124
18. Augustine, as quoted by J. S. Stewart from Hastings *Dictionary of the Apostolic Church* T. and T. Clark, Edinburgh 1915 vol i 691
19. L. H. Marshall *Challenge* ... 246
20. J. S. Stewart *A Man* ... 110
21. E. Brunner *The Mediator* 592; J. S. Stewart *A Man* ... 185f
22. O. Cullmann *Baptism* ... 47; fuller discussion in R. E. O. White *Biblical* ... 213f
23. W. Sanday, A. C. Headlam *Romans* on chapter 6
24. J. S. Stewart *A Man* ... 127ff
25. L. H. Marshall *Challenge* ... 264
26. Colossians 3: 10 appears to be Paul's only reference to the *progressive* creation of the new man. For fuller exposition of Paul's teaching on Christlikeness, see R. E. O. White *Image* ... and for a discussion of some issues raised by it, see G. Berkouwer *Faith and Sanctification*, Eerdmans, Grand Rapids.
27. W. D. Davies *Paul* ... 88f, 136f, 147 citing C. H. Dodd.

CHAPTER 9
(pages 157-187)

1. L. H. Marshall *Challenge* ... 274
2. W. Lillie *Studies* ... 165
3. W. R. Inge *Ethics* ... 80
4. T. R. Glover *Paul* ... 96
5. W. R. Inge *Ethics* ... 72f
6. A. Deissmann *Paul* ... 162
7. See R. E. O. White *Apostle* ... 92f
8. J. Moffatt *1 Corinthians* 75, 95
9. W. R. Inge *Ethics* ... 81
10. J. Moffatt *1 Corinthians* 76
11. H. Rashdall *Conscience* ... 230
12. L. H. Marshall *Challenge* ... 338
13. L. H. Marshall *op cit* 339
14. W. Lillie *Studies* ... 106
15. L. H. Marshall *Challenge* ... 328
16. H. Rashdall *Conscience* ... 233
17. Josephus *War* II viii 7
18. W. Lillie *Studies* ... 87
19. L. H. Marshall *Challenge* ... 278

CHAPTER 10
(pages 188-195)

1. E. G. Selwyn *1 Peter* 64f
2. E. G. Selwyn *op cit* 67
3. C. Bigg *S Peter* ... 235
4. A. Lillie *Studies* ... 89
5. E. G. Selwyn *1 Peter* (above) 87, 90
6. C. E. B. Cranfield *1 Peter* 70
7. C. E. B. Cranfield *op cit* 73
8. E. G. Selwyn *1 Peter* (above) 91

CHAPTER 11
(pages 196-203)

1. L. H. Marshall *Challenge* ... 349
2. W. R. Inge *Ethics* ... 83
3. Irenaeus *Adv. Haereses* I xxiv 5
4. Irenaeus *op cit* I vi 2, 3
5. Clement Alex. *Stromateis* III i, iv
6. Ignatius *Ad Smyrnaeans* vi 2
7. C. H. Dodd *1 John* 41f
8. W. Barclay in Expository Times vol 1xxi 280-284
9. N. Alexander *Epistles* ... 63
10. A. E. Brooke *1 John* 1ii, cf 1, xxviii
11. Fuller exposition in R. E. O. White *Open Letter* ... Essay 3

CHAPTER 12
(pages 204-206)

1. E. F. Scott *Pastoral* ... *xxxviii* – significant, even assuming as Scott does that Paul was not the author.
2. E. F. Scott *Varieties* ... 195

3. E. F. Scott *op cit* 196
4. E. F. Scott *op cit* 205
5. M. H. Shepherd *Epistle of James* 98ff
6. E. F. Scott *Varieties* ... 211
7. James 5:6. This is a common interpretation since Oecumenius in 6th century. Cf H. S. Songer *James* ... who cites J. H. Ropes *James* ... 291f. See also J. Moffatt *General Epistles* who says that the generic singular represents a class; and C. L. Mitton *James* who thinks it very doubtful that the words refer to Jesus.
8. J. Moffatt *General Epistles* 31
9. A. J. B. Higgins in *Peake's Commentary,* Nelson, London 1961 *ad loc*
10. See (RSV) 1 Timothy 6:4, 2 Timothy 2:23; 1 Timothy 1:3-7, 6:20, 2 Timothy 2:16; 1 Timothy 4:3; 1 Timothy 1:4, 4:7, 2 Timothy 4:4, Tit 1:14, compare 10; 2 Timothy 2:18; 1 Timothy 4:3-5; 1 Timothy 1:19f; 2 Timothy 3: 1ff; 2 Timothy 2:16, 23; 1 Timothy 4:1, 2, 6:3ff, Tit 3:10
11. Compare for example, H. Rashdall *Conscience* ... 234, 236
12. E. F. Scott *Varieties* ... 214
13. E. F. Scott *op cit* 213
14. Cf G. Barth, in G. Bornkamm, G. Barth, H. J. Held *Tradition* ... 36
15. G. Barth *op cit* 85
16. W. Barclay *Gospels* ... vol i 209
17. E. F. Scott *Revelation* 27, 130 citing such comments without endorsing all of them
18. M. Kiddle *Revelation ad loc;* C. A. Scott *Revelation* 256; M. Ashcraft *Revelation ad loc;* G. B. Caird *Revelation* 179
19. E. F. Scott *Revelation* 132; W. Lillie *Studies* ... 89f
20. O. Cullman *The State* ... 86

INDEX OF SELECTED SCRIPTURE REFERENCES

INDEX OF SUBJECTS

INDEX OF MODERN AUTHORS

INDEX OF OTHER ANCIENT SOURCES

INDEX OF OTHER ANCIENT SOURCES